THE NEW MADRID

FAULT FINDERS GUIDE

KNOX & STEWART

What People Say About This Book . . .

"*The Fault Finders Guide* is a treasure trove. An invaluable resource. If you have ever been in the New Madrid area looking for signs of the earthquakes (as I have) or if you want to visit the scene of one of nature's greatest wonders and lay your hands on the face of an earthquake landscape—there is nothing like this book!

"In addition to detailed information on the locations and appearances of faults, sand boils, landslides, and other seismic features—the authors also explain the enormous forces that molded these landforms and place them in their historical and social context. Skillfully and sensitively presented, they also talk about responsibility—which is part of living in or near an active fault zone.

"I had already found their other two books inspiring and great eye-openers. *The Fault Finders Guide* takes you another dimension further—right down to the grit of the sand and the smell of the soil where you can feel and walk on these awesome formations—creations of nature we would never have been able to know or appreciate without the work of this dedicated pair.

"These world class scientists have once more demonstrated their remarkable gift for presenting technical information in a way that is clear, enlightening, entertaining, and thought provoking—all at the same time!

A trip down Interstate 55 will never be the same again. Thank you Dr. Knox and Dr. Stewart for your continued and successful efforts to enlighten both professionals and the public."

John F. Townsend, M.D., Chairman,
Department of Pathology and
Anatomical Science, University of Missouri
School of Medicine, Columbia

"Great work! A masterpiece of organization! My wife and I are both geology enthusiasts as avocations. When we recently drove through the New Madrid area, we had very little time. *The Fault Finders Guide* allowed us to see the most in the shortest time. It was great!

"We could easily have spent a month with this clearly written, well illustrated book—yet it was especially helpful when we were in a hurry.

"You are definitely going to miss most of the earthquake features without this guide. This is subtle geology—not like the obvious structures we see here in the West where vegetation is sparse and rocks are exposed.

"We have enjoyed all of the publications by Dr. Stewart and Dr. Knox. But this one is special. An ideal text and field trip manual for students and earth science teachers.

"We plan to go back again—with *The Fault Finders Guide* as our mentor—only this time we'll stay longer. Thanks for this fantastic resource which serves both the lay public and the geologic community so well.

Robert Ziprick, Attorney
Loma Linda, California

"I was in the Navy for 31 years and Commanding Officer of a U.S. Nuclear Submarine for five years. It is easier to find the North pole under the Arctic ice than to find earthquake features in the New Madrid Seismic Zone without this superb book. I know. I have done both!

"I have spent many hours driving and walking around the New Madrid area and have thoroughly enjoyed exploring the features described in *The Fault Finders Guide* . . . But believe me, you need this book.

"There are hundreds of fascinating features to discover there, but you won't find many of them without *The Fault Finders Guide*. It is the most useful guidebook to the area available—a welcome and totally unique addition to the literature on these historic earthquakes.

"I have traveled the world several times over, but this book makes the New Madrid Seismic Zone one of the most fascinating places of all."

John D. Peters,
Retired Captain, U.S. Navy
Longmont, Colorado

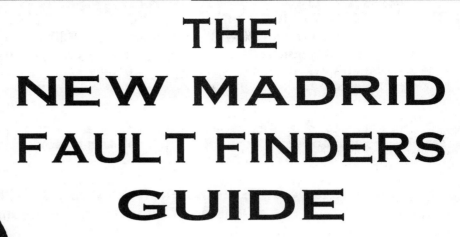

THE
NEW MADRID
FAULT FINDERS
GUIDE

BY
DR. RAY KNOX &
DR. DAVID STEWART

A Set of Self-Guided
Field Tours in the
*"World's Greatest Outdoor
Earthquake Laboratory"*
The New Madrid Fault Zone
of Arkansas, Illinois, Kentucky,
Missouri , and Tennessee

GR
GUTENBERG-RICHTER
PUBLICATIONS
MARBLE HILL, MISSOURI

1995

63345482

THE NEW MADRID FAULT FINDERS GUIDE   **by Ray Knox & David Stewart**
   *Cover Design by David Stewart & Kate Schaefer
   Figures & Maps by David Stewart and others as indicated
   Photographs by Ray Knox & David Stewart
   Fault Finders Logo by David Stewart

* The peculiar orange color of the cover is intended to simulate the color of the sands found in sand boils, sand fissures and explosion craters. Fault Finders will learn to recognize this distinctive color even at a distance with a little experience in the field.

Copyright © 1995 by GUTENBERG-RICHTER PUBLICATIONS
         a Division of Napsac Reproductions, Marble Hill, Missouri

GR
GUTENBERG-RICHTER
PUBLICATIONS
Rt. 1, Box 646
Marble Hill, MO 63764 U.S.A.
Phone: (800) 758-8629
or (573) 238-4273

*See back of this book for information on books, slides, services, and literature available from Gutenberg-Richter Publications.

Publishers Cataloging in Publication
(Prepared by Quality Books, Inc.)

Knox, B. Ray, 1931 -
   The New Madrid fault finders guide: a set of self-guided field tours of the New Madrid fault zone/by Ray Knox and David Stewart.
      p. cm.
   Includes bibliographical references and index.
   Preassigned LCCN: 91-91374
   ISBN: 0-934426-42-2

   1. New Madrid Region (Mo-Ark-Tenn-Ky). 2. Earthquakes--Missouri/Arkansas-New Madrid Region 3. Geology--Morpho-seismology. I. Stewart, David (David Mack), 1937 - II. Title.

E472.N4K66 1995   917.78'985'04'43
                                   QBI95-20327

DEDICATION

We dedicate this book to the many friends who stood by David and Lee Stewart through a long period of trial. Don and Joy Froemsdorf, Bob and Ann Parkinson, and Ed and Pat Williams stand out among those who showed their moral backbones while too many others were proving to be "Earthquake Christians."

DISCLAIMER

Almost all of the features described and/or photographed in this book can be seen from a motor vehicle, and do not require you to enter private property. Should you desire to investigate any of these features closer, where you must enter private property, you should obtain permission first.

THIS BOOK IN NO WAY GIVES ANYONE AUTHORITY TO TRESPASS.

We have encountered scores of landowners while researching for this book. We have yet to have our request to enter their property denied. This is all the more reason to stop, talk to these nice folks, and get their permission before entering their property. They will be very friendly and will volunteer many interesting historical details, greatly enriching your experiences. Visit with them awhile! You'll be glad you did!

THE NEW MADRID FAULT FINDERS GUIDE

BY

DR. RAY KNOX & DR. DAVID STEWART

TABLE OF CONTENTS

What People Say About This Book ii
Dedication & Disclaimer v
List of Maps, Photos, & Figures ix
Acknowledgements xi

INTRODUCTION   THE FUN OF FAULT FINDING   1

Nature is Generous to a Fault 1
What You See Depends on the Season 2
An Appetizer of What You Shall See 3
The Smell of Sulfur, the Taste of Wood 4
Talk to a Tree 5
A Help to Planners and Property Owners 5
Beneath This Highway Lies a Turbulent Past 6
High Speed Geology 7
A Trilogy of Books 7
Once a Fault Finder, Always a Fault Finder 9

CHAPTER ONE   SUMMARIZED HISTORY OF THE GREAT EARTHQUAKES   11

Precursory Events: Both Political and Natural 11
The Quakes Begin 12
The Modified Mercalli Scale 14
The Destruction of the Waterways 16
A National Event 16
Reading Nature's Handwriting For Yourself 16

CHAPTER TWO   HALF A BILLION YEARS IN FIVE MINUTES   19

Ancient Happenings in the "Basement" 19
The Big Rivers Take Over 26
The Mississippi River and the Ice Age 26
The Ohio River and Sikeston Ridge 29
The Mississippi River and Sikeston Ridge 29
The Wind Adds its Signature 32
Where the Mississippi River Has No Flood Plain 32
More Hot Air 33

CONTENTS CONT'D

CHAPTER THREE   RECOGNIZING SEISMIC LANDFORMS   35
  About Liquefaction   36
  Liquefaction from Light Earthquakes   38
  Calling Cards of the Big Quakes   39
  Most "Seismic" Landforms Are Really Hybrids   40
  What to Call These Things   40
  Morphoseismic Features in the New Madrid Seismic Zone   42
  Definitions and Descriptions   43
    Extrusive Sand Features   43
    Intrusive Sand Features   46
    Lateral Spread Features   46
    Differential Subsidence Features   49
    Uplift and Secondary Fault Features   52
    Slope Failure Features   57
    Historic Seismic Sites   59
    Pseudoseismic Landforms   60
  Destruction and Preservation of Earthquake Features   64

CHAPTER FOUR   THE MOST INCREDIBLE DAY ANY RIVER EVER EXPERIENCED   67
  The Cause: A Magnitude 8.8 Earthquake   67
  The Order of Events   68
  Effect #1:   Uplift of Tiptonville Horst   69
  Effect #2:   Subsidence of Reelfoot Basin   70
  Effect #3:   Violent Flooding in Missouri   71
  Effect #4:   Retrograde Motion of the River   72
  Effect #5:   Flooding in Kentucky and Tennessee   72
  Effect #6:   Waterfalls on the Mississippi   73
  The Possibility of Seiches   73

CHAPTER FIVE   INTERSTATE 55 FAULT FINDERS GUIDE   77
  How to Use This Guide   77
  Introduction to the I-55 Section   78
  The Benton Hills   78
  The Mississippi Alluvial Valley   79
  Sikeston Ridge   79
  Sand Dunes and Erosional Remnants of Sikeston Ridge   80
  I-55 Road Log   80
  Arkansas-Missouri State Line   94

CONTENTS CONT'D

CHAPTER SIX   **OVERVIEW OF FAULT FINDING SIDE TRIPS**   **99**

    Side Trip A: The New Madrid Loop   99
    Side Trip B: The Benton-Sikeston Loop   100
    Side Trip C: The Portageville-Point Pleasant Loop   100
    Side Trip D: The Boekerton-Hayti-Caruthersville Loop   100
    Side Trip E: The Caruthersville-Reelfoot Lake-Hickman Loop   101
    Side Trip F: The Steele-Blytheville-Big Lake Loop   101
    What to Do if a Big Quake Happens During Your Visit   101

CHAPTER SEVEN   Side Trip A: The New Madrid Loop   **105**

CHAPTER EIGHT   Side Trip B: The Benton-Sikeston Loop   **113**

CHAPTER NINE   Side Trip C: The Portagevillle-Point Pleasant Loop   **119**

CHAPTER TEN   Side Trip D: The Boekerton-Hayti-Caruthersville Loop   **123**

CHAPTER ELEVEN   Side Trip E: Caruthersville-Reelfoot Lake-Hickman Loop   **133**

CHAPTER TWELVE   Side Trip F: The Steele-Blytheville-Big Lake Loop   **141**

HOW YOU CAN BECOME A "CERTIFIED NEW MADRID FAULT FINDER"   **149**

Bibliography of Recommended References   151
Glossary   154
Index   164
Books, Slides & Other Items Available from Gutenberg-Richter Publications   171
Ordering & Shipping Information   176
The Exclusive GR Earthquake Hazard Warranty   177
Order Form   180

About the Authors   **178**
Your Fault Finding Certificate   (See Instructions on pages 149-150.)   **181**

LIST OF TABLES, PHOTOS, MAPS, & FIGURES

TABLES

Table 1.	The Modified Mercalli Scale of Earthquake Intensities	14
Table 2.	Morphoseismic Features in the New Madrid Seismic Zone	42
Table 3.	Primary & Secondary Effects of the 8.8 Event of February 7, 1812	68

PHOTOS, MAPS, & FIGURES

Figure 1.	Most Active Portion of the New Madrid Seismic Zone (NMSZ) Today	xii
Figure 2.	Map of Epicentral Locations of the Great New Madrid Earthquakes	10
Figure 3.	Intensity Map of the Great New Madrid Earthquakes of 1811-12	15
Figure 4.	What Trees Tell Us About the New Madrid Earthquakes	17
Figure 5.	Block Diagram of Present Configuration of the New Madrid Rift Complex	18
Figure 6.	Maps Showing Evolution of New Madrid Rift Complex	20
Figure 7.	Cross Sections Showing Evolution of New Madrid Rift Complex	21
Figure 8.	Shape and Configuration of the Continents 200 Million Years Ago	22
Figure 9.	The Plates of the Earth's Crust Today	23
Figure 10.	Map of the New Madrid Rift Complex Today	24
Figure 11.	Photos of Selected Faults in the New Madrid Rift Complex	25
Figure 12.	Map of North America Rivers Before the Ice Age	26
Figure 13.	Geologic Time Scale	27
Figure 14.	Terraces of Mississippi Now and Through the Ice Ages	28
Figure 15.	Physiographic Features Related to Course Changes of the Major Rivers	30
Figure 16.	Geologic Section of Missouri Bootheel	31
Figure 17.	How the Courses of the Mississippi & Ohio Rivers Have Changed	33
Figure 18.	Fuller's First Map of Seismic Features in the NMSZ—A.D. 1905	34
Figure 19.	Extrusive Sand Features	44
Figure 20.	Intrusive Sand Features	46
Figure 21.	Lateral Spread Features	48
Figure 22.	Types of Faults	54
Figure 23.	Map of Secondary Faults and Slope Failures in Reelfoot Lake Area	55
Figure 24.	Geologic Section and Topographic Profile of Chickasaw Bluffs	57
Figure 25.	Slope Failure Features	58
Figure 26.	Areal View of NMSZ Over Interstate 55 Between Cooter & Steele	61
Figure 27.	Chartreau Explosion Crater Before it Was Filled In	65

CONTINUED ON THE NEXT PAGE

TABLES, PHOTOS, MAPS, & FIGURES Cont'd

Figure 28.	New Madrid Bend in 1810 and in 1990	66
Figure 29.	Primary Effects: Uplift and Subsidence, Horst and Basin	70
Figure 30.	Secondary Effects: Waves, Retrograde Flow, Lakes & Falls	72
Figure 31.	Superposed Views of New Madrid Bend—1810, 1905, 1990	74
Figure 32.	New Madrid Area Today (c. 1995)	75
Figure 33.	Fault Finder's Map of Earthquake Alley (Interstate 55)	76
Figure 34.	Photos of Morphoseismic Features Visible from Interstate 55	96
Figure 35.	More Photos of Morphoseismic Features Visible from Interstate 55	97
Figure 36.	Fault Finding Side Trip Map	98
Figure 37.	Snapshot from Side Trip A	99
Figure 38.	Snapshot from Side Trip B	100
Figure 39	Snapshot from Side Trip C	100
Figure 40.	Snapshot from Side Trip D	100
Figure 41.	Snapshot from Side Trip E	101
Figure 42.	Snapshot from Side Trip F	101
Figure 43.	Aerial View of NMSZ Over the Bootheel Fault West of Steele, MO	103
Figure 44.	Map of Side Trip A	104
Figure 45.	Photos from Side Trip A	111
Figure 46.	Map of Side Trip B	112
Figure 47.	Photos from Side Trip B	117
Figure 48.	Map of Side Trip C	118
Figure 49.	Photos from Side Trip C	121
Figure 50.	Map of Side Trip D	122
Figure 51.	Satellite Image of the Boekerton Star	130
Figure 52.	Photos from Side Trip D	131
Figure 53.	Map of Side Trip E	132
Figure 54.	Photos of Side Trip E	139
Figure 55.	Map of Side Trip F	140
Figure 56.	Photos of Side Trip F	147
Figure 57.	More Photos of Side Trip F	148

Photos of Authors
Dr. Ray Knox	178
Dr. David Stewart	179

ACKNOWLEDGEMENTS

Many of the earthquake features described in this book would not have been discovered without the help of numerous friendly property owners. Few of these unique morpho-seismic landforms would have been mapped, described, and identified without the cooperation of those who own them. In six years of field research for this book, we never once encountered a landowner who was not cordial and helpful. If "Southern hospitality" is a reality anywhere, it is in the New Madrid Fault Zone. This, alone, makes it a place worth visiting.

During the six years it took to complete this book, many people provided encouragement, insight. and key information. Several students from the Geoscience Department at SEMO State University also traveled with us from time to time to assist in the field work and subsequent analysis. So many have helped us, it would truly be impossible to remember and acknowledge everyone. Some of those who helped are mentioned by name and acknowledged in the text of this book. We also wish to express our appreciation to the following for contributing information, aiding us in our research, providing encouragement, and for helping in other important ways:

The New Madrid Historical Museum: Virginia Carlson, past Museum Director; Glenda Hunter, immediate past Director; Dot Halstead, present Director; the Museum Board of Directors; Friends of the Museum; and everyone who works there whose dedication, cordiality and enthusiasm have always been an inspiration and kept us going.

The Center for Earthquake Studies at SEMO State University; Linda Dillman, Former Director; and Mark Winkler, Southeast Missouri Area Coordinator for the State Emergency Management Agency who have assisted in innumerable ways, including the locating of many facts and references.

We also want to thank Mike Aide, Faith Bailey, Lynn and Marian Bock, Riley Bock, John and Sue Bormuth, Iben Browning, Charles Carpenter, Dan Cicirello, Mike Coe, Katherine Cochran, Clement Cravens, Ed and Jacquelyn Close, Libba Crisler, Marshall Dial, Ann Elledge, Mark Ellerbusch, Bill Emerson, William B. Fowler, Arzine French, Don Froemsdorf, Evelyn Garris, Ruby German, Charles Hatley, Grant and Marcella Hedgpeth, Dave Hoffman, Tony and Pat Holmes, Brenna Holt, Angie Holzhouser, Andrew Jenkins, DeAnn Kincey, Norman Lambert, Fannie Langdon, Ed LaValle, Mark Meatte, Kim Myers, Bob Parkinson, John Peters, Shamsher Prakash, Leroy and Elaine Proctor, Scott Readnour, Don Rhodes, Robert Riley, Vonnie Snelling, Phyllis Steckel, J.K. Swilley, John Townsend, Dan and Joyce Webb, Ed Williams, and just about everybody living in and around New Madrid. Some of you may not have directly contributed to this book, but your encouragement and support during the six-year process of writing it has helped see it through.

And finally, we want to thank our wives, Karen Knox and Lee Stewart, for their input. Writing a book can be an all-consuming activity. We apologize for being distracted and inattentive at times and appreciate their patience and support.

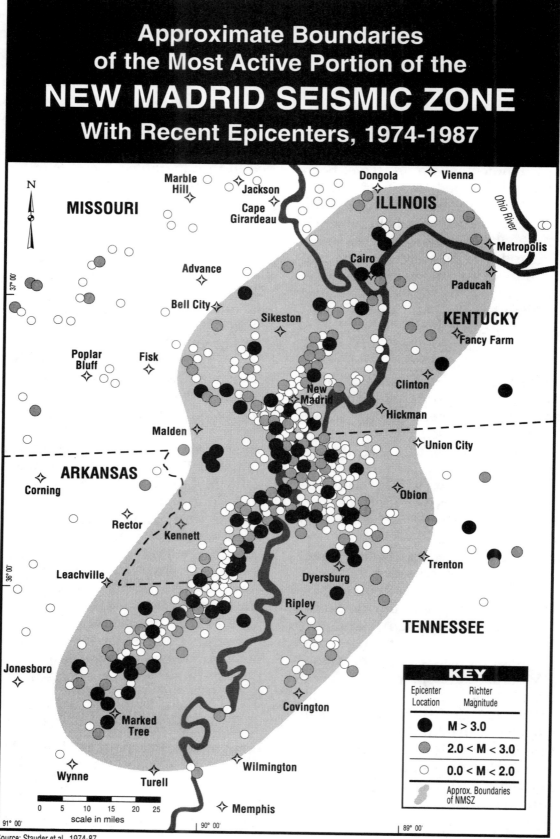

Approximate Boundaries of the Most Active Portion of the
NEW MADRID SEISMIC ZONE
With Recent Epicenters, 1974-1987

Source: Stauder et al., 1974-87

FIGURE 1

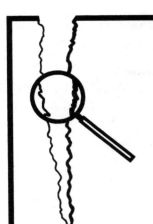

INTRODUCTION

THE FUN OF FAULT FINDING

Nothing like this book has ever been written on the New Madrid Fault Zone. This is it—the only set of self-guided earthquake fault field tours ever published for the Midwest. With maps, road logs, photos, and narrative notes, this book can bring you many days of fun and pleasure. While the book is carefully written to satisfy the rigor of the professional, it is meant for everyone with or without any background in the earth sciences. Professors and educators at all levels from high school, college and graduate studies, will find this book to be an excellent resource for a variety of class field trips. This book, and the others associated with it, could form the basis for an entire semester's course at the University level.

However, while this book can be used as an effective educational tool by teachers and students, it is really meant to bring enjoyment and appreciation to the public at large for one of nature's most dramatic displays. It is meant to be fun. "Laugh while you learn" is a maxim both of us have regularly used in our teaching.

Things you enjoy, things you smile and laugh about, things that seem crazy or zany, things that are pleasant or exciting—these are things you never forget. We think fun and humor are among the most effective educational devices ever employed. We have found that if students can relax and enjoy their education (instead of tensing up and dreading it), they learn far more with less effort and retain far more than they ever could have otherwise. So if we occasionally joke in our writings, that's just our teaching style. Don't let that detract from the solid foundation of science, fact, and field observation upon which our books are based.

Mother Nature Is Generous to a Fault

For a five month period beginning on December 16, 1811, more than 2,000 earthquakes originated from the New Madrid Seismic Zone. Five of them are thought to have been magnitude 8.0 or greater on the Richter scale. One was probably a magnitude

8.8—the largest in the history of the lower forty-eight states. These five months of almost continuous ground shaking represent the greatest outburst of seismic energy in American history. According to an article in *Scientific American*, March 1990, a survey of the great global seismic events of history does not reveal a series of earthquakes of such major magnitudes and duration anywhere else in the world for at least the last 2,000 years.

The purpose of this book is to enable you to visit the region and see for yourself some examples of the multitude of physical evidence still recognizable today. There are more than 5,000 square miles (3.2 million acres) of seismic features in the New Madrid Fault Zone. Nature has been generous.

Sand boils, explosion craters, secondary faults, earthquake lakes, seismic sand fissures, landslides, broken stream channels—this book will lead you to more than two dozen different kinds of morphoseismic features—landforms created or modified by earthquakes. These zits and blemishes on the face of the earth are the "faults" this book will guide you to find and recognize.

At the same time, we hope you will realize some of the human feelings those early pioneers must have experienced during these sudden and violent transformations of the earth.

Fault finding is for everyone. It is an affirmative action that can be enjoyed by all—without regard to sex, race, religion, handicap, date of birth, or national origin.

What You See Depends on the Season

When you visit the fault zone, don't expect to see everything described in this book during one trip. The visibility of these features varies from month to month, even from day to day. A sand boil or sand fissure that appears as an obvious mark in the land surface today may be virtually invisible next week. This is because they are not readily apparent unless they contrast in color with the soils adjacent to or around them. Maximum contrast for seeing a seismic sand feature occurs when they are bare and free of vegetation and when the sand is dry while the surrounding clay soils are still wet. Dry sand and dry clay are both light in color. Wet sand and wet clay are both dark in color. Sand dries out more quickly than clay or silty soil. Hence, there is a period of time following a rain when the sand is dry (and light in color) while the clay is still wet (and dark). In the summertime, this period of contrasting shades following a rain may last only a day or two. In the winter, it can last a week or more after a period of precipitation.

Vegetative cover is another factor that can make a seismic feature more visible or less, depending on circumstances. When crops first sprout after farmers have planted them, seismic sand features are almost impossible to see. However, when dry hot weather sets in during mid-summer, the crops over sandy areas wilt and become stunted. In this stage, seismic sand features become easily recognizable by the anomalies in plant growth. You will see circular bare patches in the middle of bean fields, or streaks of stunted stalks criss-crossing cotton fields.

During the fall, crops have been harvested, the fields are relatively bare, but the sand features usually develop a veneer of certain wilt-resistant weeds. Hence, at this stage one can recognize seismic features by the patches of light-covered grasses unique to sandy soils.

During winter, after farmers have disked and harrowed their land, many acres are completely bare. This is when seismic sand features become quite visible when soil moisture conditions are right.

As for landslides, they are harder to distinguish during summer months because of the thick foliage of trees and brush. Summer is also the time of maximum tick, chigger, and mosquito activity. The best time to see earthquake landslides is during the cooler months—October through April.

As for exploring and fishing the earthquake lake features (Reelfoot Lake and Big Lake), the warmer months of spring, summer and fall are the best. These lakes, and their abundance of water fowl, are also beautiful in the winter, too.

The earthquake museums at Reelfoot Lake and New Madrid are open the year round. The New Madrid Seismic Zone has something different to see and enjoy in every season. Consider a "Fault Finding Vacation" or a "Fault Finding Weekend." Consider taking such trips at different times of the year. A little time spent in the New Madrid Seismic Zone along with this and the other books mentioned and, who knows,

you could learn so much you would become "educated to a fault."

When you visit New Madrid, be sure to get an official "Fault Finder's T-Shirt" at the museum. You may also want to sample the peerless "Fault Finder's Wine," which can be purchased nowhere else in the world but in New Madrid, Missouri. Caution: **Fault Finder's wine is not to be shaken**.

An Appetizer
Of What You Shall See

You can take the tour two ways: (1) Vicariously, in your favorite armchair, via this book and the other two books of the trilogy; or (2) In reality, by an actual visit to the area. There are motels and campgrounds scattered in and around the New Madrid Fault Zone, so finding a place to stay is no problem.

If you visit in person you will see where New Madrid used to be—under the Mississippi River. You will see the site where the village of Little Prairie disappeared. You will drive over the stretch where terrified townspeople waded through waist–deep water on a cold winter day to escape the fate of their sinking village. You can walk over land that turned to quicksand during the quakes and feel, with your own feet, the soft and mushy texture of the soil in these places.

You can fall into an earthquake crevasse if you wish. During the long sequence of quakes the ground repeatedly cracked open into yawning fissures. The people's greatest fear was to fall into one of these during a tremor and be buried alive. A few did actually die this way. Some of these crevasses are still there. By using this guide you can find them and climb down into them, using your imagination to experience what it must have been like back then. You will walk across surface faults and step into explosion craters—visualizing the violence by which they were born.

You may find Indian artifacts in some of the bigger boils. These sand boils appear to have been present prior to 1811-12—the result of seismic liquefaction not only in 1811-12, but from previous episodes of major earthquake activity during centuries past. Native Americans seemed to prefer these sites for their villages. They have advantages. Because the boils came from below, flowing up through a vent from the water table, they are still connected with the groundwater and the permeable aquifers below. Hence, when heavy rains fall, the runoff soaks into the surface of a sand boil almost as rapidly as it hits the ground—draining through seismically formed vents into the underground. Hence, villages on sand boils were protected from runoff flooding. They were also free from the sticky clays that most other soils contain. The only problem is that during major earthquakes, such features can liquefy again, swallowing up whatever rests upon them.

Some of these sand features are so permeable and transmit surface water so readily into the ground they act as drains to the subsurface. Some farmers in the fault zone, in attempting to flood their fields with irrigation waters, have to build dikes around some earthquake features to prevent losing all of their irrigation water.

The Smell of Sulfur
The Taste of Wood

You will find coal, lignite, carbonized wood, black shale pieces, and petroliferous nodules in some of the fissures, blows and boils. You will smell sulfurous and carboniferous odors emitted by these natural substances when you "scratch and sniff."

You will visit sites of earthquake lakes and former earthquake lakes. These are large bodies of water formed by massive subsidence during deep areal liquefaction induced by the shaking. (Side Trips E & F) Of the dozen or more lakes formed in 1811-12, only two remain. The rest have been drained for agricultural purposes and mosquito control. (Side Trip B)

You may view the place where the Mississippi ran backwards and overlook the site of one of the temporary waterfalls where, perhaps, more than a hundred people drowned in 1812.

You will discover the world's largest sand boil: over a mile long and 136 acres in extent. It is an awesome breach in the landscape, even if you don't realize the dynamic upheavals that caused it. Having the appearance of a long desert strand, students have dubbed this feature "The Beach." (Side Trip D)

A Landmark for Thirty Miles

The towering 812-foot-tall smokestack at the Associated Electric Company can be considered as an approximate marker for the epicentral area of the greatest of the New Madrid earthquakes—the 8.8 event of February 7, 1812. It (or its plume) can be seen up to thirty miles away even from across the river in Tennessee and Kentucky. It can be clearly seen from the New Madrid Historical Museum and Observation Deck—six miles upstream. (Side Trip A)

One of the trips (Side Trip E) takes you across the river between Caruthersville, Missouri, and Dyersburg, Tennessee, where you will take I-155 and drive over the north flank of a massive landslide. From the top of this landslide you usually see the Associated Electric smokestack, epicenter of the quake that caused the landslide more than twenty miles away.

You can also see the smokestack from Reelfoot Lake and from Hickman, Kentucky. By orienting yourself to this outstanding landmark throughout your tours, you can gain a perspective on where the epicenter was that may have created the particular seismic feature you may be viewing at the time—even though several miles away.

Talk to a Tree

One of the favorite seismic sites you'll want to visit is the "Witness Tree." (Side Trip A) It is about seven miles northwest of New Madrid, near Kewanee, and within sight of the Associated smokestack some twelve miles to the south. The tree is a southern red oak (Quercus falcata) and is five feet in diameter at chest height. It is a 300-year-old Senior Citizen today. That means it was about 120 years old at the time of the earthquakes. Since southern red oaks are considered to have reached

maturity at age 120, it had just passed through arboreal puberty a decade or two before the tremors. We don't know if it is a southern gentleman or a southern belle, but imagine this tall tree, having just survived adolescence, when its tranquil existence was suddenly interrupted by the tumult of the New Madrid earthquakes—trapping it in a huge 200-foot-diameter sand boil. Its massive trunk leans slightly to the south—probably tilted when the soil turned to quicksand and seethed through its roots. Its bent branches, like giant biceps and forearms gesture grotesquely, as if to say, "Look what the earthquakes did to me." If only it could talk, what tales it would tell. Perhaps, if you stand by quietly and attentively, it will commune with you—whispering its secrets in silence.

A Help to Planners and Property Owners

While the contents of this, and our other books, are of interest in and of themselves, there is also much practical information here, too. Seismic sand boils, sand fissures, earthquake-induced landslides, and explosion sand blow craters are dynamic features. They were formed by past earthquakes, but will become active again in future quakes—causing major damage to structures that reside upon them. Some are also hydrologically active when water tables and river levels are high. Hence, being able to identify such features and avoid building on them could save you a lot of trouble and money.

Before this trilogy of books there were no published guides generally available by which to recognize morphoseismic features. Because of this, many buildings and structures, not only here but around the world, have unknowingly been built on unstable ground when it could have been avoided. To this point, even professional geologists, seismologists, architects and civil engineers have virtually no training in how to recognize such features. Morphoseismology is on the frontier of new knowledge. It hasn't yet made the textbooks. Being able to identify seismic landforms is essential if one wants to avoid problems with a building or structure later on. Realizing the nature of such a site in advance means that it can either be avoided or modified to reduce the hazard.

For example, the Sikeston Power Plant, which you will see on one of the tours, was unknowingly built across a huge earthquake sand fissure. At the time it was built, the science of morphoseismology did not exist. The civil engineers surveying the land for that plant did not know what that long strip of sand meant. (Side Trip B)

In Malden, an electric substation was built over a sand boil. The price of the real estate was cheap because the farmer couldn't farm it anyhow. But the real price in siting that substation may not come fully due until the next major earthquake. If the substation had only moved over 100 feet, it could have avoided that potentially liquefiable feature.

In December of 1991 a 700-foot-high cable TV transmitting tower was erected over a large explosion sand blow crater near Matthews, Missouri. You will see it on the Interstate 55 "Earthquake Alley" tour. This tower is visible for twenty miles and exerts a downward force of 300,000 pounds at its base resting on a concrete pad only two feet thick and fourteen feet square. An earthquake or even a sustained high river stage could cause this area to become temporary quicksand again.

No one would deliberately build on such features if they understood what they were. We hope that this, and our other two books, will help prevent such mistakes in the future.

Beneath This Highway Lies a Turbulent Past

The central core of this travel guide is a 101-mile strip of Interstate 55 from Exit 53 south of Blytheville, Arkansas, to Milepost 84 near Benton, Missouri. Millions of people pass through this corridor every year, but how many realize the drama preserved in the earth over which they pass? Who feels the history and senses the presence of the people of the past, both native and immigrant, who lived there during the great upheavals? Beneath that ribbon of concrete lies a story. Peaceful farm and forest that are calm and stable today were once a chaos of motion—waving, writhing, churning, jerking, spewing, splitting, splintering, boiling, heaving, hissing, rumbling, sinking, shifting, twisting, tossing, tumbling in turmoil from grinding faults wrenching the bedrocks miles below ground.

This book will take you on an intellectual oddessy, and an emotional and aesthetic one as well. You will gain a new appreciation of just how special this piece of the earth's crust really is. It is the greatest outdoor earthquake laboratory in the world. It is the world's premier collection of liquefaction, landslide and lateral spreading features. Scientists, engineers and visitors have come to visit this place from all over the world to explore its vast uniqueness. There is not another place known like it anywhere on this planet. And it has only been partially explored.

Countless fascinating discoveries remain to be found. Perhaps you will find some of them. So many interesting studies could be done, there is a master's thesis in every square mile and there are thousands of square miles to study. When we repeatedly went to the field to map the features of this book, we almost never made a trip without making another new, exciting discovery, heretofore unknown to us and to others. Even after six years of field work, we are still making new and exciting discoveries. So consider yourself an explorer as you probe into these partially charted territories.

High Speed Geology

This book presents only a small sample of what is to be found in the New Madrid Seismic Zone. You can take this book and spend an hour or two or you could spend days. If all you do is to drive the 101-mile "Earthquake Alley" along Interstate 55 at 65 miles per hour without stopping, you can see plenty if you know what to look for. You could become a "Mile-A-Minute Geologist," but please drive safely. Be considerate to both yourself, to your passengers, and to other travelers on the road.

When you slow down, pull over. When you pull back onto the road, please be careful. The greatest danger in the New Madrid Fault Zone is not earthquakes. It is traffic accidents.

If you aren't in a hurry, stop at some of the mile markers and take a photo or two. Take a side trip to Big Lake or Reelfoot Lake. Visit Sikeston, Caruthersville or Dry Bayou Baptist Church.

There used to be a ferry across the Mississippi between Hickman, Kentucky, and Dorena, Missouri—not far from New Madrid. If it is running, take it. There is no better way to gain an appreciation of the size, the wild, untameable power, and swiftness of the river than to cross it within inches of the swells and wave crests that heave and ripple across its breast—like the muscles of a weightlifter.

A Trilogy of Books

This book is one of a set of three works by the same authors—all concerning the New Madrid earthquakes of 1811-12 and the associated fault zone.

The title of the first book is *The Earthquake America Forgot, 2,000 Temblors in Five Months . . . And It Will Happen Again*. It is the most complete history of the New Madrid earthquakes ever written. It also presents the human side of these epic events. If you are fascinated by the historical, social, religious, Native American, and political events of the time of these earthquakes, you will love this book. Adventure, romance, politics, religion, Indians, pirates, steamboats, slavery, racial prejudice, murder, suicide, war, peace, science, superstition, treachery and tragedy, heroes and villains, even sex scandal—all these themes are played out in historical fact against the backdrop of the great New Madrid earthquakes of 1811-12. You would also be interested to learn of the famous people associated with these earthquakes: John James Audubon, Daniel Boone, William Clark, Jefferson Davis, Robert Fulton, Thomas Jefferson, Meriwether Lewis, Abraham Lincoln, Dolly Madison, Nicholas Roosevelt, William Henry Harrison, and the great Shawnee Chief and Prophet—Tecumseh. More than 100 anecdotes spice the pages of this work. Historically accurate and scientifically correct, *The Earthquake America Forgot* reads like a novel.

The second volume of the set is entitled *The Earthquake that Never Went Away . . . The Shaking Stopped in 1812, but the Impact Goes On*. This book addresses the fact that 200 years after these great earthquakes, the landscape still bears countless visible scars from the trauma. And what's more, these morphoseismic landforms are not all passive. Old earthquake landslides still creep—breaking apart highways and buildings. Old sand boils can still turn to quicksand when water tables are rising—the bane of farmers who have many times gotten their tractors stuck in these features. Old seismic liquefaction features under modern railroad tracks can be induced to liquefy again by the mere vibrations of a passing train—resulting in derail-

ments throughout the seismic zone. Old explosion sand blows act as conduits between surface and groundwaters—sometimes making it impossible to flood a rice crop or to get irrigation ditches to flow across a field.

Imagine! Modern streets and houses breaking apart, farm equipment sinking into quicksand, trains being derailed, irrigation waters being lost into the ground—all happening today because of an earthquake that happened 200 years ago. That's why we call it "*The Earthquake that Never Went Away*." This book contains 150 photos and figures, a vicarious visual tour viewed from both ground and air—a perfect adjunct to the self-guided field tours of *Fault Finders Guide*.

While the first book emphasizes the historical and human aspects of the earthquakes, the second book of the trilogy, *The Earthquake America Forgot*, emphasizes the geotechnical. Both, however, were written for the general public. *The Earthquake that Never Went Away* contains a glossary, like this book does. It makes an excellent college text for studying the way earthquakes sculpture the landscape. The photos, figures, maps, tables and classification of morphoseismic features presented here are not found in any other publication. While the book is published in black and white, there is a magnificent set of 150 colored slides also available corresponding to each of the 150 photos and illustrations in the book. An excellent classroom resource.

The third book of the trilogy, of course, is this one, *The New Madrid Fault Finders Guide*, which focuses on providing a detailed set of field guides for those who actually want to visit the region and see these astonishing landforms for themselves. To fully appreciate and make the most use of this guide, you really need to be familiar with the other two books as well. Together they form a complete package on the fault—its history, its current seismicity, and its potential for future major earthquakes.

All three of the aforementioned books and the slide set are available from Gutenberg-Richter Publications, as well as several other books on the New Madrid earthquakes and fault zone. Turn to the back for more details. An opportunity is provided to obtain a "Complete New Madrid Earthquake Library" at a special discount price. Make your purchase before the next major earthquake in your area and receive the special "Pre-Earthquake Sale Price!" Everything has a money-back guarantee and, of course, all purchases from Gutenberg-Richter Publications carry the "Exclusive Earthquake Hazard Warranty." Any Gutenberg-Richter product damaged in an earthquake will be replaced free of charge.

See the pages at the end of this book for details of where and how to order these publications, as well as information on special discounts, guarantees, and warranties.

Also see the end of this book for information on how you can become a "Certified Fault Finder." It's a real certificate that you'll surely want to hang on your office or living room wall. No doubt, it will also be an item you will want to include in your *Curriculum Vitae*. Most employers already have a plethora of "fault finders" on their staff, but few have a real, genuine, bona fide *Certified Fault Finder* validated for advanced levels of fault finding. You could be the first.

Once a Fault Finder, Always a Fault Finder

One thing is certain. After reading even a portion of any one of these three books, the landscape in this area will never look the same to you again. When passing through by land, air, or water you will notice things you never noticed before—even if you have lived a lifetime in the region. And things you had noticed before will look different.

Your perspective on the landscape will have been permanently changed—sensitized and made more appreciative to subtle detail. It will be like viewing the world through a new set of glasses. Your vision will have been sharpened and expanded.

Whatever the case, we hope this book will help make all your visits to or through the New Madrid Seismic Zone more interesting and enjoyable—be they vicarious or real. With this book, you can do either or both.

Happy Fault Finding.

Burnal Ray Knox,
Cape Girardeau, MO

David Mack Stewart
Marble Hill, MO

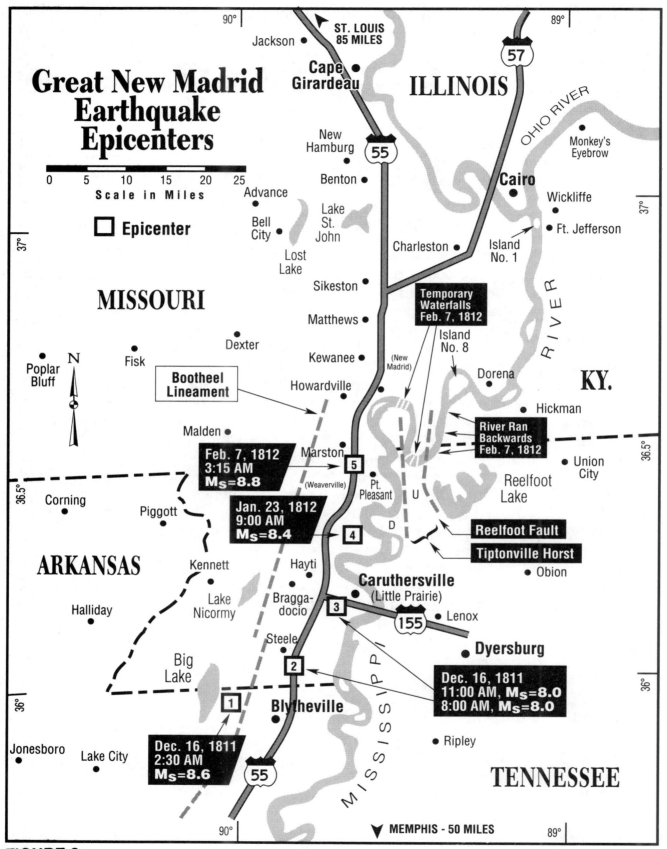

Great New Madrid Earthquake Epicenters

Scale in Miles
0 5 10 15 20 25

☐ Epicenter

ST. LOUIS 85 MILES

Jackson ●

Cape Girardeau ●

New Hamburg ●

Benton ●

Advance ●

Bell City ●

Lake St. John

Lost Lake

MISSOURI

Dexter ●

Fisk ●

Poplar Bluff ●

N

Malden ●

Booteel Lineament

Corning ●

Piggott ●

ARKANSAS

Kennett ●

Halliday ●

Lake Nicormy

Big Lake

Jonesboro ●

Lake City ●

ILLINOIS

OHIO RIVER

57

55

Cairo

Wickliffe ●

Ft. Jefferson ●

Monkey's Eyebrow ●

Charleston ●

Island No. 1

Sikeston ●

Matthews ●

Kewanee ●

Howardville ●

(New Madrid)

Temporary Waterfalls Feb. 7, 1812

Island No. 8

Dorena ●

KY.

Hickman ●

River Ran Backwards Feb. 7, 1812

Union City ●

Reelfoot Lake

Reelfoot Fault

Tiptonville Horst

Obion ●

Marston ●

5

(Weaverville)

Feb. 7, 1812 3:15 AM $M_S=8.8$

Jan. 23, 1812 9:00 AM $M_S=8.4$

4

Pt. Pleasant

U

D

Hayti ●

Bragga-docio ●

Steele ●

1

Blytheville ●

Dec. 16, 1811 2:30 AM $M_S=8.6$

Caruthersville (Little Prairie)

3

155

Lenox ●

Dyersburg

Dec. 16, 1811 11:00 AM, $M_S=8.0$ 8:00 AM, $M_S=8.0$

Ripley ●

2

MISSISSIPPI

55

▼ MEMPHIS - 50 MILES

TENNESSEE

FIGURE 2

CHAPTER ONE
SUMMARIZED HISTORY OF THE GREAT EARTHQUAKES

The winter of 1811-12 was not your average humdrum winter! If someone had been able to keep a complete journal of the geologic and historic events that occurred in that few months beginning in mid-December, and the manuscript of that account had somehow gotten misplaced into a proposed publishers fiction file, that manuscript would probably have been rejected as being just too fanciful for good fiction. And no wonder!

Earthquake seismologists call it the greatest release of seismic energy in so short a time ever witnessed and recorded by human beings. A few individual earthquakes have been bigger. In a few instances perhaps they have been more numerous within a short span. But never so many that were so big in so short a time.

Consider how unusual the New Madrid Earthquakes were. A Richter ground magnitude 8 earthquake is quite rare. In fact, of the tens of thousands of earthquakes that occur on our planet each year, only one will be that large in an average year. Often, two or three years pass without a single earthquake that strong anywhere. But 1811 and 1812 were not average years!

Precursory Events
Both Political and Natural

On March 26, 1811, a comet appeared. It was quite visible almost anywhere in the northern hemisphere on both sides of the Atlantic. It had two tails. Many folks saw this as a bad omen. It streaked across the sky for more than a year attaining its greatest brilliance during the months of the earthquakes.

There was also a total eclipse of the sun on September 17, 1811. It was visible throughout the midsection of the states—painting its dark shadowy path right across the region of the New Madrid Fault Zone like a giant finger marking the spot for some future cataclysm soon to come. The eclipse, combined with the appearance of the comet, prompted many to prophecy imminent doom and destruction.

And there were wars and rumors of wars in almost every part of the globe. There was a lot of "cussedness" going on in the United States and adjacent territories too. The British and the French and the Spanish were having their nasty conflicts. Many Indians participated in some of these skirmishes, sometimes aided by the British, more often on their own.

Slavery, with whites lording over blacks, was an ugly fact of life in most of the new states of the nation. Slaves were even being "bred" in our nation to help supply the demand, as the African slave traffic was winding down.

There were also movements afoot by some of the leaders of the Indians to organize a united resistance to the western movement of the European-Americans. The story of the great Shawnee leader Tecumseh and his brother, Tenskwatawa, is a fascinating one in the context of this point in history—including their role in the earthquakes.

All in all, it appeared that Satan was having a good time testing our new nation. The evangelists of the day certainly had their work cut out. But the people living in the midcontinent area hadn't seen anything yet!

The Quakes Begin

Starting in mid-December of 1811, and continuing through the spring of 1812, there were hundreds of earthquakes generated from the New Madrid Fault—any one of which would make front-page news today. At least three of these, and probably five, had surface wave magnitudes 8.0 or higher. Five more were 7.7's. Ten were 6.7's. Thirty-five were in the range of 5.9. Sixty-five were estimat-

ed at 5.3, eighty-nine at 4.3, and 1800 or more in the 3.0-4.3 range.

Pack all these into a three or four month period and it is easy to understand the eyewitnesses comments about "almost continuous" ground shaking. If they were averaged out over, say, four months, then there would need to be sixteen earthquakes every day—two every three hours! But they weren't averaged out. In some weeks, earthquakes occurred more frequently than this.

The great series of earthquakes started at the unholy hour of 2:30 A.M., December 16, 1811. It was a new moon, and the bright stars contrasted with the coal-black background of sky. There was no warning at all. A few miles west of the present site of Blytheville, Arkansas, and a few miles below ground, the New Madrid fault violently shifted, rocks on the west side moving north, on the east side moving south—relative to each other. This was followed at 8:00 A.M. by another large shift, this time under the vicinity of the present sites of Steele and Cooter, Missouri. Then around 11:00 A.M., beneath the present site of Caruthersville, the rocks shifted again.

The three great jolts of December 16, Richter surface wave magnitudes of 8.6, 8.0, and 8.0, ruptured the entire southern segment of the New Madrid fault, totalling some 90 miles. Each episode of slipping eased the pressure along that particular part of the fault, but shifted some of this pressure further northward, overstressing that zone even more. How long would these now overloaded areas further north hold?

Big Lake, a few miles west of present-day Blytheville, (see Side Trip F) was formed by the first quake of this triple-header. Already wet and low, it included the flood plain of the Little River. A good deal of the saturated sand below the area liquefied, and differentially settling material over the liquefied zone created the basin. Water from the Little River, and from ejected sand features all over the area, drained into and soon filled the basin.

The town of Little Prairie was lost during this time. It was shaken and subsided so badly, and there was so much water from ejected sand, that its terrified citizens had to flee for their lives. (See Side Trip D).

The New Madrid fault "held" only about five weeks before another really big earthquake occurred. The next segment of the fault, involving an estimated 45 miles, was ruptured. This one, an estimated 8.4 surface magnitude, hit around 8:00 A.M. on January 23, 1812, centered underneath a point about half way between present day Caruthersville and present day Point Pleasant. The original Point Pleasant, five miles southeast of today's town of the same name, was lost in this one. Fortunately, the residents of Point Pleasant had all fled shortly after the quakes began in December. The town was perched on a point of land that projected into the Mississippi River. During the shock of January 23rd, the whole point collapsed, town and all, crashing into the river, swept away without a trace. The Mississippi River has migrated to the west more than a mile since then, placing the location of the original site of Point Pleasant now on the Tennessee side.

But the granddaddy quake of them all happened about two weeks later. At 3:15 A.M. on February 7, 1812, a surface magnitude 8.8 earthquake occurred. It is thought to have originated in a region between Boekerton and New Madrid, Missouri, although its exact location is still a matter for research.

The truth is that a considerable length of fault would have had to rupture to produce an earthquake that large. The epicentral region of such a giant earthquake would be enormous—perhaps as big as a whole county. The energy released on February 7, 1812, was equal to more than 8,000 atomic bombs. To produce that much force the fault would have to rip through many miles of bedrock. Hence, the epicentral region for this quake is probably an elliptical area at least 25 miles long and 10 miles wide with its long axis extending from New Madrid to the vicinity of Boekerton with Marston near the center. Thus, Marston and St. Jude Industrial Park serve as a convenient marker for the epicentral region of the largest earthquake in American history.

According to Nuttli (1990) the megaquake of February 7, 1812, caused 60 miles of the New Madrid fault to rupture. It produced the most dramatic events of the entire series of earthquakes. This is the one that caused waterfalls on the Mississippi, and made the river run backwards. This is the quake that resulted in the destruction of thousands of acres of mature forest, and the creation of Reelfoot Lake. It was the violence of the Mississippi River—the rapids, the falls, the caving banks, the near-

Table 1. The Modified Mercalli Scale of Earthquake Intensities

Intensity Value	Description Of Damages & Effects
I.	Not felt. Recorded only by instruments. Some marginal and long period effects for large earthquakes.
II.	Felt by persons at rest, on upper floors, or favorably placed.
III.	Felt indoors. Hanging objects swing. Vibration like passing of light trucks. Duration estimated. May not be recognized as an earthquake.
IV.	Hanging objects swing. Vibration like passing of heavy trucks; or sensation of a jolt like a heavy ball striking the walls. Standing cars rock. Windows, dishes, doors rattle. Glasses clink. Crockery clashes. In the upper range of level IV, wooden walls and building frames creak.
V.	Felt outdoors; direction estimated. Sleepers awakened. Liquids disturbed, some spilled. Small unstable objects displaced or upset. Doors swing, close, open. Shutters, pictures move. Pendulum clocks stop, start, change rate.
VI.	Felt by all. many frightened and run outdoors. Persons walk unsteadily. Windows, dishes, glassware broken. Knickknacks, books, etc., off shelves. Pictures off walls. Furniture moved or overturned. Weak plaster and masonry D cracked. Small bells ring (church, school). Trees, bushes shaken visibly, or heard to rustle.
VII.	Difficult to stand. Noticed by drivers. Hanging objects quiver. Furniture broken. Damage to masonry D, including cracks. Weak chimneys broken at roof line. Fall of plaster, loose bricks, stones, tiles, cornices, also unbraced parapets and architectural ornaments. Some cracks in masonry C. Waves on ponds, water turbid with mud. Small slides and caving in along sand or gravel banks. Large bells ring. Concrete irrigation ditches damaged.
VIII.	Steering of cars affected. Damage to masonry C; partial collapse. Some damage to masonry B; none to masonry A. Fall of stucco and some masonry walls. Twisting, fall of chimneys, factory stacks, monuments, towers, elevated tanks. Frame houses moved on foundations if not bolted down; loose panel walls thrown out. Decayed piling broken off. Branches broken from trees. Changes in flow or temperature of springs and wells. Cracks in wet ground and on steep slopes.
IX.	General panic. Masonry D destroyed; masonry C heavily damaged, sometimes with complete collapse; masonry B seriously damaged. General damage to foundations. Frame structures, if not bolted, shifted off foundations. Frames racked. Serious damage to reservoirs. Underground pipes broken. Conspicuous cracks in ground. In alluviated areas, sand and mud ejected, earthquake fountains, sand craters.
X.	Most masonry and frame structures destroyed with their foundations. Some well-built wooden structures and bridges destroyed. Serious damage to dams, dikes, levees, embankments. Large landslides. Water thrown on banks of canals, rivers, lakes, etc. Sand and mud shifted horizontally on beaches and flat land. Rails bent slightly.
XI.	Rails bent greatly. Underground pipelines completely out of service.
XII.	Damage nearly total. Large rock masses displaced. Lines of sight and level distorted. Objects thrown into the air.

Definitions of Masonry Quality: Stone, Brick, Tile, or Concrete Block

Masonry A. Good workmanship, mortar, and design; reinforced, especially laterally, and bound together by using steel, concrete, etc.; designed to resist horizontal forces.

Masonry B. Good workmanship and mortar; reinforced, but not designed in detail to resist horizontal forces.

Masonry C. Ordinary workmanship and mortar; no extreme weaknesses like failing to tie in at corners, but neither reinforced nor designed against horizontal forces.

Masonry D. Weak materials, such as adobe; poor mortar; low standards of workmanship; weak horizontally.

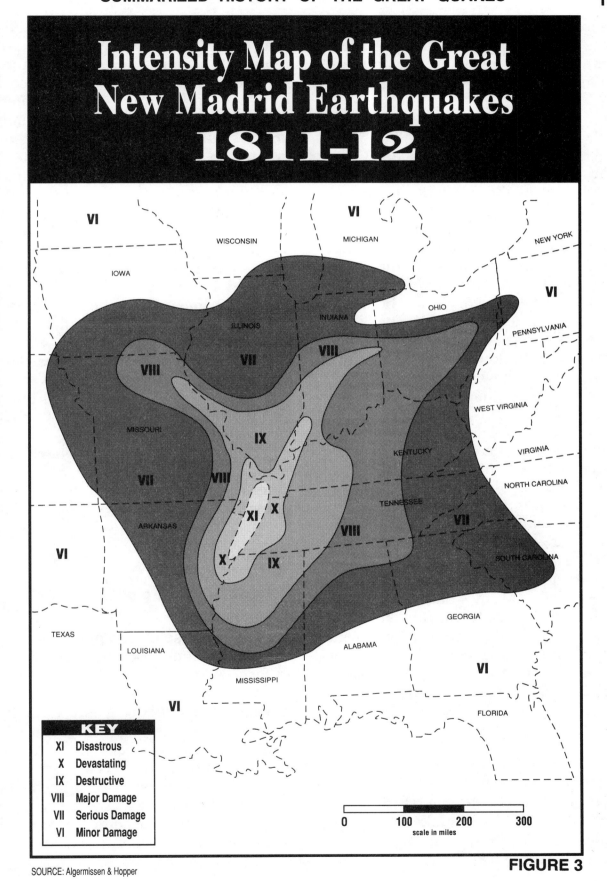

Intensity Map of the Great New Madrid Earthquakes 1811-12

KEY

XI	Disastrous
X	Devastating
IX	Destructive
VIII	Major Damage
VII	Serious Damage
VI	Minor Damage

scale in miles
0   100   200   300

SOURCE: Algermissen & Hopper

FIGURE 3

shore flooding, log jams and the hazards of thousands of floating trees that caused most of the human deaths from these earthquakes.

The Destruction of the Waterways

But the Mississippi wasn't the only stream drastically affected and permanently altered by these quakes. Land that was raised a few feet, or sunk a few feet, completely fouled up the drainage of the area. Land that had been dry became swamp while land that had once cradled ponds and lakes became dry, their bodies of water heaved up and emptied out. Stream channels that once flowed freely were broken up into discontinuous pieces, never to flow again. No longer could canoes and keelboats navigate from the Mississippi to the Little River and St. Francis or vice versa. Before the quakes, there were at least four connections where this was done, criss-crossing the Bootheel with commercial boat traffic.

Practically every stream in the entire area was altered, not just the Mississippi. In a great many cases, stream gradients were increased or decreased. Many channels were closed by laterally moving slabs or flows of bank material, or by violent explosions of sand, water, and air, or by sand boils that quietly piled sand up, sometimes damming the streams.

A National Event

Do not think of the New Madrid earthquakes as occurring only close to that town. The late Dr. Otto Nuttli, the esteemed earthquake seismologist from whom the magnitudes cited above were determined, estimates that 800,000 square miles (more than half a billion acres) of territory experienced Mercalli intensity effects rated VI or greater. An estimated 100,000 square miles (64 million acres) suffered intensity VIII or greater. In the epicentral zone, intensities were X, XI and XII—the maximums for which the scale is defined. (For definitions of Mercalli intensities see Table 1 and Figure 3 on pages 14-15.) Eighteen of the quakes were felt as far away as Washington, D.C., and did minor damage there, more than 800 miles from the epicenters. These quakes were felt from Mexico to Canada, from the Rocky Mountains to the Island of Cuba. The great New Madrid earthquakes were felt by every man, woman and child living in the Unites States at that time. It was a national event.

There has been no such earthquake in American history before or since. But it will happen again. The subject of future quakes, however, is covered in one of the other books of this trilogy.

Reading Nature's Handwriting For Yourself

The purpose of this publication is to take you back to 1811-12 in a face-to-face encounter with the land and the vegetation to see for yourself the physical evidence of what actually happened so long ago. The story is written in the hillsides and in the soils and also in the trees. There are many living witnesses who speak to us in their own way. Countless trees were killed by the quakes and in some places their shattered stumps remain to this day—mute, yet eloquent testimony to the terrors that took their lives.

Some oaks and cypress survived the quakes and still stand today. Some are giants permanently warped by traumatic experiences of earthquakes in their childhood and youth. Others have been dwarfed, injured for life, submerged in waters too deep to flourish, yet they still survive. Amazingly they have come through the centuries to beckon to us, and demonstrate their tenacity for life.

Even young trees, current crops, and recent vegetation growing on old seismic features can talk to us, sharing insights as to the nature and origin of the soils and slopes that clasp their feet.

No book made by man can capture what nature has written for herself. To comprehend the past, present and future of the New Madrid Fault Zone, one must go there and learn to read directly from nature's pages as inscribed in her mother tongue. This book will help you do that. When you see nature's own handwriting on the face of the land and comprehend what she is saying to you—then you will know, first-hand, a little of what happened in 1811-12. Realizing the past is the first step toward forecasting the future and preparing for what will come.

FIGURE 4. What Trees Tell Us About the New Madrid Earthquakes. These huge stumps on the banks of the Mississippi are what's left of some trees that were alive before the earthquakes. (Note the boat on the left.) Their splintered tops tell us of the violence by which they were broken in February of 1812. (See Chapter 4.) This virgin stand of vertical cypress by Dry Bayou Baptist Church all sprouted since 1812. They tell us that the bayou in which they stand was created at the time of the quakes. (See p. 126, Trip D.) This row of dwarfed cypress in deep water tell us that they once lined a small stream before the quakes drowned them in Reelfoot Lake. (See p. 135, Trip E.) The Bait Shop in Hickman, Kentucky, sits on an earthquake landslide from 1811-12. Notice how the street has pulled away from the curb and the trees beside the shop all lean downslope to the left. That tells us that the slide is unstable and slowly creeping. In the 1980's the hill behind broke loose, shoved in the back wall, and filled the building with mud. It was then shoveled out and reoccupied. As of 1995, it was still in business. (See p. 138, Side Trip D.)

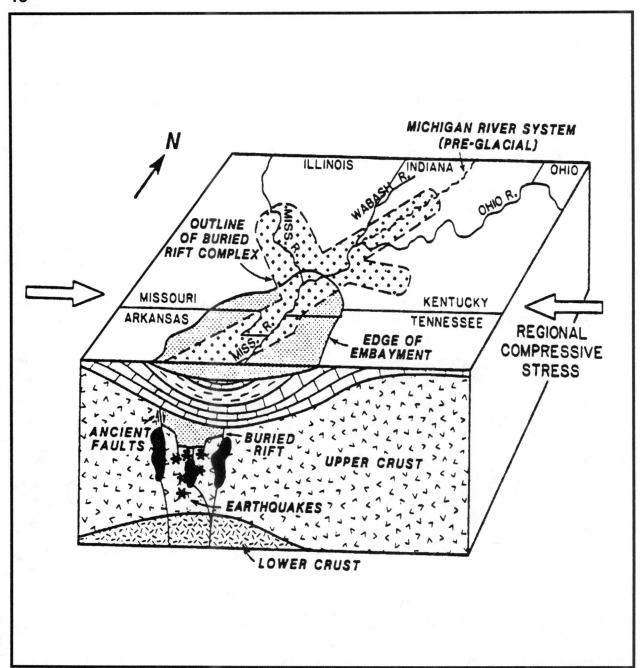

FIGURE 5. Block Diagram Showing Present Configuration of the New Madrid Rift Complex. The structurally controlled rivers, Paleozoic rocks in cratonic sedimentary basins, and the Mississippi Embayment, all associated with the buried rift complex, are also shown. Dark areas indicate intrusions of magma near the edge of the buried rift. An uplifted and possibly anomalously dense lower crust is suggested as the cause of the linear positive gravity anomaly associated with the upper Mississippi Embayment. (After Braile, et al., 1984.) Also see Figures 6 and 7 as they relate to this diagram.

CHAPTER TWO

HALF A BILLION YEARS IN FIVE MINUTES

Some fault finders may wonder why the New Madrid Seismic Zone is so unique and how it came about. If you are **not** one of these, then you may skip this chapter without becoming a failure as a human being. But if this whets your curiosity, then this chapter is for you. We have tried not to get too technical, but not too simplistic either. As the chapter title suggests, we must fly low and fast. We're trying to condense a semester's geology into a few minutes of reading time for you. So, fasten your safety belts! Here we go!

Ancient Happenings In the "Basement"

Long before there was any life on land anywhere, geologic forces and processes were already at work. The rocks that make up the earth's crust have been (and continue to be) subjected to tremendous pressures, not just from above or below, but from the sides also. The strongest of these pressures comes from great 100-mile-thick slabs of rock (**called tectonic plates**) moving sideways, sometimes banging into each other,

sometimes diving beneath each other, and sometimes just crunching the edges of both slabs. 200 million years ago, the plates of the earth were all stuck together in one great continent called **"Pangaea."** (See Figures 8-9.) We are talking about solids here, not liquids. On the scale of geologic time (Figure 13), however, solids can behave like very slow-motion liquids! Ocean basins, mountain ranges, and major faults are formed when tectonic plates collide.

The scientific theory that puts all this together was once called **continental drift**, but is now more appropriately called **plate tectonics**. This is because we once thought that the continents **were** the **plates**, but now we know that most plates are both part continental crust and part oceanic crust. At any place on earth's surface, at times, pressures (stresses) have been tensional, attempting to pull the crust apart. At other times, they have been compressional, attempting to push slabs toward each other, or make one move beneath the other. If you still think "solid" rock is something permanent and immovable, forget it!

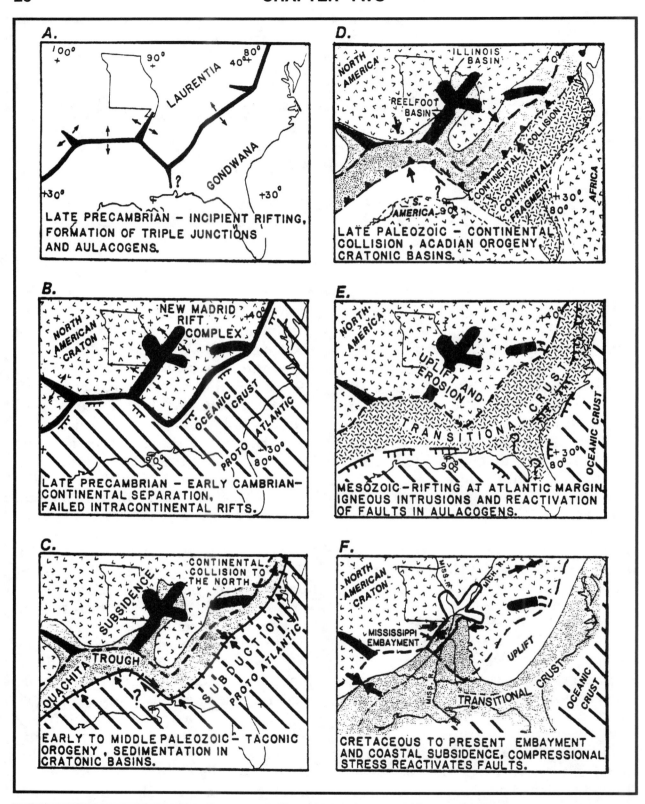

FIGURE 6. Schematic Maps Showing Evolution of New Madrid Rift Complex. See next page for discussion. (Figures 6 & 7 both after Braile, et al., 1984.)

FIGURE 7. Schematic Cross Sections Showing Evolution of New Madrid Rift Complex.

The sectional sketches of Figure 7 show stages of geologic development for the New Madrid Rift Complex in parts A through F which relate to the map views A through F of Figure 6 on the previous page. The orientation of the cross sections is approximately northeast-southwest.

Figure 6 shows plate reconstruction of the North american Craton. Interactions with adjacent plates are indicated. The New Madrid Rift Complex has evolved over at least the last 600 million years.

The maps of Figure 6 are meant to be studied with the sections of Figure 7 shown to the right. The outline of the state of Missouri is shown for location and approximate scale.

Terms like "Precambrian," "Paleozoic," and "Mesozoic" are eras of geologic time. A geologic time scale defining these terms is given by Figure 13, page 27.

Map F and Section F correspond to the block diagram of Figure 5 on page 18.

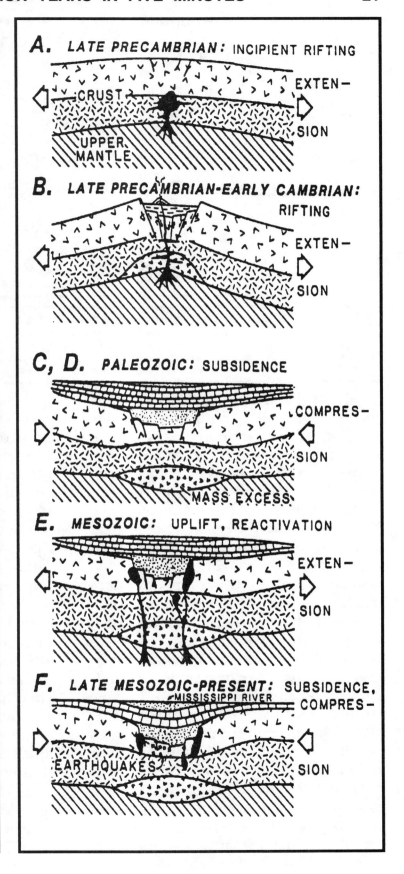

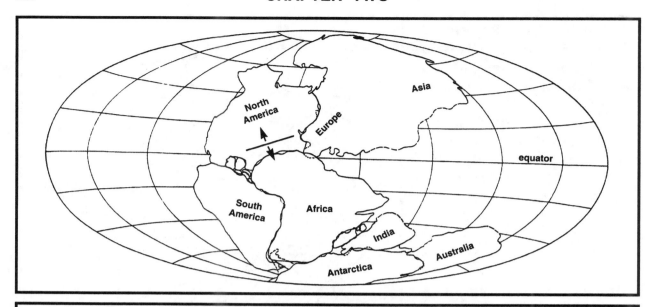

FIGURE 8. Shape and Configuration of the Continents 200 Million Years Ago. All of the continents were once joined into one great land mass called Pangaea. Global forces in the early Mesozoic (Age of Dinosaurs) tried to split Pangaea along the zone identified today as the New Madrid Rift Complex which actually stretched from present-day Louisiana to Canada along the St. Lawrence Seaway. The Rift Zone is shown in tension, as it was then, as a line with arrows on the map above.   (After Deitz & Holden, *Journal Geophysical Research* 75:4943.)

The New Madrid area was almost pulled apart 600 million years ago and again 200 million years ago. If those forces would have succeeded in breaking North America along that zone, New Madrid would have been on the Atlantic coast and the Eastern U.S. would have been part of Africa. Although the continent **did not** separate there a weak zone was created that persists to the present where quakes occur. Scientists call it a **"failed rift"**. As Pangaea stretched, the rift evolved into a long basin to become a sea creating what geologists call the **"Protoatlantic Ocean"**.

The Protoatlantic was a narrow trough of seawater through the heart of North America from Texas to Nova Scotia. It lasted "only" a few hundred million years (three eyeblinks to a geologist!) when compressive stresses brought the plates together, closing it off. When two plates come together, one of them usually "dives" beneath the other. Geologists call this "sub-

duction." The plate that dives under gets recycled back into the earth's innards—melted into magma. The crunch caused by the collision of two plates plus the melted rock (magma) working its way up from the plunging plate creates mountain ranges. This particular collision created the Appalachian and Ouachita Mountains. Most of the world's long mountain chains were made this way.

Some of the hot, rising magma plastered itself to the "bottom" of the tectonic plate above. This added weight, which is still there, is thought to have caused that large region to sink. This subsidence invited ancient seaways to flood a large area of what is now the midcontinent area. The limestones, sandstones, and shales that can be found outcropping in the hills of western Tennessee, western Kentucky, southern Illinois, and southeast Missouri around the present-day alluvial valley were produced from calcareous oozes, silts,

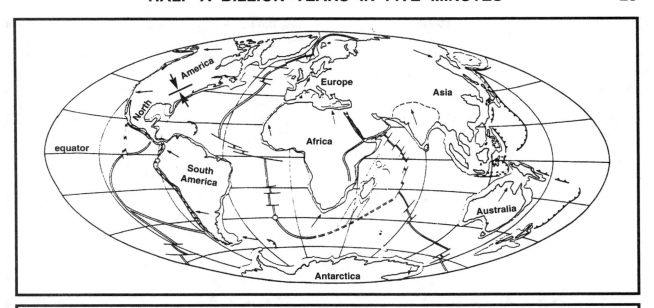

FIGURE 9. The Plates of the Earth's Crust Today. After Pangaea broke up into plates, the New Madrid Rift Complex ended up in the middle of the North American plate which is bounded by the Mid-Atlantic Ridge on the east and by the San Andreas Fault Complex in California on the west. North America is moving away from Europe an inch or two a year—about the same rate your fingernails grow. The Rift Zone is shown in compression, as it is today, on the map above. (After Deitz & Holden, *Journal Geophysical Research* 75:4943.)

and muds deposited on the ocean floor of this subsided area.

Interstate 55 road-cuts north of Cape Girardeau reveal a good assortment of these rock types. (See Figure 11.) Many of these same marine (ocean floor) deposits can also be found with the drilling bit when deep wells encounter them where they have been buried by younger marine rocks of the ancestral Gulf of Mexico. The youngest sediment, the alluvial layers deposited by streams, overlie this entire sequence. (See Figure 16.)

The next major event was renewed tension and pulling apart associated with the creation of the **modern Atlantic Ocean**. The land masses that were to become Europe and Africa pulled away from the land masses that were to become North and South America. Geologists call this "plate divergence", where new plates are created at plate boundaries and spread both ways. This is still happening today, and the boundary

of the plate on which most of North America is riding is located at the **Mid-Atlantic Ridge**. In the New Madrid Rift Complex area, these new stresses caused the area to rise (uplift), caused the old areas of weakness to break again (faulting), and allowed molten rock (magma) to force its way into (intrude) some of the faults near the margins of the rift zone.

Finally, for the last few tens of millions of years, compressive stresses caused by the plate motion of the North American Plate moving from the Mid-Atlantic Ridge westward have caused the old rift zone to subside again. The old faults tend to "give" when stresses build up to certain levels. (See Figures 5 & 10.)

Geologists believe that present-day earthquakes in the New Madrid Seismic Zone are caused by slippage along these pre-existing zones of weakness inherited from this past. (See Figures 1, 5, 6, 7, 8 & 9.)

Figure 10: THE NEW MADRID RIFT COMPLEX

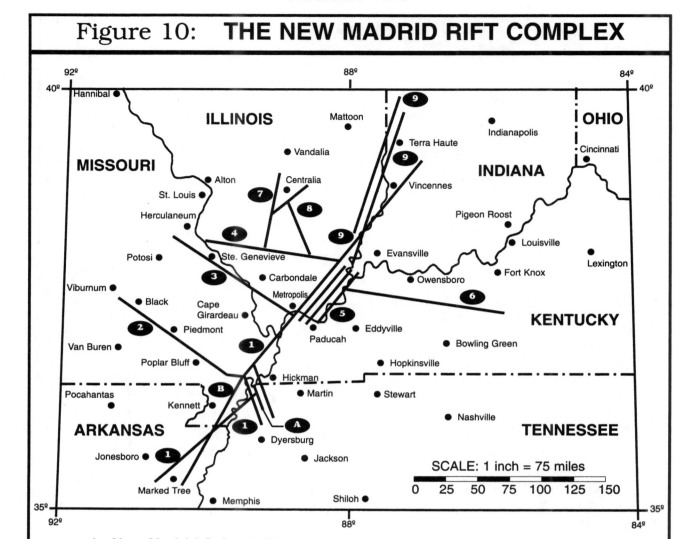

1. **New Madrid Seismic Zone**
   A. **Reelfoot Fault**
   B. **Bootheel Lineament**
2. **Black Fault**
3. **Ste. Genevieve Fault Zone**
4. **Cottage Grove Fault System**
5. **Shawneetown Fault Zone**
6. **Rough Creek Fault System**
7. **Centralia Fault**
8. **Rend Lake Fault System**
9. **Wabash Valley Fault Zone**

• There are many faults in the central United States, but those shown above are the major ones. As you can see, all of these faults are interconnected as a single complex system. The term "New Madrid Seismic Zone" or "New Madrid Fault" usually refers to the southern end of this complex which generated the events of 1811-12. The two largest events of the 20th century, however, were on the northern or Wabash Valley end of the system. Braile, et al. (1984 & 1986) refer to the entire midwestern fault system shown above as "The New Madrid Rift Complex." Johnston & Nava (1985) and Nishenko & Bollinger (1990) refer to the southern end of the rift complex as "The Small New Madrid Source Zone" and entire region of faults shown above as "The Large New Madrid Source Zone." The media has been confused by this. The fact is that when authorities quote probabilities for New Madrid earthquakes they mean the entire complex, not just the southern end or "Small Source Zone." When we say there is a 50% chance of a 6.0-6.9 quake in the next 10 years in the "New Madrid Fault System," this could be for an epicenter anywhere from Marked Tree, Arkansas, to Terra Haute, Indiana. This is important in determining how close you actually are to a potentially destructive earthquake source.

FIGURE 11. Photos of Selected Faults in the New Madrid Rift Complex. The sign along southbound I–55 reads "Exit 141, Hwy Z, St. Marys, 1 mile." Across from the sign by the northbound lane is a roadcut of horizontally bedded grey limestone—Mississippian in age or 340 million years old. As you continue southward from here the outcrop bedding remains horizontal until you approach the St. Marys exit where the rocks are upturned chaotically. (2nd photo) This is the Ste. Genevieve Fault. On the southeast side of the exit you will see orange-stained sandstones of the St. Peters formation—Ordovician in age or 460 million years old. (3rd photo) The bridge in the distance is Hwy Z at the St. Marys Exit. Note how the horizontal beds of the sandstone bend downward as they approach the fault zone at the overpass. The sandstone is on the upthrown side. This high angle fault has moved vertically 1,800 feet, producing many earthquakes during its long history but no large ones in recent times. Photo 4 is another example of disturbed bedding in or near a fault zone. This is the Jackson Fault as seen between mileposts 101 & 102 on I-55. The fault, itself, runs through the valley just to the south of this slump feature. At the bottom left we see an aerial view of the Bootheel Fault near Braggacodio, Missouri. It is a strike-slip fault which sweeps diagonally across the photo. The light colored patches are huge sand boils that are common on the east side of the fault, but not on the west. A 161,000 volt power line from Associated Electric at New Madrid crosses the fault in the center of the picture. The last photo shows Reelfoot Fault—seen here as a grassy escarpment in the distance completely across the picture. This is a normal fault—the east boundary of the Tiptonville Horst. The field in the foreground with people is on the downthrown side of the fault—about 20 feet lower than the top of the horst. The fault in this photo is about 1/4 mile away.

The Big Rivers Take Over

Subsidence also has had a direct influence on the location of one of the world's great river systems, the Mississippi-Missouri-Ohio river system. Deposits of these rivers are superimposed over the old marine rocks, which are in turn superimposed over the ancient volcanic rocks and granites. When an earthquake occurs in the ancient rift far below, vibrations shake all overlying rocks. Now you might think that the poorly consolidated, water-saturated alluvial deposits on top of this sequence might not be affected as much by earthquakes as would the more rigid, solid rocks. But just the opposite is true! The loose, wet sands and silts are affected most of all. And on top of these alluvial deposits sets New Madrid! The block diagram (Figure 5) on page 18 summarizes the tectonic setting of the New Madrid area and shows the location of earthquake foci relative to this region.

The Mississippi River and the Ice Age

The New Madrid Seismic Zone underlies a large part of the Mississippi Embayment, that portion of the Gulf Coastal Plain that loops northward up the Mississippi River valley as a big inverted "V" with Cairo, Illinois, setting about at the point of the "V".

As we have seen, this great allu-

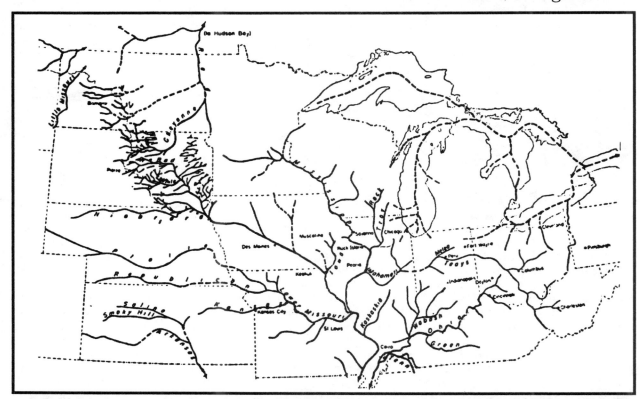

FIGURE 12. Map of North American Rivers Before the Ice Age. Prior to the Pliestocene Ice Age, much of the area now part of the Mississippi River watershed drained to the north, northeast, or east. During the Ice Age the Mississippi drainage area decreased and increased, respectively, with ice advances and retreats. With the retreat of the last continental ice sheet, the area of the Mississippi River basin was doubled. (After Flint, 1957.)

vial valley is a product of the Mississippi River and its tributaries. The Mississippi River system has reacted through geologic time to changing conditions, controlled not only by uplifts and subsidences, but also by widely changing climates. The most dramatic climate changes occurred during the Ice Age.

The Ice Age spanned the interval between about 1.6 million and 11 thousand years ago. Geologists call this the Pleistocene Epoch (See Figure 13.) Before this, the Mississippi River system drained a much smaller area than it now does. (See Figure 12.) Much of the surface runoff in the north and east parts of the present-day Mississippi drainage area then flowed to the north or to the east. We know a lot about this because these old river valleys are well-preserved under thick deposits left by the Ice Age glaciers. Water well drillers seek these valleys, because they are usually good sources of groundwater. So we know where most of them are.

Streams and rivers of the upper and middle Mississippi Valley were permanently changed by the Ice Age glaciers. Actually, there were several major ice advances, (glacials), separated by long periods of retreat (interglacials). The present-day course of the Missouri River was established by one of these ice advances. The Missouri River was at one time an ice-marginal stream, and its course pretty well marks the southernmost ice advance in the western part of the Mississippi drainage basin. Although caused by a later glacial advance, in a similar way, the present course of the Ohio River approximates the

southernmost ice advance in the eastern half of the Mississippi drainage basin. The combined effect of these events was to suddenly (geologically speaking) double the area drained into the Mississippi River. All of this added runoff as well as the sediment carried by these tributaries was funneled into the lower Mississippi Valley. The "neck" of the funnel was the upper Mississippi Embayment.

During each of the major glacial episodes, relatively low temperatures and high precipitation persisted. The glaciers grew and advanced southward. Stream flows were high and the humid climate caused the plant cover to be dense and this in turn controlled sediment erosion. Sea level

GEOLOGIC ERAS, PERIODS & EPOCHS	MILLIONS OF YEARS TO BEGINNING OF	FOSSIL SIGNS OF LIFE
CENOZOIC ERA		
Quaternary		
Recent	.01	Recorded history
Pleistocene	2.5	Humans
Tertiary		
Pliocene	7	
Miocene	26	Primates
Oligocene	38	
Eocene	54	
Paleocene	65	Mammals
MESOZOIC ERA		
Cretaceous	136	Birds
Jurassic	190	Flying reptiles
Triassic	225	Dinosaurs
PALEOZOIC ERA		
Permian	280	Small reptiles
Pennsylvanian	310	Large Plants
Mississippian	345	Insects
Devonian	395	Amphibians
Silurian	430	Land plants
Ordovician	500	Fish
Cambrian	570	Multicelled life
PRECAMBRIAN ERA	3400	One celled life
Oldest Known Rocks	4000	No sign of life

FIGURE 13.   Geologic Time Scale

GLACIATED AREA		LOWER MISSISSIPPI VALLEY	
GLACIAL STAGES	INTERGLACIAL STAGES.	INTERGLACIAL TERRACE DEPOSITS	
Each glacial stage characterized by accumulation of ice upon continents and lowering of sea-level with resultant entrenchment of streams and valley cutting.	Each interglacial stage characterized by retreat of ice sheets from continents and rise of sea-level with alluviation of valleys cut during previous glacial stage.	Each terrace deposit is of interglacial age, fills valleys cut during preceeding glacial stage, and constitutes a geologic formation. Continued uplift during Quaternary Period has raised terrace deposits above level of present floodplain.	

Left axis labels: QUATERNARY PERIOD — PLEISTOCENE OR GLACIAL EPOCH — RECENT EPOCH

Glacial Stages	Interglacial Stages	Interglacial Terrace Deposits	
		RECENT ALLUVIUM (RA)	
Late Wisconsin (youngest)		------ Valley cutting VC-5	
	Peorian	------ PRAIRIE FORMATION (PF)	
Early Wisconsin		------ Valley cutting VC-4	
	Sangamon	------ MONTGOMERY FORMATION (MF)	
Illinolan		------ Valley cutting VC-3	
	Yarmouth	------ BENTLEY FORMATION (BF)	
Kansan		------ Valley cutting VC-2	
	Aftonian	------ WILLIANA FORMATION (WF)	
Nebraskan (oldest)		------ Valley cutting VC-1	

IDEALIZED RELATIONSHIP OF TERRACES

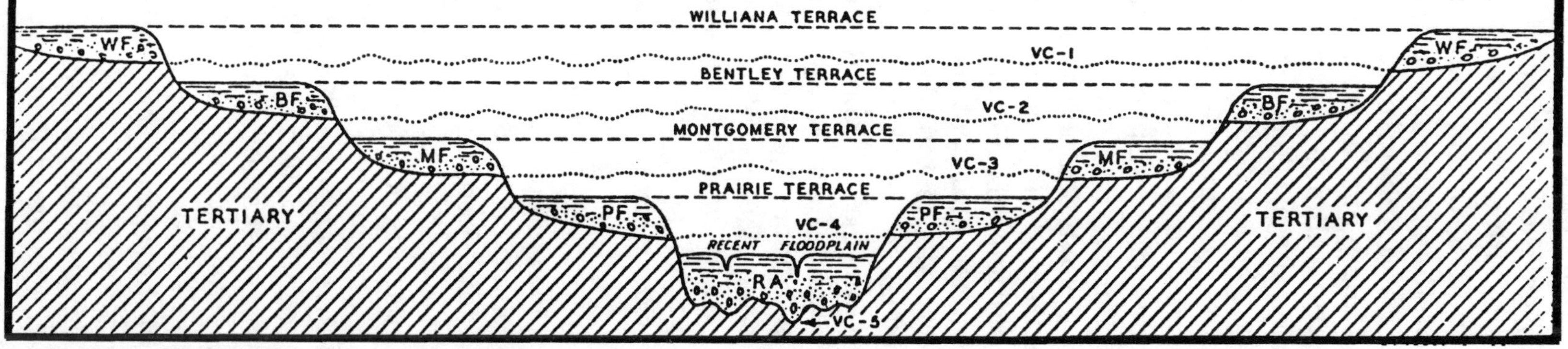

Cross-section labels: WILLIANA TERRACE, BENTLEY TERRACE, MONTGOMERY TERRACE, PRAIRIE TERRACE, RECENT FLOODPLAIN; VC-1, VC-2, VC-3, VC-4, VC-5; WF, BF, MF, PF, RA; TERTIARY.

FIGURE 14. Terraces of the Mississippi River Now and Through the Ice Ages. Fisk believed that the alluvial valley alternately cut and filled, correlating with Pleistocene glacial and interglacial stages. Though probably too simplistic, it does illustrate the development of fluvial terraces in response to changes, probably both tectonic and climatic, that controlled sediment availability in the Mississippi River Drainage basin. (This idealized cross section is from Fisk, 1944.)

was low, because the great glaciers took water from the oceans. Because sea level was low, the rivers had to "drop" a greater distance, thus had a steeper gradient. The increased gradient plus the high flow rate caused the rivers to vigorously erode their channels.

On the other hand, during each of the major interglacials, temperatures were warmer and precipitation was relatively low. This starved the glaciers, spilling the water back into the oceans, causing sea level to rise once again. Because the dryer climates caused a less-dense plant cover, sediment was more available to stream erosion. Decreased gradients and increased sediment supply caused the rivers to fill their valleys with their deposits.

The numerous cut-fill cycles resulted in the many terrace remnants so conspicuous in the alluvial valleys of the big rivers. When depositing, the rivers were braided and choked with their own sediment loads. When eroding, they were meandering and downcutting. (See Figure 14.)

During the Ice Age the big rivers reacted to the numerous ice advances and retreats by alternately cutting and filling the lower Mississippi Valley. If we could see through these great masses of river deposits, which average nearly 125 feet thick, we would see that they bury two great canyons or trenches, averaging about 200 feet deep. The ancestral Mississippi and Ohio rivers cut these trenches, in a time when they paralleled each other and when their junction was south of the present location of Helena, Arkansas!

The Ohio River and Sikeston Ridge

Among the terrace remnants are the **Sikeston Ridge** and the **Malden Plain**. They owe their existence to both the Ohio and Mississippi rivers. When the course of the Ohio River ran east to west it eroded the south edge of the Benton Hills. It then turned southward for a long time and scoured out the deepest part of its trench. A segment of this trench underlies the present location of Sikeston Ridge. (See Figures 15-17.)

The Ohio later became a depositing river, and built a tremendous alluvial fan that spanned completely across the valley east of Crowley's Ridge. It ranged from Kennett, Malden, and Dexter on the west to Cairo, Wickliffe, and the Chickasaw Bluffs on the east. Later, the Ohio River abandoned the Cache Valley and took its present course which left the alluvial fan intact—at least until the Mississippi River took it over!

The Mississippi River and Sikeston Ridge

Next the Mississippi got into the act! It abandoned its course in the Western Lowland past Poplar Bluff for a new course through the Morehouse Lowland—between Bell City and Oran. During this time the Mississippi laid its sediments atop the Ohio River deposits across much of the same area. Later, the Mississippi changed its personality from braiding and depositing to meandering and downcutting. It removed the middle portions of the old fan, thus separating it into two parts—the Malden Plain on the west and the

FIGURE 15. Physiographic Features Related to Course Changes of the Mississippi and Ohio.
The Mississippi occupied the Advance Lowlands, then the Morehouse Lowlands, and finally the present course through Thebes Gap. The Ohio River occupied the entire area east of Crowleys Ridge before moving eastward and giving it up to the Mississippi. Sikeston Ridge is an Ohio River Terrace. At one time the junction of the Mississippi and Ohio was as far south as Natchez, Miss., 400 miles from the present junction at Cairo, Illinois.

After Grohskoph, 1955.

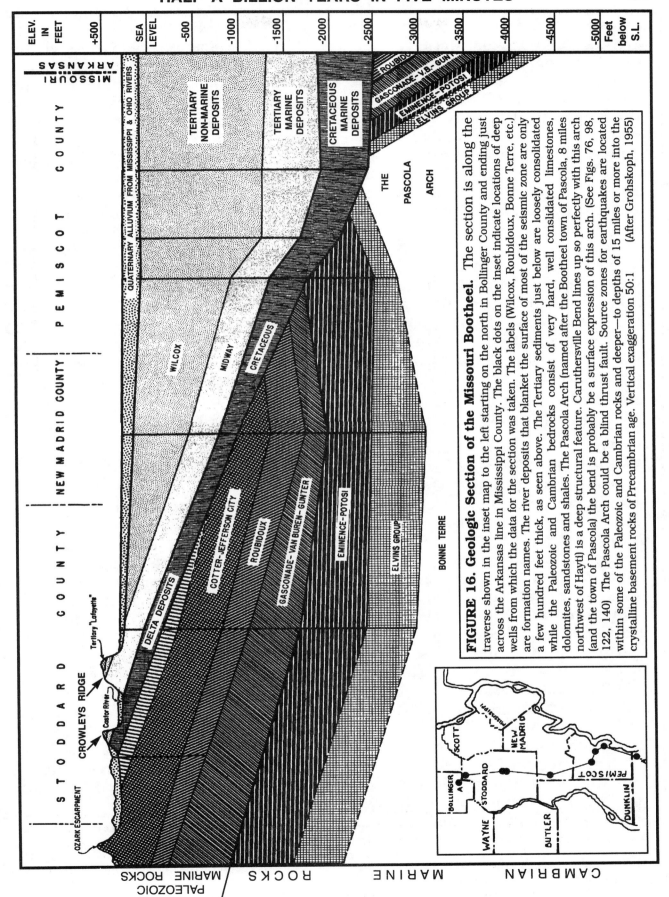

FIGURE 16. Geologic Section of the Missouri Bootheel. The section is along the traverse shown in the inset map to the left starting on the north in Bollinger County and ending just across the Arkansas line in Mississippi County. The black dots on the inset indicate locations of deep wells from which the data for the section was taken. The labels (Wilcox, Roubidoux, Bonne Terre, etc.) are formation names. The river deposits that blanket the surface of most of the seismic zone are only a few hundred feet thick, as seen above. The Tertiary sediments just below are loosely consolidated while the Paleozoic and Cambrian bedrocks consist of very hard, well consolidated limestones, dolomites, sandstones and shales. The Pascola Arch (named after the Bootheel town of Pascola, 8 miles northwest of Hayti) is a deep structural feature. Caruthersville Bend lines up so perfectly with this arch (and the town of Pascola) the bend is probably be a surface expression of this arch. (See Figs. 76, 98, 122, 140) The Pascola Arch could be a blind thrust fault. Source zones for earthquakes are located within some of the Paleozoic and Cambrian rocks and deeper—to depths of 15 miles or more into the crystalline basement rocks of Precambrian age. Vertical exaggeration 50:1   (After Grohskoph, 1955)

Sikeston Ridge on the east. (See Figures 15-16.) Thus, these two terraces were once joined.

During the latter stages of the Mississippi River's tenure in the Morehouse Lowland, it occupied the eastern part of the lowland. This caused the west side of the Sikeston Ridge to be straight, and allowed the Mississippi to "jump" across its north end during extra large floods. Some of this excess flood water ran along what is now the east edge of Sikeston Ridge, eroding channels that can be seen today. One of these was used by Lake St. John (Figure 2) as a spillway. Remnants of Sikeston Ridge that escaped this erosion can be seen along I-55 from mile markers 58 to 79 in Missouri.

Wind Adds It's Signature

The last major ice advance, the Wisconsinan, contained a relatively arid interlude within it. During this time of relatively low precipitation and high temperatures, around 20,000 years ago, wind erosion was especially active. Wide, braided streams provided an abundant supply of sand and silt, and the sparse plant cover did little to prevent wind erosion. Wind picked up much of this and redeposited it. The silt-sized material (dust) became a loess "blanket". Much of it became incorporated into the soil, adding valuable nutrients to the already-rich soils that make this region's farms so successful. The intermediate-sized material, primarily sand, was moved closer to the ground, being redeposited as sand dunes. Both loess deposits and sand dunes are common features in the alluvial valley.

As the last glacial ice melted away, the great trenches were filled for the last time. At first, gravels from glacial outwash filled in the lower parts. Then sediment from nonglacial sources was added. As the valleys became more and more filled, diversions of the courses of the major rivers began to occur. The Ohio River diverted from the Cache Valley (Figures 15-17) to the present course through the Metropolis Lowland. The Mississippi diverted from the Western Lowland to the Morehouse Lowland. This course change left the combined flows of the Whitewater, Castor, St. Francis, Black, and Current Rivers in the Western Lowland. Most geomorphologists estimate that these course changes occurred between 17,000 and 11,000 years ago.

Where The Mississippi River Has No Flood Plain

The most recent major river diversion, involving the Mississippi, is thought to have occurred around 9500 years ago. This was the abandonment of the Morehouse Lowland in favor of its present course through **Thebes Gap**. (Figure 17.) Notice that though the wide valley and flood plain of the Mississippi turns southwest, the river continues south! Travellers who wish to visit this impressive landform may drive to Thebes, Illinois. The court house at Thebes is located high above the river, providing the best observation point from which to view this feature. The court house itself is a historic museum. One of the Lincoln-Douglas Debates took place here.

More Hot Air

The period around 7500-4500 years ago was another relatively warm and dry episode. Trees and shrubs declined, allowing herbs to increase. This **"Altithermal"** interval allowed wind to once again become a more effective erosion agent. Sand dunes became reactivated because of the thinning plant cover, and mounds of dust (loess) settled in the patchy clumps of grassy vegetation which stalled the wind. This is the combination of factors which probably produced the **"prairie mounds"** that once existed by the hundreds of thousands in several states. It should be noted that there are at least twenty-four hypotheses in the scientific literature on the origin of these mounds—including earthquakes!

Relatively minor course changes have occurred since the Thebes Gap diversion. Most of these were probably caused by slightly uplifted areas in some places and gentle subsidence in others. Major prehistoric earthquakes prior to 1812 may have contributed to some of these changes. Today, we see the results of this long history of geologic and geomorphic processes at work in the Upper Mississippi Embayment. The clues are there, if only we can interpret them!

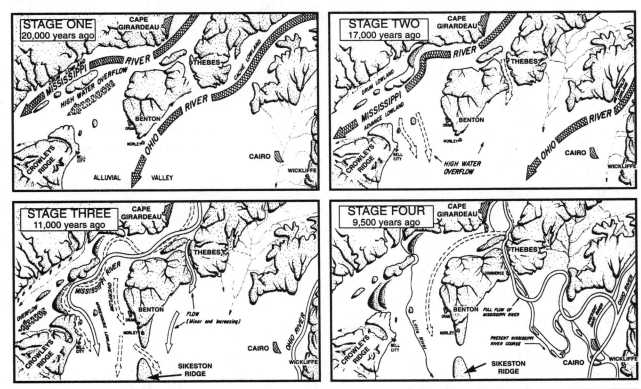

FIGURE 17. How the Courses of the Mississippi & Ohio Rivers Have Changed Over Time.
1. EARLY STAGE. Braided Mississippi flows thru Drum lowland and west of Crowleys Ridge. Braided Ohio in Cache lowland. 2. INTERMEDIATE STAGE. Braided Mississippi diverted from Drum lowland to Advance lowland but still flows thru Western lowland. Braided Ohio in Metropolis lowland. Mississippi highwater overflows into lowlands east of Crowleys Ridge thru Bell City-Oran Gap and also overflows through notch at Thebes Gap. 3. INTERMEDIATE STAGE. Mississippi diverted from Advance lowland to Morehouse lowland while partial flow is maintained in Thebes Gap. 4. LATE STAGE. Mississippi established through Thebes Gap. Flood waters flow through Morehouse lowland. River develops meandering channel between Commerce and Ohio river junction.   (After Fisk 1944; Thacker & Satterfield 1977; Beveridge & Vinyard 1990.)

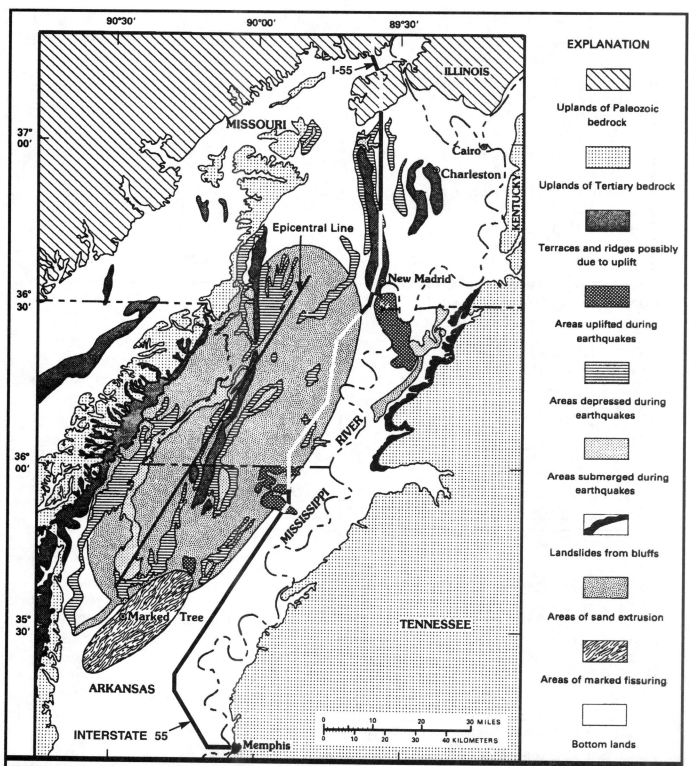

FIGURE 18, Fuller's First Map of Morphoseismic Features in the New Madrid Seismic Zone-1905
Myron Fuller, a geologist with the U.S. Geological Survey, made the first map of seismic landforms in the New Madrid area in 1905—which was published in 1912. While his map is incomplete, generalized, and inaccurate in a few places, it is amazing what he did on horseback, by boat, and on foot without the benefit of good roads, detailed maps, satellite imagery, or aerial photos. We added I-55 to Fuller's map which confirms an observation we also made. From Fuller's map you would expect to find seismic features along I-55 from the Benton Hills of Missouri to a point just south of Blytheville, Arkansas. This is exactly what we found 90 years after Fuller—except we had the comfort of an air-conditioned car.

(After Fuller 1912;

CHAPTER THREE

CHAPTER THREE

RECOGNIZING SEISMIC LANDFORMS

The New Madrid Seismic Zone (NMSZ) includes some 5000 square miles of area in parts of five states. Tens of thousands of surface features still remain from past super-large earthquakes—most of which were created or modified in 1811-12. The best "hunting" for earthquake features is probably in the immediate area around New Madrid, Missouri. This book can take you to many of the best of these, but serious "fault finders" need to do some "homework" to be able to recognize and interpret them. This chapter, along with the appropriate maps, photos, and help from the glossary, is your homework assignment! But hey! It'll be worth it! In the process of preparing for and actually visiting the fault zone, yourself, you'll acquire a new skill—how to read the past from the pages of nature in her own handwriting. Of all the books in the world, nature's own is by far the most fascinating. Developing the skills and sensitivities of a "Fault Finder" will enhance your satisfaction and pleasure in travel everywhere you go from now on! The world around you will become a more inter-

esting place—everywhere.

The NMSZ is an extremely unique place where people can see a wide variety of seismically-related (morphoseismic) features from the comfort of motor vehicles. Morphoseismic features are numerous here because the essential ingredients, conditions, and forces to create them are all present in abundance.

First: There are plenty of loose sediments. Most of the natural surface material throughout this zone have been carried and spread by streams and rivers. This sediment (alluvium) is loose and porous.

Second: The water table is close to the surface, so that most of the pore spaces between sediment grains are full of water.

Third: A lot of big earthquakes have happened here. These water-saturated materials lie above one of the most active seismic zones anywhere.

These are the ideal prerequisites for the creation of seismic features and the NMSZ has them all. There is probably no place in the world quite like it!

About Liquefaction

Most of the seismic features encountered in the New Madrid area are at least partly caused by liquefaction. Before going further, this term needs to be defined and explained. The only way loose sand can have any strength is if the grains touch each other—supporting each other's weight and whatever burdens may rest from above. When sand is saturated with water, as is the case below the water table, earthquake waves can generate pressures in the ground water that cause the grains to separate. What had been solid earth suddenly becomes a viscous fluid mixture of water and suspended sand grains—like a cement slurry when freshly poured. Liquefaction is the term that geologists and earthquake engineers use when referring to this sudden loss of rigidity of water-saturated, sandy or silty soil.

You might wonder why the term **"liquefaction"** (four syllables) is used instead of **"liquification."** (which has five syllables) That is because these two terms don't mean the same thing. Liquification refers to "melting from heat." Most solids becomes liquid if they get too hot. Metals melt. Plastics melt. Cheese melts. Ice melts. All of these solids melt when enough heat is applied, turning into liquids. Even sand can melt. When we melt sand, remold it into sheets, and let it cool, we call it glass. In every example, here, heat is involved. That is "liquification."

In the case of "liquefaction" there is no heat involved—only pressure. Whereas most solids can **liquify**, only very special combinations of materials can **liquefy**. With few exceptions, liquefiable materials have to be bodies of sand, silt, gravel, or certain clays saturated with water. When pressures are applied to the water—the sand, silt, gravel, or clay particles can separate and become suspended creating a thick mush that acts like a liquid. But there was no heat involved. Nothing melted.

The pressures necessary to create "quicksand." "quicksilt," "quickgravel," or "quickclay" can be generated by a variety of sources including artesian ground water conditions, high river stages next to levees, vibrations of heavy traffic, explosions, and earthquakes. Even you can cause liquefaction with your feet and hands, and have probably done so.

Most of us made "pattycakes" when we were kids. Remember how the more we "patted", the more liquid it became? Or maybe we remember how we would jump up and down on a sandy beach near a lake shore or a riverside. The more we jumped, the larger the area that became "quicksand." You might remember how water filled the depression we caused—sometimes even spouting up from below an inch or two. Earthquakes can do the same thing—only on a larger scale.

Liquefaction is more likely to occur if the sediment consists of sand or silt, is loosely compacted, and if the spaces between grains are filled with water. Liquefaction is not as likely to occur if there is a lot of clay in the sediment, although in special instances, even clays can liquefy and have done so—causing destruction to houses and property. Liquefaction from earthquakes is more likely if ground motion is strong, and if the motion lasts a relatively long time. The larger the earthquake, the sooner liquefaction can occur.

Duration of ground motion is one of the most important of the variables. The 1906 San Francisco earthquake is reported to have lasted about 65 seconds and did cause some liquefaction near the seashore. But the 1964 Anchorage, Alaska, earthquake lasted four minutes and was accompanied by far more liquefaction and liquefaction-induced slope failures than the San Francisco event. While the Alaskan quake was larger, the main reason more liquefaction resulted was because it was longer. The liquefaction in the Anchorage area reportedly did not begin until 90 to 120 seconds after the earthquake started. Had it lasted only 65 seconds, like San Francisco, liquefaction effects would have been minimal.

Besides the size of the earthquake (big quakes last longer), another factor that controls the duration of ground motion is distance from the epicenter. The further you are, the longer it lasts. The intensity of the shaking usually decreases with distance, but duration of the shaking increases. As a "rule of thumb", duration of significant ground motion doubles about every 100 kilometers (60 miles) distance from the epicenter. Hence, an earthquake lasting 20 seconds at an epicenter near the town of New Madrid would last 40 seconds at Cape Girardeau, 60 miles away. The same 20-second quake at New Madrid would lengthen to more than a minute at St. Louis—160 miles away.

For strong earthquakes 6.0 or greater, liquefaction can occur at the epicenter or for considerable distances—more than 100 miles away. For light to moderate earthquakes (magnitudes 4.0-5.9) there may be no liquefaction damage within 40 miles of the epicenter, but liquefaction has been observed in a ring or "doughnut" area from 40 to 150 miles away from the source.

For example, on June 10, 1987, a Richter 5.2 earthquake occurred near Lawrenceville, Illinois, close to the Indiana state line at Vincennes. There was damage from the shaking in the epicentral region, but no liquefaction was reported. However, 150 miles to the west near Advance, Missouri, five cases of liquefaction damage were observed by Stewart.

• A below-ground swimming pool in Advance was heaved upwards four inches, breaking a concrete patio.
•Near Bell City, Missouri, the soil beneath two half-filled grain bins subsided—cracking their concrete pads and buckling the metal bins.
•Near Morehouse, Missouri, an L-shaped house slightly sank on one end causing structural damage.
•Near Painton, Missouri, a concrete carport sank down while the back yard heaved upwards. • A neighbor a half-a-mile away found concentric fissures in his yard encircling his house while his foundation on the end opposite the carport sank down four inches, breaking his basement in two. A test hole near this last house verified the presence of liquefiable sands starting four feet below his basement floor and extending to a depth of sixty feet.

An oddity about this last example

is that 21 years earlier, on March 23, 1976, this same house had received no damage at all from a 5.0 magnitude quake only 85 miles to the south! While in 1987 this house had suffered $35,000 in damages from a broken basement by a quake 150 miles away—it, again, suffered no damage whatsoever in 1990 from a 4.6 magnitude earthquake only 20 miles away. Fifteen miles from the house with the broken basement, there was a two-story commercial building that was not damaged by the quakes of 1976 or 1987, but it was split from top to bottom by the 1990 quake. This last example was due to vibratory ground motion, however, and not liquefaction.

How is it that quakes nearby can do no damage while quakes at a distance can do serious damage to the same building? Why does one earthquake of small magnitude seriously damage one area while a larger quake brings no harm at all? Why do some buildings receive damage in one quake and not from others as close or as big? The "hit or miss" damage patterns of light to moderate earthquakes are almost as random and inexplicable as the aimless striking of a tornado that can totally destroy one side of the street and leave the other untouched. Earthquake forces are far more complex than we understand.

Another set of variables, which we are just beginning to understand, involves a whole suite of wave phenomena. We are beginning to realize that trains of seismic waves may interfere with other trains of waves, at times causing combined effects to be magnified, and at times causing them to be at least partly canceled.

We suspect that at times, something akin to resonance or standing waves may form wave harmonics when subsurface features are favorable.

Liquefaction from Light Earthquakes

There is a rule of thumb used by seismologists, geologists, and earthquake engineers that says that liquefaction does not occur for earthquakes less than 5.0 on the Richter scale. This is not a hard and fast rule, however, but only a guideline. In the New Madrid Seismic Zone the water table is so near the surface and the deposits of sand are so ubiquitous that at least ten instances of liquefaction have been observed by Stewart for light earthquakes only 4.6 Richter in size.

The Richter 4.6 quake near New Hamburg, Missouri, on September 26, 1990, caused landslides in the epicentral area and serious landslide damage up to 70 miles away. While there was no observed liquefaction within 48 miles, damage due to liquefaction was observed in a "doughnut" shaped area from 48 to 107 miles away. • A water well was destroyed and filled with sand near Grand Tower, Illinois, 48 miles away. • The floor of an old brick building was cracked at Piggott, Arkansas, at 67 miles distance. • Foundations and concrete floors settled and cracked at Reyno and Marmaduke, Arkansas, 82 and 85 miles away. • A brick chimney and fireplace settled and cracked at Halliday, Arkansas, 90 miles away. • And at Lake City, Arkansas, 107 miles away, the end of a house opposite its carport settled, cracked, and caused the north wall to lean outwards.

The Risco, Missouri, earthquake on May 3, 1991, was also measured as a 4.6 event and also caused liquefaction—not in the epicentral area, but at a distance. At least five houses in the little town of Keiser, Arkansas, were damaged due to liquefaction—65 to 70 miles from the epicenter. In every case, the houses were single story dwellings with no basement and a poured concrete floor. • In all cases the houses sank slightly on the end opposite the car port. • The street also subsided in front of two of the residences showing characteristic arcuate crack patterns from liquefaction and lateral spreading beneath. •A slight ridge was heaved upwards between two of the damaged homes that sank. In one home, the back yard subsided four inches under a tool shed leaving a circular, dish-shaped depression approximately 25 feet in diameter. •The cracked flooring in this house also broke the plumbing, resulting in water damage to the structure. A test hole was drilled between two of the damaged dwellings at Keiser which verified, by **Standard Penetration Test (SPT)** data, that all of the conditions for liquefaction were present—i.e. soft, water-saturated sand. (See glossary for discussion of SPT as a test for liquefaction potential.)

These recent examples of liquefaction from relatively small earthquakes prove how liquefaction-prone the New Madrid Seismic Zone really is. Hence, when a series of truly large earthquakes measuring 6.0, 7.0 and 8.0 points on the Richter scale occurred in back in 1811-12, it is no wonder that the liquefaction phenomena was so extensive that thousands of traces can still be seen.

While light to moderate quakes (Richter 4.6 to 5.2 in size) have been observed to cause liquefaction at a distance (between 40 and 150 miles) but not close to the epicenter, larger quakes, 6.0 and above, can cause liquefaction both in the epicentral region and at a distance—sometimes hundreds of miles away.

Calling Cards of the Big Quakes

Some of the earthquakes in the New Madrid Seismic Zone have been extra large. The effect of large quakes upon the surface muds, silts, sands, and bluffs of loess has transformed the landscape, pocking it with thousands of permanent scars still visible today—many decades after the last great cataclysm. Clues of still more ancient seismic upheavals are preserved in older sediments and in ancient rocks below the alluvium, and several teams of modern researchers are busy digging trenches, studying soils, and running seismic profiles to try to find out more.

The seismically-related features of the New Madrid Seismic Zone can be classified into seven general categories with subcategories totaling more than twenty different types of landforms. These broad categories are as follows: (1) Extrusive sand features; (2) Intrusive sand features; (3) Lateral spread features; (4) Differential subsidence features; (5) Uplift and Secondary fault features; (6) Slope failure features; and (7) Seismically historic sites. Table Two details the subcategories for each of these general classes and adds an eighth category—(8) Pseudoseismic features, which tabulates natural and man-made landforms that can be mistakenly identified as seismic in origin.

Most "Seismic" Landforms Are Really Hybrids

It will also be a good idea to keep in mind that practically all landforms that existed in the New Madrid Seismic Zone before the giant earthquakes of 1811-12 were effected and changed by them. On the other hand, practically all seismic features produced in 1811-12 have been altered in the decades since 1812 by streams, wind, vegetation, and humans. Technically, practically all these landforms are "polygenetic", that is, more than one geologic agent is responsible for their development. Nevertheless, we will continue to classify landforms into these seven categories as if they are "pure" seismic, but we realize that few of them are "pure"!

The first four categories are all directly related to seismically-induced liquefaction (SIL). Category (6), slope failure, is also often related to SIL processes, while category (3), lateral spreading, is actually a form of landsliding or slope failure except that lateral spreading can happen in flat areas with no slope.

What To Call These Things?

The terminology used to name and describe SIL features varies from author to author. There has not yet evolved a common set of terms agreed upon by geologists, seismologists, engineers, and others who study and deal with seismically-induced liquefaction. The terms "sand boil" and "sand blow" are good examples. Some scientists use one of these terms for all extrusive sand features, and some scientists use the other.

We find both terms useful in distinguishing various types of visible sand features that are extruded through a vent. There are apparently a whole family of these things, ranging from most violent to most quiet. The violent ejection types leave explosion craters, and earn the term "sand blows", because air, sand, and water are, literally, blown out of the ground, sometimes high into the air, during an earthquake. After the earthquake, a funnel-shaped hole, originally about half as deep as wide, and surrounded by a rim of sand, remains. The more quiet ejections are apparently more common. These "sand boils" are produced where liquefied material, mostly sand and water, quietly boils out from its vent, sometimes for two or three days following the earthquake. After the earthquake, a mound of sand remains, surrounding its vent. It is also quite likely that many, perhaps most, extrusive sand features start as sand blows and finish as sand boils.

We have learned that we must be careful with the term "sand blow" in the New Madrid area. A lot of local folks use this term when referring to wind-blown sand! "Blow sand", to them, means dune sands, and other situations where sand is transported by wind.

"Sand boil" also has a local meaning. When the Mississippi, Ohio, St. Francis, and other rivers of the region rise to high stages on their levees, the protected land inside the levee is sometimes lower than the water level in the stream. Because water seeks its own level, this situation produces pressure, a hydraulic head from the higher stream to the lower level on the other side of the levee, causing ground water to move toward the ground surface and producing boiling cones of water and sand. The suggestion has been made, for good reasons, to restrict the term "sand boil" to these hydrologically-induced liquefaction features (HIL).

We have a problem with this, however. The underground routes that ground water takes to produce HIL features are the same ones that become active during earthquakes. Thus, SIL and HIL would effect the same materials in the same way in the same places. The same boil could sometimes be an example of HIL while at others an example of SIL. For example, artesian springs that boil from the hydraulic pressures of a groundwater gradient are also likely to boil from the pressures generated by an earthquake. In fact, changes in the flow of springs is a commonly reported earthquake effect. It is impossible to tell in all cases whether or not a vented sand feature was originally created by ground water hydraulics or by seismic stresses. The point is that once established, the channels by which ground water and liquefied sand move will respond to either or both kinds of forces.

Yet another comment is needed concerning definitions of terms. Some researchers have used the term "sand volcano", to describe the cones with central vents that can build up during the extrusion of liquefied sand in response to earthquakes. When the term "volcano" is used, even when preceded by the word "sand", many people think of flowing lava and fiery eruptions. Myron Fuller, in his classic book (1912), writes: "of the various explanations offered by those who speculated on the causes of the shock the volcanic theory was, as usual, by far the most popular". Some eyewitnesses reported seeing visible light glowing from the ground—a phenomenon called "seismoluminescence". Others noted the extrusion of warm ground water. The odor of sulfur was commonly experienced. Indeed, it is not difficult to imagine that some of the sights, sounds, and odors described by eyewitnesses during the big earthquakes actually came from accompanying volcanic eruptions. We think, therefore, that it is best if we do not use the term "volcano" in connection with any seismic or hydrologic feature. It is too misleading to the public because it suggests an associated volcanic activity when there was none. We are avoiding the term altogether.

We recognize that complete agreement on descriptive terminology does not exist at this time. In fact, the entire subject of liquefaction is relatively new, especially to geologists. Most of the classic scientific papers on the subject are found in engineering, not geological journals. So it is not surprising that standardization of nomenclature has not yet occurred. Even so, we must apply a set of terms to the features described in this book.

Table Two:
Morphoseismic Features in the New Madrid Seismic Zone
From the 1811-12 Series of Great Earthquakes

I. Extrusive Sand Features
  A. Sand Blows
    1. Explosion Craters
    2. Filled Explosion Craters
    3. Earthquake Ponds
    4. Channel Blowouts
  B. Sand Boils
    1. Simple (Circular or Elliptical)
    2. Compound (Elongated or Irregular)
    3. Mounded (Convex)
    4. Flat
    5. Depressed (Concave)

II Intrusive Sand Features
  A. Sand Dikes (Discordant Intrusions)
  B. Sand Sills (Concordant Intrusions)

III. Lateral Spread Features
  A. Sag Features
  B. Linear Crevasses
  C. Graben Fissures
  D. Sand Fissures
  E. Seismic Sand Ridges
  F. Seismic Sand Sloughs

IV. Differential Subsidence Features
  A. Sunk Lands
  B. Earthquake Lakes
  C. Discontinuous Channels

V. Uplift and Secondary Fault Features
  A. Strike-Slip Faults
  B. Normal Faults
  C. Domes or Horsts
  D. Altered Stream Gradients
    1. Reversed (Temporary Retrograde Flow)
    2. Accelerated (Temporary Rapids or Waterfalls)

VI. Slope Failure Features
  A. Translational Block Slides
  B. Earth Flows
  C. Rotational Slumps
  D. Incoherent Landslides

VII. Historic Sites
  A. Former Site of New Madrid
  B. Former Site of Little Prairie
  C. Former Site of Big Prairie
  D. Former Site of Point Pleasant
  E. Site of Broken Stumps

VIII. Pseudoseismic Features
  A. Natural
    1. Sand Dunes
    2. Dune Ponds
    3. River Terraces
    4. Erosion Remnants of Terraces
    5. Natural Levees
    6. Braided-Bar Islands
    7. River Sandbars
    8. Small Stream Channels
    9. Oxbow Lakes
    10. Gravity Landslides
    11. Prairie Mounds
    12. Sun Boils
    13. Hydrologically Induced Liquefaction
  B. Made by Humans
    1. Indian Mounds
    2. Borrow Pits
    3. Canals and Drainage Ditches
    4. Sand Mine Pits
    5. Sand Piles
    6. Spoil Banks
    7. Small Dug Ponds
    8. Leveled or Displaced Land
    9. Mechanically Induced Liquefaction

We will use the terms as given in the Table on the previous page. Whenever possible, we have tried to conform to terms appearing in recent scientific publications or to terms that seem the simplest, most descriptive, and least likely to mislead lay readers. The terms are first classified and listed in Table Two. Then each is defined, described and discussed in the order given in the Table in the text that follows.

Definitions and Descriptions of Landforms from Table Two

Section I.
Extrusive Sand Features

Sand Blow Explosion Craters. These are circular conical pits 15-200 feet in diameter and 2-6 feet deep. At the time of formation, eyewitnesses reported these to be 15-20 feet deep. Few of these features remain because of natural sedimentation processes and because of deliberate filling in by humans. Many have been used as dumps. Since these features were violently explosive during their formation, they could become so again during a future shock, thus regurgitating back into view the masses of trash and human artifacts they were intended to hide. In addition to broken brick, concrete blocks, metal bed frames, old radios and television sets of modern times, some of these "seismic dumps" may also contain rusty rifles and other civil war artifacts from 1860-65.

Filled Explosion Craters. These landforms are circular, ranging from 15-200 feet in diameter, and currently at the grade of the surrounding land, or slightly lower. The sandy material now filling the crater could have been carried by wind, water, or people. When filled by natural processes, the sediment generally grades in size from coarse in the bottom to fine near the top. The material at the surface is usually dark-colored, organic-rich, and damp or covered with a few inches of water. Often, various growths of water-loving plants are seen as "circular green spots" in fields that are otherwise cultivated for crops. Farmers avoid these patches because they lack the strength to support a tractor, or even a person on foot in some cases.

Earthquake Ponds. These are sand blow explosion craters that intersect the water table. They are circular, range from about 15 to about 200 feet in diameter, and range 4-10 feet deep. Since these ponds were not dug by humans, they have no spoil banks or dams. They are not recharged by rainfall and surface runoff, but by ground water from beneath. Their water levels rise and fall seasonally with the fluctuations of the water table. These, and several other morphoseismic features such as explosion craters, sand boils, and sand fissures, act as points where ground water is recharged and discharged. There is a need for a whole new specialty within hydrogeology called "seismohydrology"—the relationship between earthquakes, aquifers, and surface flow before, during and following seismic activity.

Sectional Views of Extrusive Sand Features

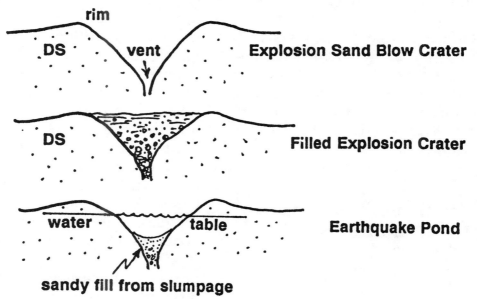

Explosion Sand Blow Crater

Filled Explosion Crater

Earthquake Pond

sandy fill from slumpage

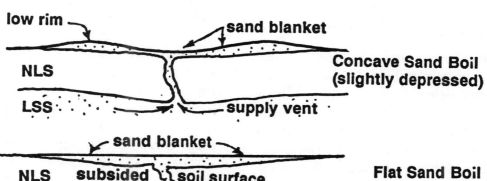

Concave Sand Boil (slightly depressed)

Flat Sand Boil

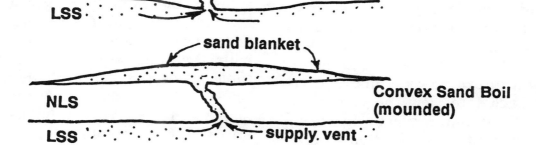

Convex Sand Boil (mounded)

DS =
Dry Sand

NLS =
Non-Liquefiable Soil

LSS =
Liquefiable Saturated Sand

FIGURE 19. Extrusive Sand Features

Channel Blowouts. These are sand blow explosion features that involve segments of surface streams. Most are small, measured in tens or hundreds of feet, but some may have involved stream segments of a mile or more. Even parts of the Mississippi River were involved. Numerous eyewitnesses to the big earthquakes reported large, noisy, frightening examples where stream channels literally exploded. Compressed air, water, and sand were sometimes blasted "as high as tall trees." Stream channels have the perfect combination of loose, saturated sand--prerequisites for liquefaction.

Simple Sand Boils. These landforms are circular to elliptical, sometimes elongated, and range widely in diameter from as little as three feet to well over 300 feet. Although usually composed of sandy material, sometimes medium to fine gravel is seen mixed with the sand.

Because of the fluid state of the rising sand slurry, a variety of light materials float to the top to be deposited on the surface of the sand blanket. These include coal, lignite, carbonized wood, limonite nodules, fragments of black shale, and petroliferous nodules (also called "seismic tar balls). Particles of lignite and carbonized wood are often be found. Seismic tar balls are less common, but have been found in larger sand boils from Arkansas to Missouri. Try lighting one of these. Some will burn readily with a hot flame, yielding a petroliferous or bituminous odor. A diligent search may also reveal lignite particles coated with sulfur compounds or with limonite.

Simple sand boils are extruded from a single vent. Sand boils visible today, 180 years after the New Madrid earthquakes of 1811-12, are the larger ones of more than 12 feet or so in diameter. Most sand boils are slightly mounded or convex, but few are more than three feet high. Sand features higher than three feet are almost always sand dunes, or erosional remnants of a terrace, or old natural levees. We know that more than 100 quakes of the 1811-12 New Madrid series were large enough to produce liquefaction, and that at least 50 were large enough to have caused sand to be ejected.

Compound Sand Boils. All of the comments about simple sand boils also apply to compound boils except for shape, size, and number of vents. Most simple sand boils are circular or elliptical. The more elongated and irregular the shape, the more likely that the boil is compound—formed by the coalescence of two or more simple sand boils. Compound sand boils can grow to huge dimensions as more and more simple boils merge into a single compound boil, or if more than one earthquake has caused liquefaction and sand ejection. Several compound sand boils in the NMSZ are ten acres or more in size. The largest we have discovered to date may be the biggest boil in the world. It is about eight miles west of Hayti. Over a mile long, it is 136 acres in size— almost pure sand throughout. We think this one is compound both in the sense that many vents are involved, and that it has been activated several times by several earthquakes. (See Side Trip D.)

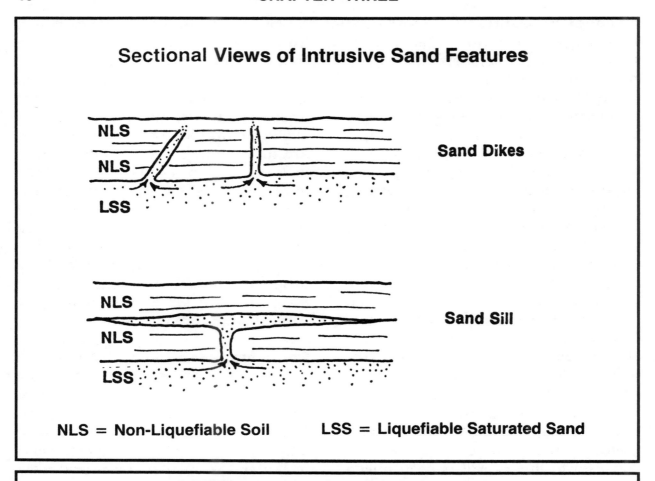

FIGURE 20. Intrusive Sand Features

Section II.
Intrusive Sand Features

Sand Dikes and Sand Sills. Sand dikes are sand-filled crevasses that may or may not reach the surface but which are vertical or nearly so, cutting across (discordant with) the layers of sediment. A few sand dikes, when viewed from above (airphotos), have a circular or concentric pattern, and the term **"seismic liquefaction ring dikes"** may be appropriate. Sand sills are lenses of sand which were forced between and parallel to (concordant with) layers of sediment. Sand sills and sand dikes have dimensions that range from a few inches to a few feet. Most are usually not visible from the surface, but sometimes a drainage canal or ditch may cut through them. Trenches dug by researchers working in the NMSZ have exposed many more.

Section III
Lateral Spread Features

Lateral Spread Sags. When liquefied sand moves beneath layers of sediment and soil, and the overlying layers have not liquefied, the ground surface becomes wrinkled. This is especially true when liquefied sand spreads away from a central area or line. The loss of volume beneath causes the sag. The areas between the sags are sometimes called ridges (the guy that came up with that term for these things couldn't be from the Ozarks!). The sags often catch and hold water forming sag ponds.

Linear Crevasses. In the cases where laterally spreading, liquefied sand causes the non-liquefied layers above to crack instead of sag, crevasses are formed. The opened crack through the more brittle, less liquefied material above is usually linear, or nearly so. Linear crevasses are often parallel to nearby stream channels, indicating that the flow of the liquefied layer of sand was in the direction of the stream valley. This is to be expected, because the stream has removed layers of material that would have resisted lateral spreading. Stream valleys, then, "invite" lateral spreading to occur in their direction. Linear crevasses contain no ejected sand, but usually contain sediment trapped since they were formed. They are relatively narrow, from a few inches to a few feet wide, and have narrow bottoms. Most of those formed in 1811-12 have been filled in by natural processes. Thousands of crevasses and fissures (discussed later) formed during the 1811-12 earthquakes and were the source of the greatest fears to the inhabitants. Many accounts tell of their terror at the prospect of being "swallowed alive". In spite of all these fears, however, we have found only one recorded instance where loss of human life was attributed to a crevasse. In that incident, "seven Indians were swallowed up" in one of these chasms, six of whom perished. The seventh Indian survived to tell

the story. This fascinating and frightening episode is told in the book, *The Earthquake America Forgot.*

Graben Fissures. These landforms are perhaps the next level of lateral spreading. Instead of a sag or crevasse forming, under certain conditions a down-dropped "block" sinks, replacing the liquefied material which has moved out. The non-liquefied sediment and soil, instead of bending and sagging downward, breaks and sinks as a unit. The block is bounded on each side by normal faults. These features can be only a few feet in length, or extend more than a mile. Their widths range from 10 to 100 feet. They contain little or no sand and sometimes hold water during wet weather. Their depths average around 1-10 feet. Another characteristic of graben fissures is their "canoe shape". They "pinch out" on both ends, having no natural surface outlet. Some witnesses to the 1811-12 events reported that the flat bottoms of these features remained horizontal after sinking. Trees, sometimes very large ones, would be as vertical after they were lowered down as they were before! Graben fissures are not the same as "grabens" which are discussed later.

Sand Fissures. Sand fissures may be linear, curvilinear, or show a circular and concentric pattern from above. They are simply crevasses that opened deeply enough to allow the liquefied sand below to gush upwards, filling them with sand. These are usually at or near grade and can be more than a mile long. Their widths range from a few inches

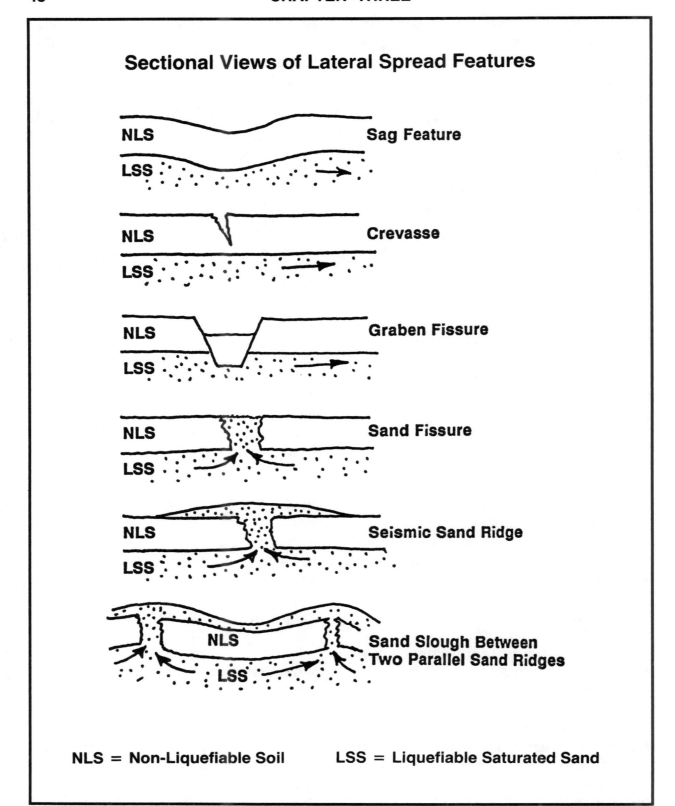

FIGURE 21. Lateral Spread Features

to more than 30 feet. More properly, they could be called "sand-filled fissures", but "sand fissure" is shorter and we prefer to use the more succinct term. Sand fissures have many of the same liquefaction-prone sensitivities as sand boils, and, like boils, fragments of carbonized wood and lignite can often be found. Farmers do not cross sand fissures during wet seasons, because their machinery tends to bog down. Hundreds of these features mark the landscape between New Madrid and Blytheville, and are especially numerous between Portageville and Hayti. They will liquefy again in future earthquakes.

Seismic Sand Ridges and Sand Sloughs. When a linear crevasse opens deeply enough, it can be filled with liquefied sand from below forming a sand fissure. If the liquefied sand keeps coming, and continues to flow after the crevasse is filled, then it flows out on both sides forming a seismic sand ridge. We use the term "seismic sand ridge" because the term "sand ridge" has been used by some scientists to designate old river terraces or old natural levees. Seismic sand ridges can be several miles long and as much as a mile wide. Most are smaller. They are usually linear and often found in parallel with other ridges with intervening sandy troughs between. These troughs have been named "sand sloughs", (pronounced "sloo") a local term used by Fuller (1912). They often formed linear intermittent lakes or seasonal swamps with trees and vegetation growing in the sloughs but little or no vegetation growing on the ridge crests.

Section IV
Differential Subsidence Features

Sunk Lands. Sunk lands are depressions, covering large areas, that formed during the New Madrid (or earlier) earthquakes. They usually drain well enough not to become permanent lakes, but they may act as catchment basins for rainwater runoff and become intermittent lakes. The subsidence that creates sunk lands is due primarily to the behavior of the ancient rocks far below. The very cause of the earthquakes are the great "fault blocks" moving upward, downward, or laterally. Rock and sediment layers above these moving blocks are raised, lowered, or moved laterally in response. Another factor causing subsidence may be **deep areal liquefaction (DAL)** where wet, porous sandy sediments are very near the deep source zone of the quake or in direct contact with, or very close to, the moving fault blocks. Near the focus of the earthquake, waves may be strong enough to "free" pore water in spite of the great weight of material at these depths. The liquefied material is then able to move, causing differential settling of the loose, shaken sediment above. (See Stewart & Knox 1995, reference #44.)

Myron Fuller (1912) discusses sunk lands at length and shows the locations of many such areas on his regional map published in 1905 and included with his 1912 publication as a pocket insert. These features were sometimes several miles in extent and of all shapes--linear, elliptic, and irregular. Sunk lands flanked both sides of the Sikeston Ridge. The large, low area south of the New Madrid

High School was covered with water enough of the time to be named **Lake St. Anne.**

Earthquake Lakes. These landforms are sunk lands deep enough to intersect the water table. They hold water perennially and differ from other low areas, such as lateral spread sags or sand sloughs, that hold water intermittently. Earthquake lakes differ from earthquake ponds in that the ponds result from explosive sand expulsion during intense near-surface liquefaction (Figure 19) while the lakes are due to deep areal liquefaction (DAL). The most famous of the earthquake lakes is **Reelfoot Lake.** This lake covered 65,000 acres in 1812, but has silted in to only 14,000 acres of open water today. Reelfoot is about 18 miles long and 3-5 miles wide with maximum depth of 20 feet The terrain that was to become Reelfoot Lake was already low and swampy before the quakes. The area was a large former meander loop of the Mississippi, a landform called an oxbow lake. A small stream, Reelfoot creek, drained the area. It is reported that an extrusion of sand along the downstream part of this creek contributed to the ponding of Reelfoot Lake. Evidence for additional sinking, "partly due to a general depression and partly due to faulting", is cited by Fuller. We think that the causes were renewed upward movement of Tiptonville Dome, concurrent downward movement of the lowland, and areal subsidence from deep liquefaction.

A large earthquake lake is located in Mississippi County, Arkansas, on the Arkansas-Missouri state line just west of Blytheville. This is **Big Lake.** Before the earthquakes, the Big Lake region was a hardwood and cypress forest. Afterwards the area became a new lake whose bottom was covered with fallen deciduous trees—species that commonly grow on dry ground and cannot survive submergence in water. Many of the cypress trees survived the inundation and can be seen to this day—some standing in water up to eight feet deep. Big Lake is presently a fishing and wildlife area.

At least eight more earthquake lakes were created, at least partly, by the big earthquakes, but they have since been drained. Only Big Lake and Reelfoot Lake remain. The site of one of the largest of the drained lakes is found twenty miles north of Sikeston. This is the basin of the former **Lake St. John**. It was drained in the early 1900's to create more farmland. Other large ones include **Lake Nicormy**, which was located between Hayti and Kennett, and **Cagle Lake**, near Cooter. The largest of all the earthquake lakes was **Lake St. Francis** which resulted from a combination of subsidence and the temporary doming of the St. Francis River north of Marked Tree, Arkansas. This lake was 40 miles long, extending as far north as Senath, Missouri, and Leonard, Arkansas. It was still there in 1905 when Fuller did his field work and mapped the lake for his 1912 publication. Fuller also mentions **Flag Lake**, northwest of Kennett, Missouri, and **Lake Tyronza**, near Tyronza, Arkansas. **Lost Lake**, just east of Bell City, Missouri, is also shown on one of Fuller's maps. (See Figures 2 & 18.) The proneness to liquefaction in earthquake lake areas was well illustrated in 1987 when a Richter 5.2 earthquake occurred near Lawrenceville, Illinois, and caused liquefaction damage to several homes in the Lost Lake area—150 miles from the epicenter! This interesting incident is described in more detail in the book, *The Earthquake America Forgot*. Examples of liquefaction from light earthquakes (magnitudes 4.0-4.9) are also discussed in that book.

Discontinuous Channels. These landforms usually meander and usually "pinch out" on both ends. Most of them are rarely more than 6-8 feet deep or 12-15 feet wide. At first glance, they appear to be remnants of old drainages that farmers have had trouble filling and leveling. On closer inspection, however, it becomes apparent that they are more than this. They do not have a consistent gradient as does an unmodified surface drainage channel. In fact, it is not unusual to find evidence that they gather water from both directions. When investigating them up close, it becomes apparent that water enters both ends and disappears into the ground.

We believe discontinuous channels were produced by some combination of at least three processes. In many cases, streams that were running on the ground surface when the big quakes hit were modified by the strong ground motion, including violent channel explosions. In other cases, buried channels, near the surface, were "reactivated" by the ground motion. In fact, buried sand bars and sandy natural levees probably supplied much of the sand that is ejected onto the surface as sand blows and sand boils. In other instances, channels became "discontinuous" when terrain over or toward which they were flowing were raised or lowered, sometimes reducing or even reversing their gradients.

In any case, both surface streams and buried stream channels are very susceptible to seismically-induced liquefaction. During strong earthquakes, they are easily modified by liquefaction of the saturated sediment. Sand ejected from below probably invites differential subsidence into the vacated spaces. On the surface, the ejected sand often disrupts drainage directions, or dams it entirely in small streams. Subtle upwarped surfaces resulting from raised lands undoubtedly disrupts many streams, especially when they try to flow in the direction of the upwarp. Add to this scenario the effects of some lateral spreading and we probably have a pretty good picture of why so many discontinuous streams exist in the NMSZ to this day. The most-subsided segments induce surface water to flow toward them. Less-subsided segments can be filled in and claimed for farming. The net result is thousands of stream segments or channel segments, cut off from other segments, not "going anywhere".

The landforms we are calling "discontinuous channels" might also include subsided oxbow lakes. The subsidence and filling of the oxbow lakes in the sunk land east of the Tiptonville Dome would then be the prime example of this species. We call it Reelfoot Lake!

These features illustrate a couple of principles that we have become aware of while researching SIL features in this area:

Principle One could be stated something like "all landforms in the NMSZ have been effected and modified by the big earthquakes". The question is not whether or not, but rather, how much.

Principle Two is that in order to understand almost any SIL feature, we must see how it ties in to the water table. For example, how far above the water table is the feature? Where were the saturated and unsaturated zones in 1811? An understanding of the local and regional hydrology is an absolute must.

Section V.
Uplift and Secondary Fault Features

Raised Lands. Land areas were warped upward, as well as downward, during the big earthquakes. Raised lands are the opposites of sunk lands. Several contemporary accounts describe the occurrence of land that was higher after the earthquakes than before. One account states that "the numerous large ponds which covered a large part of the country were nearly dried up. The beds of some of them were elevated above their former banks several feet, producing an alteration of 10 to 20 feet from the horizontal surface". Another account says that "previous to the earthquake keelboats would come up the St. Francis River and pass into the Mississippi (through Little River) three miles below New Madrid. The bayou is now dry land". One of the most conspicuous of the uplifts (to geologists!) is the

Tiptonville Dome, (also called the Lake County Uplift), south of New Madrid Bend. This structure has a surface area of some 250 square miles. The central part of this uplift appears to be a horst, a "block" raised up between two faults. The name of this feature is the Tiptonville Horst. We visualize the Tiptonville Dome as a large area which has been repeatedly pushed upward, probably responding to faulting in the ancient rocks far beneath the soft alluvium seen at the surface. This overlying material responded by bending in most places, but it was forced to break (fault) in others.

Primary and Secondary Faults. As far as we can tell at the present time, there is no location on the surface where we can definitely say "here is the New Madrid Fault". The Bootheel Lineament is the best candidate for this "honor". The Bootheel Lineament is a feature that can be seen on satellite images. It is at least 50 miles long, and possibly as much as 70 or 80 miles long, and stretches from near Blytheville to near New Madrid. Marked by massive SIL sand features, it is currently under study by researchers. Early and inconclusive evidence suggests that it may be a strike-slip fault. (See Figure 22.) It might be primary - that is - it might be an extension to the surface of actual faulting in ancient rocks below. Movements along this fault plane may have been the cause of at least one of the earthquakes.

However, it is more likely that the Bootheel Lineament is an expression of a secondary fault, one that was caused by (not a cause of) the earthquakes. Perhaps the data present researchers are collecting will show whether this lineament is primary, secondary, or neither of the above!

Another feature on the Bootheel Lineament can be seen on satellite imagery near the lineament's northern end. It has been called **"The Star."** The center of this feature is located a mile or two south of the community of Boekerton. Distinct "rays" appear to radiate outward from a center. (See Figure 51, page 130.) Does this feature predate 1811-12? Is it the intersection of three or more lineaments? Can faults actually radiate outward? Is this unusual feature related, perhaps, to the epicenter of the 8.8 magnitude megaquake on February 7, 1812? Or is the explanation cultural and non-geologic? We really don't know what to make of it.

The most impressive of the secondary faults in the NMSZ is undoubtedly **Reelfoot Fault**. (See Figures 11, 23 & 29.) This fault separates the raised land to the west, the **Tiptonville Dome**, from the sunk land to the east, now including **Reelfoot Lake**. The fault, then, was the shear plane along which this movement occurred. A prominent escarpment, up to 30 feet high, can be seen.

There were probably hundreds of small secondary faults produced by the big earthquakes. Natural erosion processes and human modifications have eliminated all traces of them, at least on the surface.

Accelerated Stream Gradients. A well-publicized and probably related set of phenomena were the notorious **waterfalls** that appeared during the greatest of the earthquakes, on February 7, 1812, and lasted for a few days. Do not visualize these features as great, plunging Niagara-type waterfalls. A better image is one that resembles the falls of the Ohio River, dropping 15 or 20 feet over one or two miles. Sudden movements on geologic **faults**, running across the bed of the Mississippi, almost certainly created the cascades. The falls lasted for only a few hours, or days, until the river was able to reestablish its former gradient by wearing away the deformities in its bed.

The exact locations of the waterfalls have been a matter of disagreement. Penick (1981), who researched this point, identifies "two sets of falls, one above New Madrid and the other below New Madrid." Penick's interpretation puts a pair of falls on each side of Bessie's neck. (See map on page 55.) Another interpretation puts one fall half a mile upstream from New Madrid and the other ten miles downstream. The latter location does not jibe with the account of Mathias Speed, who was in charge of two boats coming down the river. His party tied up for the night opposite Island #9, 15 miles **upstream** from New Madrid, on February 6. They were there when the first shocks came, and the danger of collapse of the bank forced them to get underway early (3:15 a.m.!) on February 7. Surviving through the remaining night, daylight found them approaching Island #10, ten miles upstream from New Madrid. Speed's account of the wild ride past Island #10 follows: "we were affrightened with the appearance of a dreadful rapid of falls in the river just below us; we were so far in the suck that it was impossible

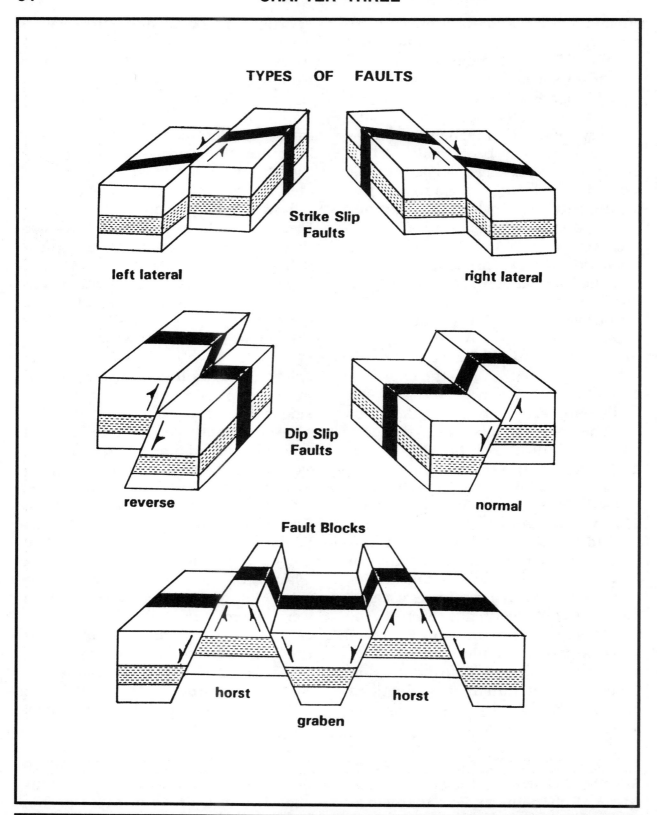

FIGURE 22. Types of Faults

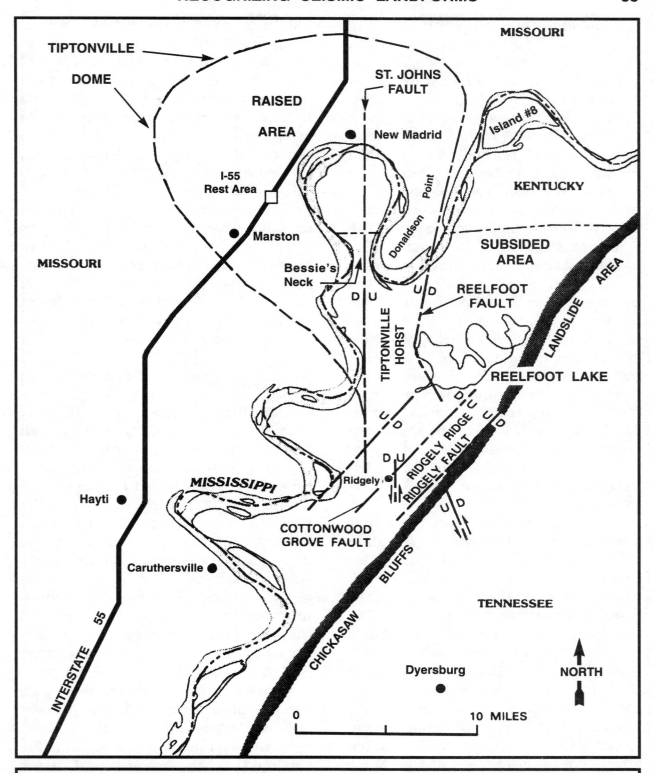

FIGURE 23. Secondary Faults & Slope Failures in the Reelfoot Lake Area. The epicentral region of the 8.8 magnitude quake of February 7, 1812, is thought to have been centered somewhere between Marston and New Madrid, Missouri—near the Rest Stop on I-55. More than 200 landslides were triggered along the Chickasaw Bluffs from Memphis to Wickliffe. Temporary waterfalls (rapids) formed on the Mississippi where it crossed the two boundary faults of the Tiptonville Horst. The river ran backwards between the tip of Donaldson Point and Island #8. As can be seen, Reelfoot Lake is only 17 miles from New Madrid "as the crow flies," but more than 70 miles by highway. See Figs 29-30.   (After Jibson & Keefer 1988)

now to land—all hopes of surviving was now lost and certain destruction appeared to await us". It is compelling to place the upper waterfall at 10 miles upstream from New Madrid for another reason. This location is on a direct line with the **Reelfoot Scarp,** which borders the eastern margin of the Tiptonville Dome. The Reelfoot Scarp is from 10 to 30 feet high, and trends in a northerly direction. It is a surface expression of the **Reelfoot Fault** that here marks the eastern side of the Tiptonville Dome.

There is good evidence that the dome and the fault have been active for a very long time. Further movements that occurred during the New Madrid earthquakes of 1811-12 were only the latest. There are a lot of confusing data regarding the amount of movement on the Reelfoot Fault in 1811-12. Evidence from trenching suggests only about 4 feet of movement occurred. Evidence from seismic profiles indicates a good possibility of much more.

The same earth movements that created this scarp almost certainly effected the land across the river, displaced the river bed, and created the rapids so vividly described by Mr. Speed. Then there is another credibility problem with the location of the lower falls reportedly 8 miles "downriver" from New Madrid. It is stated that the residents of New Madrid could hear the roar of these rapids. Penick (1981) says "the roar of the lower falls, although eight miles away, could be heard distinctly at New Madrid". We think it more likely that the roars heard were those associated with a rapids only a half-mile or so above New Madrid. We think the

falls purported to be 8 miles **down**river were actually 8-10 miles **up**river. A likely source of error is the fact that while the downstream direction from New Madrid is to the south, **so is the upstream direction!** When referring to any river location within ten or fifteen miles of New Madrid, the term "below" might mean "downstream" or it might mean "south of". We think, therefore, that the first set of falls was located a mile or so upstream from present New Madrid, but that the **second set of falls** was **also** upstream, in the vicinity of Island#10, at Donaldson Point—eight or ten miles **upstream** from New Madrid. (See Figures 29 & 30.)

Reversed Stream Gradients. An event that rivals the waterfalls as a fascinating, almost unbelievable occurrence, was the **"river that ran backwards"**. Accounts from contemporaries on this subject range from probably accurate and objective to completely fanciful. Reports of the time involved in the alleged reversal ranged from a few hours to several days. Some of the gross exaggerations prompted some scientists to dispel the entire event. One prominent seismologist attributed tales of the river flowing upstream to "hysteria and superstition." Lyell, and later, Fuller, hardly mentioned the episode. They apparently viewed the tales with considerable skepticism. Another scientist, James MacFarlane (1883), even went so far as to insist that the earthquakes themselves had never occurred! We think the retrograde movement of the Mississippi River **did** actually occur. As suggested above, we believe the **Reelfoot Fault**

extended across the Mississippi, near the east end of Island #10, northward into Donaldson Point. Movement on the fault was such as to raise the west side while lowering the east side. This raised the channel of the river several feet, perhaps even 15 or 20 feet, creating a **natural dam** that must have lasted several hours. This caused a reversal in gradient, a retrograde flow of the current, and spilling of much backed-up water both into the lowland that became **Reelfoot Lake** and into the forests on the Missouri side of the river that were overwhelmed, then buried by sediment. We therefore believe some of the dramatic accounts of huge waves causing **destruction of forests**. We discuss these dramatic events in more detail in the next chapter.

Section VI.
Slope Failure Features

Slope Failure Features. The Chickasaw Bluffs east of the Mississippi River from Memphis, Tennessee to Wickliffe, Kentucky have more than 200 identified landslide features attributed to earthquake shaking. Geologic circumstances there are particularly susceptible to slope failures. They are high. The tops are made of thick loess deposits overlying permeable glacial outwash gravel over impermeable clay. Water percolates downward, through the loess and gravel, but is forced to flow out horizontally when it hits the clay. The water lubricates the clay, and the only thing missing is a trigger, such as an earthquake. The resulting slide can be dramatic!

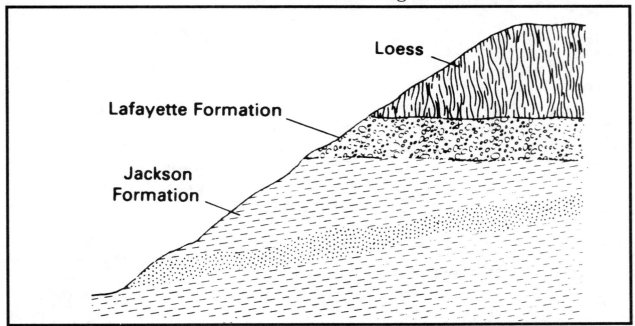

FIGURE 24. Geologic Section and Topographic Profile of Chickasaw Bluffs. These bluffs extend along the east side of the Mississippi from Wickliffe, KY, to Memphis, TN, ranging in relief from 80-200 feet above the flood plain. The Pleistocene loess that tops the bluffs is a very slide-prone material which can break away in blocks when dry, rotate as a slump when wet, or form an earthflow when saturated. The Pliocene Lafayette gravel below the loess conducts groundwater to the Eocene Jackson clay below—keeping it wet. Many springs can be found along the base of the bluffs at the Jackson-Lafayette contact. The Jackson clay is usually water saturated—providing a lubricated base plane for translational block sliding when a large earthquake occurs.　　　　(After Jibson & Keefer 1988)

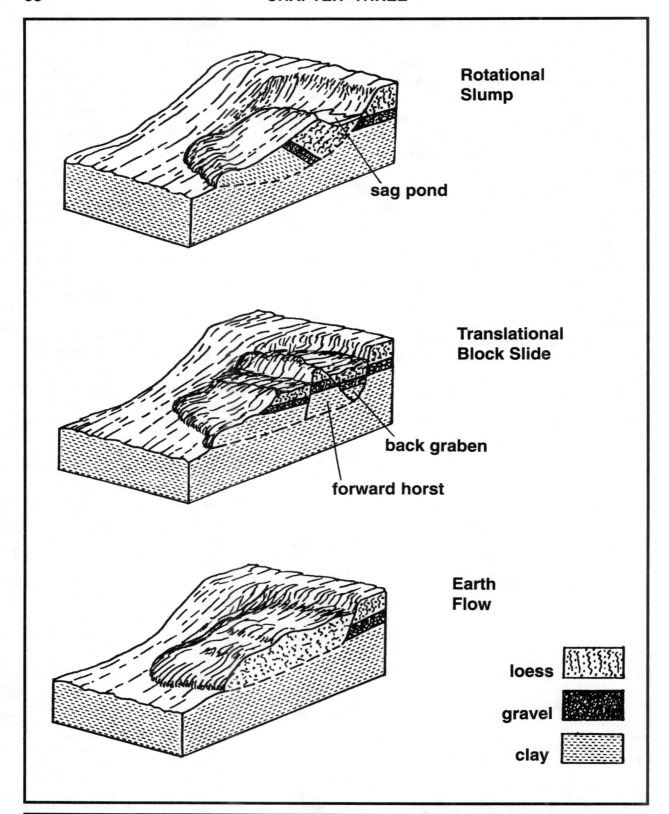

Rotational
Slump

sag pond

Translational
Block Slide

back graben

forward horst

Earth
Flow

loess

gravel

clay

FIGURE 25. Slope Failure Features

Most slope processes are much more subtle than this. Unconsolidated material on any slope is moving down that slope, when viewed from geologic time. Strong ground motion may convert the subtle, gentle forms of downslope movement into rapid, even violent forms.

Evidence exists for slope failures along the escarpments of the Benton and Bloomfield Hills segments of Crowley's Ridge. Many of these were triggered by earthquakes. The combination of factors described for the bluffs east of the Mississippi River are also operating along the escarpments of Crowley's Ridge. Loess which overlies gravel, which in turn overlies sand and silt, which overlies an impermeable clay seam, awaits a trigger. (See Figure 24.) Even a mild earthquake might provide enough ground motion to set the mass of material free.

For some really dramatic examples of slope failures and potential slope failures, the town of Hickman, Kentucky, is a good place to visit.

Section VII.
Historic Sites

Historic Seismic Sites. There are many, many historic sites in the New Madrid area that have a seismic connection. The rich history and folklore of the region is so much a part of any study of the great earthquakes. The New Madrid Historic Museum and Observational Platform are good places to start.

Former Site of New Madrid. The original site of New Madrid when the great earthquakes occurred in 1811-12 is presently occupied by the Mississippi River. Standing on the observation deck and looking straight south across the river, the viewer can see a piece of Kentucky within a tight oxbow. The large island seen to the right was deposited by a large flood in 1927. Looking due south from the deck, the river is a mile wide. Visualize a point about halfway across. This is where original New Madrid was built. On February 7, 1812, during the great 8.8 magnitude quake, much of what was left of the town (already badly damaged from the earlier earthquakes) subsided about 12-15 feet by being on the downthrown side of the fault movement that created the waterfall just east of town. The final blow to the town was the spring floods of 1812, which washed its remains away.

The epicenter of the 8.8 event is thought to be within a few miles of the Associated Electric Company smoke stack—easily visible next to the river 5.5 miles downstream. The high visibility of this smoke stack makes it an ideal marker for the epicentral area of this monster earthquake.

Looking upstream to the left (east), find where the river bends out of sight. This is the approximate place where one of two temporary **waterfalls** appeared. The falls reportedly played havoc with some of the flatboats that tried to "shoot" them, and accounts of some of these episodes are difficult to unravel. A second zone of falls and rapids appeared about 10 miles upstream, at the southern end of Donaldson Point. This is the obstruction that probably caused the **"river to run**

backwards" for several hours.

Violent waves from this episode were thrown ashore on the west bank between Islands #8 and #10. Several thousand acres of virgin trees—cypress, cottonwoods, and oaks—were broken off into stumps 3-12 feet tall. (See Figure 30.) Hundreds of thousands of tree limbs and trunks clogged the Mississippi and the devastation of these forestlands was visible to passing boatmen for many decades following the quake. We think there must be thousands of acres of this devastated forest still buried along the east side of Donaldson Point. Photos of these shattered arboreal victims of the earthquakes of 1811-12 can be seen in both of the books that are companions to this one.

Former Site of Little Prairie. Another site of great historic significance is near present-day **Caruthersville**. The present town was founded in 1857, several decades after the earthquakes. However, nearby is the site of Little Prairie. This original town, like old New Madrid, became a victim of the December 16 quake. What apparently happened is that this whole area became liquefied and fractured into thousands of sand blows, sand boils, and fissures. Tremendous quantities of water and sand were ejected. It is reported that so many crevasses and fissures opened, that people could not walk without stepping into or over a crack. Eyewitnesses also reported water shooting up from cracks "over the tops of tall trees" and that when the ground broke in some places, it also split trees that straddled the fissures.

One report states that one hundred residents of the doomed village were forced to flee for their lives, wading for about 8 miles through water which in some places was up to waist deep. Snakes, coyotes, and other creatures swam along with them. Finding some high ground near present-day Hayti, they spent the night of December 17, then trekked to New Madrid, where they arrived on Christmas Eve, 1811, to find the town a shambles. And, of course, New Madrid was to experience the great 8.8 quake 45 days later!

The site of Little Prairie is now occupied by the Mississippi River. This can be viewed by driving to the Bunge Elevator in Caruthersville, a ten-story structure visible for miles. Tennessee can be seen across the river. Stand on the Mississippi River bank at the city park here and visualize a place about half-way across the river out from the elevator. From that point to the opposite side is where Little Prairie used to be.

To learn more about the historical aspects of the New Madrid earthquakes, we recommend the books by Fuller, Penick, and Nuttli in the bibliography of this book as well as *The Earthquake America Forgot* by Stewart & Knox, which is the most complete historical account of these earthquakes published to date.

Section VIII.
Pseudoseismic Landforms

Pseudoseismic Landforms. Earthquakes are only one of the several forces and processes that modify the landscape in the New Madrid area. Streams, ranging from tiny rills to the

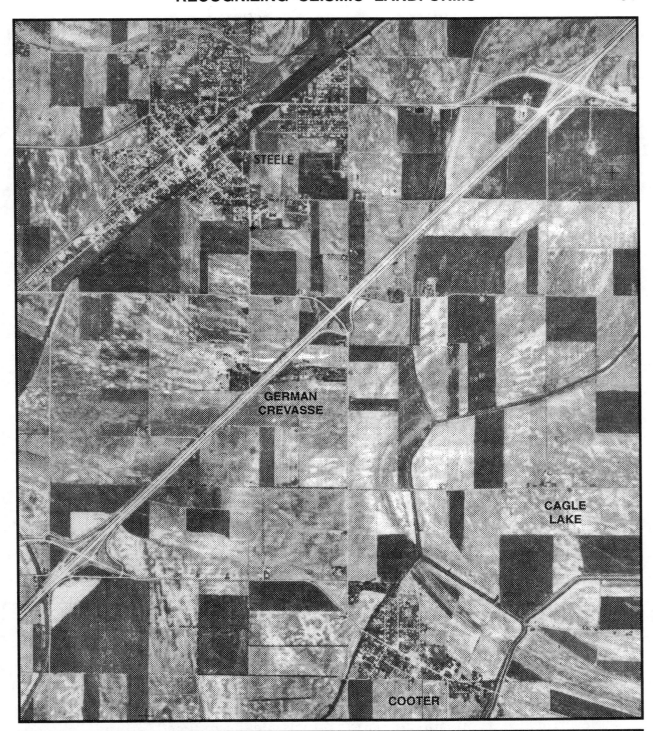

FIGURE 26. Aerial View of New Madrid Seismic Zone Over I-55 Between Cooter & Steele. This is epicentral ground zero for the Richter 8.0 earthquake around 8:00 A.M. on December 16, 1811. I-55 passes right through it. In the upper right is Exit #8, Hwy 164, to Steele. Duckies is there. (See p. 93) On the lower left is Exit #4, Hwy E, to Cooter. The numerous streaks of light grey are seismic sand fissures—places where the earth split open during the quakes and where quicksand from below filled the cracks. Midway between the two exits is a half-mile-long east-west dark zone passing under the Interstate—the German Earthquake Crevasse. (See p. 93) This is a place where the earth split but no quicksand flowed in. It is still a deep crevasse. Several sand fissures funnel into this zone from the west while one large white streak under I-55 parallels the crevasse on the north. A portion of the bed of Cagle Lake, created by the December 16 earthquake, is also seen here. (Photo U.S. Geol. Survey 1974.) Scale: 2.625 inches = 1 mile or 1 in = aprox. 0.4 mi.

great rivers, have contributed the most. Wind, slope failures, ground water, and people have added their influence. Today, the greatest changes are wrought by people, mostly to level land for agricultural purposes. Hence, countless seismic features have been obliterated. What is remarkable is that so many hundreds of seismic features can still be found in spite of the forces of man and nature working to erase them. It speaks to the incredible magnitude of these cataclysms that the landscape still bears recognizable testimony of their occurrence over 180 years ago.

Natural Pseudoseismic Features. Technically, all landforms in the core area of the New Madrid Seismic Zone have been modified to some degree by the great series of earthquakes in 1811-12. There is a broad continuum between those landforms modified ever-so-slightly on one hand and those landforms completely seismic in origin (seismogenic) on the other.

The sands and silts "used" by seismic forces to create earthquake induced liquefaction or lateral spread features come from whatever sources are available. For example, the sand ejected from explosion sand blows may have been part of a natural levee, deposited by a stream that existed thousands of years ago, or from any number of other pre-existing, non-seismic sandy features.

Nevertheless, thousands of sand features are close to the "modified ever so slightly" end of the continuum, and may be considered pseudoseismic—that is, "false seismic," and we need to take care to avoid attaching too much seismic influence on

them, and to distinguish them from the clearly morphoseismic landforms discussed above.

Sand dunes of wind origin or sand deposited by ancient streams are sometimes round or elliptical and can be mistaken for sand boils. Such features, however, are usually several feet, or tens of feet, high. Boils are rarely more than 2 feet high. Sometimes water is trapped in small irregular ponds between dunes. These **dune ponds** can be mistaken for earthquake ponds. Many dune ponds can be seen east of Newport, Arkansas.

Erosion remnants of former terraces and fans are common, especially east of Sikeston Ridge where streams have eroded some of this old terrace away, but have left remaining many relatively high places.

Braided-bar islands are remnants of the times thousands of years ago when the waters of the Mississippi and Ohio braided across these plains, in contrast to the meandering rivers of today. **River and stream sandbars** of present-day or streams of the past, can also be mistaken for seismic features, until studied close-up. **Small stream channels** can look like discontinuous channels, indeed, discontinuous channels were once segments of streams. After alteration by seismically-induced ground motion, stream channels become differentially subsided, disrupting the gradients.

Prairie Mounds. The origin of prairie mounds is still very much in doubt, but is unlikely to be seismic. Prairie mounds, also called prairie pimples or mima mounds, are found by the thousands, especially in the western and northern portions of the NMSZ. These mounds are composed of silt, not sand, and they rarely exceed 100 feet in diameter or 5 feet in height. Since they are composed of silt, the most likely origin is wind.

Sun Boils. Sometimes, when moisture and crop conditions, sun angles, and holes in clouds are just right, sun boils can be seen in fields. These sunbeams can look remarkably similar to sand boils from a distance, especially when the clouds are nearly stationary. We have learned to postpone looking for extruded sand features when these things are messing with our minds.

Alluvial features such as **terraces and natural levees**, formed by ancient rivers, can be confused with seismic or tectonic features. Old relic terraces and levees are usually found paralleling the large rivers that created them.

Sikeston Ridge is a major topographic feature stretching from north of Sikeston to southwest of New Madrid. It is composed of braided stream deposits spread across the upper Mississippi Alluvial Valley by the ancestral Ohio and Mississippi Rivers. Since its deposition, the Mississippi River has eroded the central portion of the once much larger landform, bisecting it into the Malden Plain on the west and the Sikeston Ridge on the east. Although the Sikeston Ridge "lines up" pretty well with the Tiptonville Horst, no struc-

tural relationship has yet been proven.

Hydrologically-induced sand boils are mostly due to high river levels that create a hydraulic gradient (head) from the riverside of the levees toward the protected land inside. When in the process of boiling, many sand cones are formed, some 10-20 feet in diameter and 2-6 feet high, but which erode away within a year. Seismic sand boil and fissure features will also boil from hydraulic pressures during high water on the levee. Hence, hydraulically induced liquefaction (HIL) and seismically induced liquefaction (SIL) can act upon the same places and produce the same features.

An important point to remember is that earthquakes are opportunistic. They will release their forces by the pathways of least resistance. Often these pathways are the creations of other processes of nature, such as rivers, hydraulics, wind, and human. Reelfoot Lake, as an example, was already the site of a large oxbow lake, but the earthquakes deepened and extended the water area. The landslides at Hickman, Kentucky, are active during heavy rains, but will also respond to earthquake ground motion. An earthquake will mold and modify whatever is vulnerable to its forces, taking whatever opportunities it can grab whether provided by nature or man.

Man-made Pseudoseismic Features. Various landscape modifications made by humans can be confused with seismic features, but with study and thought they can be distinguished. **Indian mounds** are normally regular and often more than 3-10 feet high. They are made of soils, not sand. **Borrow pits** are usually square, rectangular, or triangular, which helps to distinguish them from sunk lands, graben fissures, or earthquake lakes. In addition, they are nearly always near to the structures to which the soils were transported, such as highway overpasses and levees. **Canals and drainage ditches** are almost always straight, not meandering or at odd angles.

Some **sand mining operations** can be confused with sand blow explosion craters, but a quiz of the residents will tell if it is natural or man-dug. The same goes for filled explosion craters and earthquake ponds. It should also be remembered that just as earthquakes are opportunistic in the features they select for seismic reshaping, so too are humans opportunistic in their modification of the landscape. Many sand pits, for instance, occur in old seismic sand boils, sand fissures, or seismic sand ridges. A particularly outstanding example of this is a huge sand pit in Howardsville, Missouri. It could be mistaken for an earthquake pond inasmuch as it is surrounded with sand and the water table freely rises and falls in the depression. However, the property owner tells us that it is a former sand mine. The site is still seismic, however, probably a huge sand boil. There are several large nearby sand boils that have not been mined.

Spoil banks are the piles of material that line the drainage ditches and some natural channels that have been dredged for deepening and/or widening. These form levee-like features on one or both sides. Earthquake crevasses, graben fissures, earthquake ponds, or subsided channels do not have spoil banks.

Destruction & Preservation of Earthquake Features

Many of the unique landforms created by the great earthquakes of 1811-12 can be considered as natural resources—like the hot springs of Arkansas or the sculptured rock-forms in Colorado's Garden of the Gods. Thousands of remarkable features created in 1811-12 no longer exist—many destroyed by the unrelenting forces of nature, herself, others destroyed by the works of man.

In fact, several outstanding features we would have included in this guide we had to omit because they were destroyed during the six year interval during which we researched and wrote the book. Some of the features included here and which existed at the time the book was published may be destroyed by the time you go to visit them—covered by a highway, obliterated by a new housing subdivision, or scraped away by agricultural activity.

Most of the earthquake lakes created in 1811-12 were drained between 1924-1929 for mosquito control and to make land available for agriculture. The giant cypress stumps broken off by these quakes that used to be visible along the banks of the Mississippi River are now covered with stone rip-rap by the U.S. Army Corps of Engineers while other quake-shattered stumps exposed in borrow pits near levees have been uprooted and destroyed. Most of the earthquake ponds and explosion craters have also been filled in. These latter features. however, could still be dug out and restored to their 1811-12 appearance. They are not lost, just buried.

The greatest destruction of seismic features in recent decades has been caused by land leveling. The large equipment used in these operations literally scrapes off the high places and fills in the low spots until the fields are planed and graded for agricultural purposes—often for rice production.

Wouldn't it be a good idea to set aside a few hundred acres that contain some of the best remaining seismic features and save them for future generations to see? We think so. This series of earthquakes may have been one of the world's greatest cataclysms in the last 2,000 years. It ought to be remembered. In a couple of hundred years or so it will happen again.

It is important, we feel, for people to realize how powerful nature can be and how small, as mortal humans, we are in comparison. To look upon these features and realize the magnitude of the incredible forces that produced them is an humbling experience. Such appreciation and respect for the natural world helps one to keep a wholesome perspective on how we fit into the universe, at large, as well as with our neighbors nearby.

As you enjoy the trips of this field guide, take note of your favorite stops and make a mental list of the features you would like to see preserved for future generations to visit. Send us a copy of your list, if you like.

Perhaps some day an "Earthquake Park" could be created in the New Madrid Seismic Zone to commemorate one of natures all-time-great performances and to honor the brave people who witnessed and survived it.

FIGURE 27. Chartreau Explosion Crater Before it Was Filled In. This conical crater was blasted out by the earthquakes of 1811-12. It is just west of Hwy 61 and I-55 at Exit 49—just north of New Madrid. With the rustic red barn and the charming Chartreau mansion, this was always a favorite stop and photo opportunity on field trips to the NMSZ. On the left is a group of geoscientists and earthquake engineers from 15 countries who visited the site in 1991. On the right is Ray Knox (6' 2") standing in the crater while David Stewart lay with his elbows on the ground to get this angle. If you go there now, you'll find neither the barn nor the house nor the explosion crater. The buildings were torn down and the crater was filled up in 1994. However, there are still two other explosion craters only a few hundred feet north of this one and they are both still there. (See Side Trip A.) Furthermore, the large trees seen in the distance behind the house is a grove of 200-300 year-old oaks. These trees were alive during the earthquakes in 1811-12 and are still alive today. One of these majestic oaks is six feet in diameter at chest height and almost 90 feet tall. We propose that the county or state purchase this grove, dig out the filled explosion crater, restore it to the way it was in 1812, and create an "Earthquake Park" complete with earthquake explosion craters, sand boils, seismic sand fissures and a host of living witness trees. (See p. 109.)

NEW MADRID BEND in 1810

Before the earthquakes of 1811-12 there were two towns on New Madrid Bend, New Madrid and Point Pleasant. There were also three inlets to the Mississippi: St. John's Bayou, Bayou Fourche (which connected with Gut Ste. Anne) and Bayou Portage (which connected with Portage Open Bay). Gut Ste. Anne and Portage Open Bay both connected with the Little River which, in turn, was connected with the St. Francis River.

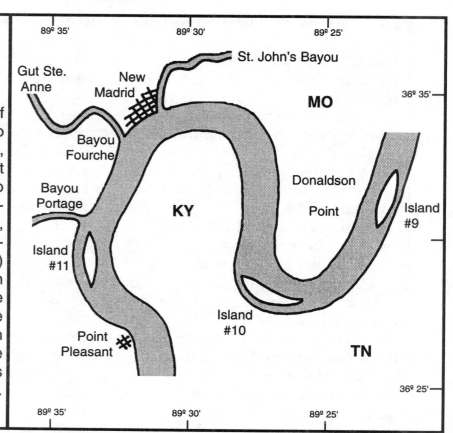

NEW MADRID BEND in 1990

By the late 20th century, the Mississippi River had migrated a mile northward at New Madrid. The waterfront of the original town is now a river bank in Kentucky. The site of Old Point Pleasant is now in Tennessee. Island #9 has been absorbed into the Kentucky mainland while Island #11 has been absorbed into the Missouri side, as has been the mouth of Bayou Portage. Island #10 is now half missing while the remaining half is absorbed into Donaldson Point.

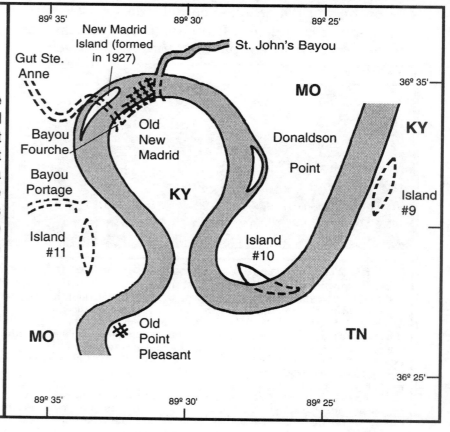

CHAPTER FOUR

THE MOST INCREDIBLE DAY ANY RIVER EVER EXPERIENCED

Now we shall attempt to tie together six incredible happenings on the Mississippi River over the weekend of February 7-10, 1812. History records the following phenomena:

1. Boats Thrown Up on Land at the Mouth of St. John's Bayou.

2. Trees Destroyed Along the East Side of Donaldson Point.

3. The River Flowed Backwards Between Islands #8 and #10.

4. Kentucky Bank Flooded Near Island #9.

5. Reelfoot Lake Created in Tennessee.

6. Two Waterfalls (or Steep Rapids) Formed on the Mississippi.

THE CAUSE:
A Magnitude 8.8 Earthquake

Around 3:15 A.M. on Friday, February 7, 1812, several miles beneath the river deposits of sand and mud at New Madrid—the basement rocks suddenly snapped, precipitating a large rupture that continued to rip for several miles and several minutes emitting great trains of shock waves that radiated outward and upward. Within seconds of the first burst of energy released from depth in the bedrock, the waves, traveling several miles a second, had propagated to the surface—heaving, rolling, shaking and lifting the land up, down, and sideways—perhaps a foot or more. The violent motions lasted several minutes, causing the ground surface to crack, fault, fissure, boil, uplift and sink. This was the greatest of the New Madrid earthquakes. It is considered to have been an 8.8 in Richter surface wave magnitude. The movements of the deep-seated primary faults from which the earthquake originated caused renewed slippages on some of the old secondary faults at the land surface—including the normal faults bounding the east and west sides of the Tiptonville Horst.

The effects and consequences of the great February 7, 1812, earthquake in the vicinity of New Madrid, Missouri, and Reelfoot Lake, Tennessee, are summarized in the Table Three below.

Table Three

Primary & Secondary Effects Of The 8.8 Event Of February 7, 1812

I. Primary Effects
  A. Uplift of Tiptonville Horst
  B. Subsidence of Reelfoot Basin

II. Effects of Uplift & Subsidence
  A. Violent Flooding in Missouri
    1. Boats Thrown up on Land
    2. Forest Broken by Waves
  B. Retrograde Motion of River
  C. Flooding in KY & Tenn.
    1. KY Flooded near Island #9
    2. Filling of Reelfoot Lake
  D. Waterfalls on the Mississippi

Primary Effects are defined here to mean those caused directly by the vibratory ground motion—namely, uplift and subsidence.

Secondary Effects, in this context, are defined to be the consequences of the uplift and subsidence.

The Order of Events

The outline above establishes a time sequence for these happenings:

1. First, the quake occurs at 3:15 A.M. on Friday, February 7, 1812—focused at depth.

2. Seconds later, strong vibratory ground motion begins disturbing the land surface.

3. In response to the ground motion, the Tiptonville Horst is uplifted, with movement along both boundary faults—east and west.

4. At the same time as the uplift, the subsidence of Reelfoot Basin begins.

5. Immediately with and as a result of the uplift of Tiptonville Horst, violent waves result on the Mississippi River—a fluvial tsunami.

6. The waves generated along the west boundary fault throw boats out of the water and onto land at the mouth of St. John's Bayou.

7. The waves along the east boundary fault of the horst destroy thousands of acres of trees along the east side of Donaldson Point—which is on the downthrown side of the fault.

8. The combined uplift and subsidence reverses the gradient of the Mississippi River between Islands #8 and Island #10 causing it to flow backwards for several hours—until around daylight of February 7.

9. The subsidence, downwarping, and reversed flow of the river cause the inundation of the flood plains on the Kentucky and Tennessee sides of the Mississippi.

10. The newly formed Reelfoot Basin begins to fill up creating Reelfoot Lake—which remains to the present day.

11. As the waters of the retrograde river back up and flood the land, more water continues to flow into the area from further upstream eventually rising to a level that can overcome the reversed gradient and

flow over the uplift of Tiptonville Horst. The River then rights itself to its normal downstream course.

12. In flowing over the newly uplifted portion of Tiptonville Horst, two temporary waterfalls (or rapids) form—one near Island #10, the other near the mouth of St. John's Bayou. These waterfalls last until Monday, February 10.

Had you been so unfortunate as to have been one of those living at that time and place, you would certainly call this "A Weekend Never to Forget." The profound and lasting impact of this earthquake on the settlers, the Native Americans, and the history of the Midwest is told in the book entitled, *The Earthquake America Forgot.* Here we shall stick to the profound and lasting impact of this earthquake on the land and the river.

Let us now elaborate a bit more on these extraordinary events—the most incredible day in the life of Old Man River!

EFFECT NUMBER ONE: Uplift of Tiptonville Horst

Tiptonville Horst is a surface feature of the **Tiptonville Dome** or so called **"Lake County Uplift."** The dome or uplift is a large, gentle feature that includes parts of Missouri, Kentucky and Tennessee. It includes most of Lake County, Tennessee, and a good portion of New Madrid County, Missouri. (See Figure 23 on page 55.) This dome predates the earth-

quakes of 1811-12 and is the reason the Mississippi River has such a large bend here. **New Madrid Bend** (also called **Kentucky Bend** and **Bessie Bend**) is actually an earthquake feature—a reflection of the ongoing uplift caused by the thrusting of a portion of the **New Madrid Fault** buried miles below beneath the sediments of the river.

This uplift has been going on for many centuries—probably thousands of years. The river flowing south along the east side of **Donaldson Point** is forced to turn 180 degrees around the point and head north again to get around this feature. As the river erodes over the centuries, the uplift continues with each renewed episode of tectonic or earthquake activity.

It was uplifted a few more feet in 1811-12. The Tiptonville Horst is a portion of the Tiptonville Dome. A **horst** is a block of the earth bounded by **normal faults** on both sides. (See Figure 22 on page 54.) As the larger area of the dome was pushed upwards from below during the New Madrid earthquakes, a portion of the surface, already broken from previous seismic and tectonic activity, shifted again as a block—the Tiptonville Horst.

The eastern fault bounding the horst is called the **Reelfoot Scarp** or **Reelfoot Fault**. The area of uplift renewed in 1811-12 included the western two–thirds of Donaldson Point and the easternmost third of land within New Madrid Bend. (See Figure 29 on the next page.)

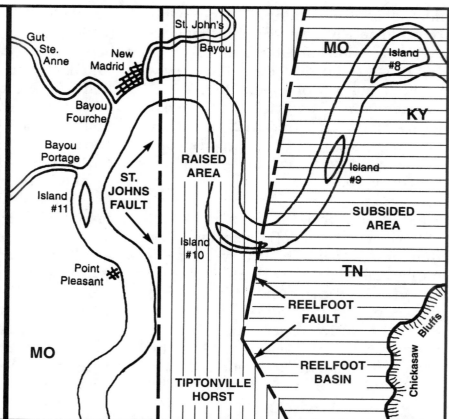

FIGURE 29

PRIMARY EFFECTS OF THE FEBRUARY 7, 1812, QUAKE: MAGNITUDE 8.8

The primary New Madrid Fault is several miles deep here. This segment strikes north-south and is a thrust fault or low angle reverse fault. This type of tectonic movement at depth produces uplift at ground surface. The uplift here is of two types: (1) A gentle upwarping and bending of the surface sediments producing a regional high called "Tiptonville Dome" and (2) a more localized raised area within the dome called "Tiptonville Horst" bounded by normal faults on both sides—Reelfoot Fault on the east and St. Johns Fault on the west. (See Figure 23, p. 55) The large subsided area is not primarily from tectonic forces, but from seismic vibration-induced deep areal liquefaction (DAL). (See Reference #44.) The configuration shown of Mississippi, tributaries, islands, and towns is that of 1811-12. (See Figures 28 & 31.)

EFFECT NUMBER TWO:
Subsidence of Reelfoot Basin

Deep areal liquefaction (DAL) induced by vibratory ground motion over a large area caused the soils to compact, densify, settle, and subside as much as twenty feet in places—creating a large bowl-shaped depression just east of the Tiptonville Horst. (See Stewart & Knox 1995, Ref. #44.)

This area is part of the Mississippi River flood plain. It was already low and swampy before the quakes, but it was not a lake. In fact, a large hardwood forest covered this land before the quakes, sprinkled with bald cypress trees along the streams and bayous that flowed across the plain. Indians lived, farmed and hunted there.

The original size of the basin that formed during the quakes was approximately 20 miles long and 5 miles wide—an area of 100 square miles or 64,000 acres. It has since silted in to an area 16 miles long and 4 miles wide or 41,000 acres—an area less than two-thirds its original size. When the land was inundated in 1811-12, most of the trees died, but many of the cypress remain and can be seen today. (See Side Trip E.)

The region of subsidence during the New Madrid earthquakes of 1811-12 included not only Reelfoot Basin, which imponds the lake, but nearly all of the area in Tennessee and Kentucky between the Chickasaw Bluffs and the Mississippi River. It also included an area in Missouri containing the eastern tip of Island

#10, the easternmost part of Donaldson Point, and several miles of the New Madrid Floodway north and northeast of Donaldson Point.

EFFECT NUMBER THREE:
VIOLENT FLOODING IN MISSOURI

The pair of faults that define the Tiptonville Horst cross the Mississippi at two places: The east side of the horst (Reelfoot Fault) crosses near or at Island #10 at the southern tip of Donaldson Point and extended up the east side of the point. The west side fault of the horst crossed the Mississippi less than a mile upstream from New Madrid—near the mouth of St. John's Bayou.

When the horst raised up, New Madrid would have been on the downthrown side while the the mouth of St. John's Bayou half-a-mile upstream was on the upthrown side. The sudden uplift of the river bed at this point hurled a huge wave which rushed up St. John's Bayou beaching boats and throwing fish onto dry land. Even today, there is a sudden change in the depth of the Mississippi River here. You can't tell by looking at the surface of the water that a cascade ever existed across this stretch, but the history of this event is still preserved in the bottom.

At the same moment, the other side of the horst had raised most of Donaldson Point, except for the eastern portion along the river bank which was on the downthrown side of the fault. The result was a violent wave rushing over a strip of forest extending several miles along the bank which snapped off the trees, reducing them split trunks, broken limbs, and splintered stumps. Boatmen coming down the river for the next fifty years remarked about the graveyard of stumps that lined this bank. Subsequent floods on the Mississippi inundated this portion of Donaldson Point and covered the remains of these broken trees with sand and mud. While the hardwood trees rotted, the cypress have been preserved by this burial. Up until 1993 we could see some of these stumps—casualties of an earthquake nearly 200 years ago. We had originally written a side trip to include in this book for fault finders to go see them for themselves. But, alas, in 1993-94 the U.S. Army Corps of Engineers covered them with stone rip-rap to keep the bank from eroding. We had to delete that portion of our *Fault Finder's Guide*. (More photos of these stumps can be found in our other two books.)

The cases of violent flooding at Bayou St. John and along the east side of Donaldson Point are the only two we know of reported in 1811-12. When faulting occurs beneath an ocean, a huge wave called a **"tsunami"** or **"seismic sea wave"** can be generated that devastates shorelines. Tsunamis are also called **"tidal waves"** in the press, even though they bear no relationship to the tides. In the case of the New Madrid earthquakes of 1811-12, the two known instances of violent waves being thrown from the river described above can be considered as **"fluvial tsunamis"** or **"seismic river waves,"** since, like their oceanic counterparts, they are the result of faulting under water.

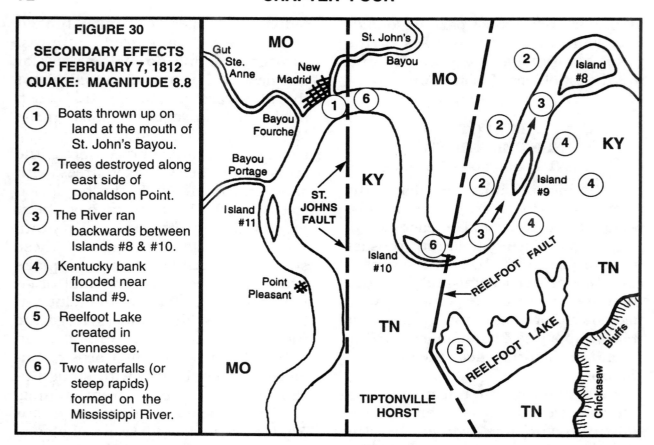

FIGURE 30

SECONDARY EFFECTS OF FEBRUARY 7, 1812 QUAKE: MAGNITUDE 8.8

1. Boats thrown up on land at the mouth of St. John's Bayou.
2. Trees destroyed along east side of Donaldson Point.
3. The River ran backwards between Islands #8 & #10.
4. Kentucky bank flooded near Island #9.
5. Reelfoot Lake created in Tennessee.
6. Two waterfalls (or steep rapids) formed on the Mississippi River.

EFFECT NUMBER FOUR:
RETROGRADE MOTION OF THE RIVER

The combined uplift of the Tiptonville Dome and the subsidence of the sunk lands to the east and northeast, reversed the gradient of the Mississippi River at least between Island #10 and Island #8, a distance of some 12 miles. The present gradient of the river is about 0.4 feet/mile to the southwest. If the Reelfoot Fault, where it crosses the river, had a movement that lifted the upthrown block (the Tiptonville Horst) and the bed of the river 10 feet, it would have locally and temporarily created a reverse gradient of about 0.4 feet/mile to the northeast in this 12 miles! If Penick's estimate of the size of the falls, on the order of "a twenty-three foot descent over a distance of

two miles" is correct, then the movement on the fault where it crosses the river might have been closer to 20 feet. The river bed raised by this much would have reversed the gradient to more than 1 foot/mile! This is a very steep gradient for a stream in flat country. At any rate, the flow of the mighty Mississippi River was temporarily halted and actually reversed for a few hours on that incredible day in the winter of 1812!

EFFECT NUMBER FIVE
Flooding in Kentucky & Tennessee

During the dark early morning hours of February 7, 1812, the current of the Mississippi River ran north from the tip of Donaldson Point (at Island #10) to at least Island #8, and probably many miles further. Following the uplift of the Tiptonville Horst, this enormous mass of water first ponded, then overspilled the banks of the river on both sides.It is not difficult to imagine the maelstrom of churning water, as the mass of water moved upstream, battling against the current of the river moving downstream. It would be quite similar to a river trying to reach the sea in spite of an incoming tide. Such phenomena can be observed today in some places in the world where the tidal range is high. The interfaces between the two opposing water masses produces some incredible raging water as currents and countercurrents collide and dissipate. To this scene on the Mississippi, add the effects of strong ground motion and possible seismic and/or water wave harmonics, (**seiches**). Imagine the effects of the east side of Donaldson Point and its trees. This bank subsided a few feet because it is on the downthrown side of the Reelfoot Fault. Then consider the slumping and sliding of the banks of the river during all this activity. At any rate, the mass of water **swamped thousands of acres of great forests** on the Missouri side between at least Island #8 and Island #10. The ponding backwaters of the river also inundated Island #9 and spilled into the newly created sunk lands of Tennessee and Kentucky as far east as the **Chickasaw Bluffs. Reelfoot Lake** was quickly filled during this process. The flow of water into the lowlands on both sides of the river would have increased the retrograde current along some segments of the river until the sunk lands were "filled".

EFFECT NUMBER SIX
Waterfalls on the Mississippi

The Reelfoot Fault extends across the Mississippi River pretty much in line with the eastern portion of Donaldson Point. The crossing was directly across the former position of Island #10. The renewed movement on this old fault suddenly raised the upthrown block a few feet. The upthrown block is downstream here. This created a temporary dam across the Mississippi. For several hours it ponded and flowed upstream, but then it cut a steep rapids through the escarpment, and for few days the "waterfall" was operative. The west flank of the Tiptonville Horst is bounded by St John's Fault—identified by Charles Lyell in 1846. This fault crosses the Mississippi half-mile east (upstream) from New Madrid, between the town and the mouth of St. John's Bayou. Movement on this fault was such that the downthrown block was downstream. This movement did not create a temporary dam, but it did greatly accelerate the flow, causing the second "waterfall." At least 28 boats were known to have crashed over these falls between the 7th and the 10th of February 1812— killing almost everyone aboard.

The Possibility of Seiches

Bodies of water throughout the New Madrid Seismic Zone and, undoubtedly, far beyond it in many cases, were effected by the intense ground motion and wave harmonics. The shapes of many lake basins and stream channels were suddenly changed by faulting, subsidence, uplift, and/or channel explosions during the earthquakes. The sudden reshaping of the water's container can cause huge waves to attack shores and banks. Thus there were inland tsunamis in both lakes and streams. Add wave harmonics to the equation and you get **seiches**. Every stream channel, slough, pond, and lake has its own natural fundamental period of vibration. The various types of ground waves have their natural periods of vibration also. When seismic waves resonate at the same frequencies as the natural periods of lakes, ponds or stream channels, the response or the water body is the generation of large waves that "slosh" over the shores and batter the banks.

This is the same phenomenon that takes place when you walk with a full cup of coffee and unintentionally match the natural frequency of the beverage with the rhythm of your steps—it suddenly splashes out! When nature does this to bodies of water with the rhythms of earthquakes, they are called **"seiche waves."** While tsunamis are due to sudden faulting beneath a body of water, seiches are due to resonance. Seiches can be as violent as tsunamis and can be generated hundreds, even thousands, of miles away.

Imagine the scene on February 7, 1812, when boats at New Madrid in the mouth of St. John's Bayou were thrown up on land, capsized and bashed against cottonwood trees. The site was near the epicenter and adjacent to St. John's Fault. Is it possible that the havoc that day at New Madrid on St. John's Bayou was a case where a seiche, a seismic river wave, and a channel explosion all took place simultaneously?

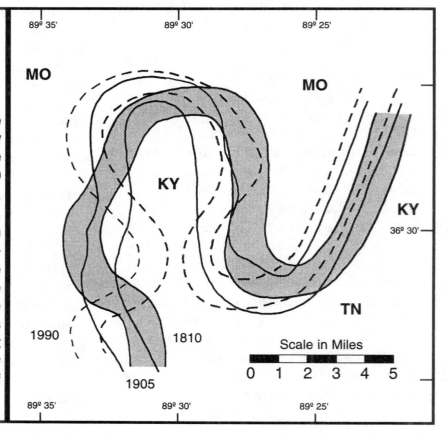

FIGURE 31

SUPERPOSED VIEWS OF NEW MADRID BEND 1810, 1905 & 1990

This composite view of the Mississippi River at New Madrid Bend shows the course of the river in 1810 (shaded), in 1905 (solid line), and in 1990 (dashed line). You can see how Donaldson Point has moved to the southwest and how the neck of the bend has narrowed to where it is less than a mile wide today. Some places, such as the original site of Point Pleasant, have actually changed to the other side of the river. (See Figure 28.)

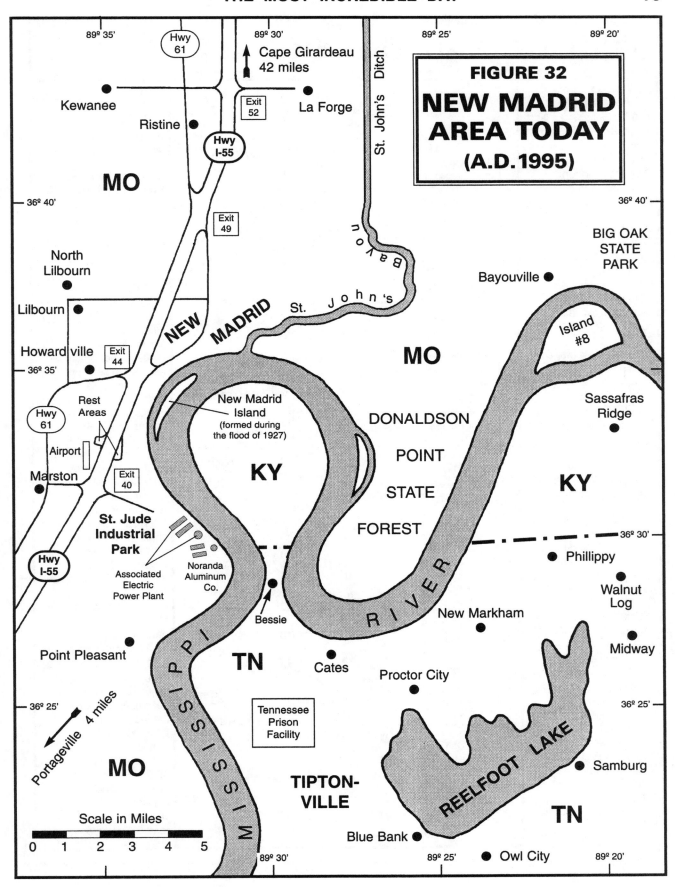

FIGURE 32
NEW MADRID
AREA TODAY
(A.D. 1995)

FIGURE 33
MAP OF EARTHQUAKE ALLEY (I–55)

WEST SIDE FEATURES

100.5 Jackson Fault
93-91 Former Mississippi River channel
91-83 Benton Hills
82.4 North boundary New Madrid Fault Zone
82.0 Sunk land & former Ohio River channel
76.0-76.2 Several large sand boils.
75.0-75.3 More large sand boils
66.6 Filled explosion sand blow crater
61.8 Seismic sand fissure parallel to I-55
60.05-60.1 Explosion craters and Richter Dip Stick
53.0 Filled explosion sand blow crater
58.6-59.7 Seismic sunk land adjacent to St. Johns Bayou
58.15-58.4 I-55 angles up Sikeston Ridge
49.3-49.6 Explosion craters and grove of living witness trees.
47.75 Des Cyprie
44.3-44.8 Lake Ste. Anne—earthquake lake and part of a seismically broken channel.
43.8 Former channel of Gut Ste. Anne causing MIL damage to shoulder and pavement of I-55.
42.2 New Madrid Rest Stop & epicentral area for 8.8 earthquake
36.4 Swilley Pond
31.8 Portage Open Bay—former channel broken up by quakes
6.0 German Crevasse
0.0 MO–AR state line
57.8 Graben Fissure
55.05 Classic sand boil 300 feet west of I-55 and just south of farm road 565.

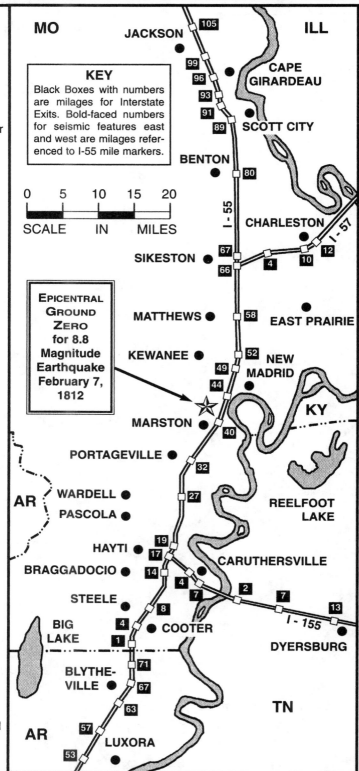

KEY
Black Boxes with numbers are milages for Interstate Exits. Bold-faced numbers for seismic features east and west are milages referenced to I-55 mile markers.

0   5   10   15   20
SCALE   IN   MILES

EPICENTRAL GROUND ZERO for 8.8 Magnitude Earthquake February 7, 1812

MO   JACKSON   ILL
CAPE GIRARDEAU
SCOTT CITY
BENTON
I-55   I-57
CHARLESTON
SIKESTON
MATTHEWS   EAST PRAIRIE
KEWANEE   NEW MADRID
KY
MARSTON
PORTAGEVILLE   REELFOOT LAKE
AR   WARDELL
PASCOLA
HAYTI   CARUTHERSVILLE
BRAGGADOCIO
STEELE
BIG LAKE   COOTER
I-155
DYERSBURG
BLYTHE-VILLE
TN
AR   LUXORA

EAST SIDE FEATURES

100.5 Jackson Fault
93-91 Former Mississippi River channel
91-83 Benton Hills
82.4 North boundary New Madrid Fault Zone and Proctor Landslide
82.0 Sunk land & former Ohio River channel
81.9 7-acre sand boil
60.05-60.1 Two explosion sand blow craters
50.2-50.5 Large linear graben fissure
47.75 Des Cyprie—A seismically disrupted stream feature
43.8 Former boat channel from Mississippi filled with sand by earthquakes causing MIL damage to shoulder and pavement of I-55.
42.2 New Madrid Rest Stop & epicentral area for 8.8 earthquakes
40.9 Sand boils near Marston exit and view of remnant of Bayou Portage, a discontinuous channel, marked by cypress trees in St. Jude Industrial Park
36.0-37.0 "Devastation Acres." Numerous seismic features: sand boils, filled crevasses and an earthquake pond
31.8 Portage Open Bay
25.4 KOA Campground with a large earthquake fissure or seismic channel explosion feature behind 1 mi to SE
6.0 2000-foot-long earthquake crevasse
0.0 AR-MO state line
55.05 Seismic sand boils and sand fissures in fields. For the best view climb up on farm road 565 overpass.

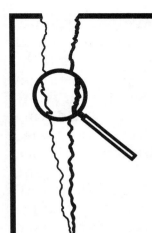

CHAPTER FIVE

INTERSTATE 55 FAULT FINDERS GUIDE

The stretch of Interstate 55, From the Benton Hills, Missouri, near Scott City, to a point just south of Blytheville, Arkansas, should be called "Earthquake Alley." This hundred-mile stretch of roadway is an approximate marker for more than 2,000 epicenters in 1811-12. It also roughly correlates with the most active portions of the New Madrid Fault today. More than 200 small earthquakes are recorded there each year along a band 25-30 miles wide through which this parkway passes. Millions of motorists annually drive through the area with no awareness of the turmoil that boils in the bedrock beneath. The evidence of great earthquakes past abounds along both sides of this thruway—if you only know where to look and how to recognize what you see. What is visible from your car, even at 65 miles per hour, will amaze you. Once you have used this guide, that portion of interstate highway will never look the same to you again. You will have acquired the eyes of a "New Madrid Fault Finder."

How to Use This Guide

The I–55 Guide is designed to lead you to earthquake features that you can observe and photograph from your car or from the roadside.

Please remember that these features are on private property

The guide is keyed to the mile markers along the sides of both the north and southbound lanes. Check a mile marker against your odometer. For northbound travelers, this will be easier than for southbound travelers, because the mileages increase from south to north. For the Missouri portion of the guide, the zero mile marker is the state line.

As you travel the Interstate looking for earthquake features you can take advantage of the many overpasses of relatively quiet country roads. Sometimes earthquake features can abound on both sides of the Interstate and yet be difficult, if not impossible, to see from the low angle at the level of the pavement. If you carefully pull over, park under an overpass and climb up to the grade above, your perspective is much better. You can see earthquake features from there that would otherwise have escaped your notice. **CAUTION**: Don't try this at I-55 exits or other places where a lot of traffic overpasses I-55.

Introduction to the I-55 Section

Interstate 55 gives a north-south slice across essentially the entire New Madrid Seismic Zone. (See Figures 3 & 32.) From north to south, travellers will observe the rolling terrain north of the flatlands and see two geologic faults that cut through rocks all the way up to the surface. The Ste. Genevieve Fault at Exit 141 cuts through the rock layers, clearly tilting and deforming them. The Jackson Fault runs through the valley between Mile Markers 100 and 101 - in fact the old fault has caused a zone of weakness prone to the erosion that is creating the valley. The tilted strata near the road cut at mile marker 101 is probably not caused by the Jackson Fault--but by a collapse into an ancient sinkhole. (See Figure 11.)

The Cape Girardeau area has lots of excellent motels and restaurants and is a good place from which to launch your adventure, or end your excursion if driving south to north. The same is true if you begin at Blytheville and work northward. Thus, Cape and Blytheville pretty much bracket at least the central part of the New Madrid Seismic Zone.

South of Cape, I-55 descends to cross a flat flood plain that has no river in it between mile 93 and 90. This is an old course of the Mississippi that was abandoned by

that river when it changed its route several thousand years ago. Flood plains without rivers and rivers without flood plains are not unusual in these parts! The reason is that many streams had course changes during the Ice Age. While rivers can change course—flood plains can't! (See Figure 17, p. 33.) I-55 traverses the Benton Hills from mile 91 to 83. From mile 83 southward the road log is quite detailed because earthquake features are numerous from here on!

The Benton Hills

The 8-mile section of Interstate 55 between Mile Markers 91 and 83 passes through terrain more rugged than either the lowlands containing Cape Girardeau's airport to the north or the Mississippi Alluvial Valley to the south. This area is known as the **Benton Hills** (Commerce Hills of some literature). On a map (such as Figure 15) you may notice that they are actually part of a string of forested hills, resembling a row of islands in an ocean, that extend southward into Arkansas. The entire string is called **Crowley's Ridge**, but each segment has its own local name.

Crowley's Ridge and Benton Hills were **not** caused by earthquakes. They are **erosion remnants**. In the last few tens of thousands of years, both the Ohio and Mississippi Rivers have been busy eroding and carrying away the rock and soil of which these hills are made. What we see today are just the few areas that the rivers haven't gotten to yet! The "core" of the Benton Hills is made of rocks of the same age and type that make up the Ozark Highlands.

The Mississippi Alluvial Valley

Persons looking southward from the escarpment of the Benton Hills from Mile Marker 83 are treated to quite a view! From this vantage point on the Interstate, and especially if you can get up on the overpass (Highway E), the great Mississippi Alluvial Valley spreads as far as the eye can see to the southeast, south and southwest. The view is similar to one seen from a seacoast, and, like the seacoast view, the earth's curvature can clearly be seen. The New Madrid Seismic Zone starts here—extending southward from these hills for more than a hundred miles.

Actually, this great flatland is caused by both the Ohio and Mississippi rivers. These great rivers have carved wide and deep gorges far below the present elevation, then they have filled these valleys by spreading their gravels, sands, silts, and muds far and wide, running over and reworking their own deposits, sometimes in great meander belts, as at present, and at times in great braided patterns. The rivers did this several times, alternating times of erosion and downcutting with times of deposition and valley filling. (See Figure 14.)

It may surprise you to learn that a lot of the alluvium (river deposits) that fills up the valley south of the escarpment of the Benton Hills was deposited by the Ohio River, when it ran east to west directly south of you, some 20,000 years ago! Where in the world was the Mississippi River at that time? It flowed southwest from Cape Girardeau, running through the lowland now occupied by the Cape Girardeau airport, continuing to near the present location of Poplar Bluff and southward, between Jonesboro and Hoxie, Arkansas. (See Figure 17.)

Sikeston Ridge

From the Benton Hills all the way to New Madrid, Interstate 55 is constructed on or just east of a low but prominent alluvial ridge known as the Sikeston Ridge. It is 35 miles long but only 2 or 3 miles wide, except near its southern end at New Madrid, where it is about 5 miles wide. It is nearly 40 feet above the bordering lowlands at the north end, but becomes closer and closer to the elevation of the lowlands at the south end, where it merges with the levees of the present Mississippi River at New Madrid.

Being higher and dryer than the lowlands both east and west, Sikeston Ridge was an early north-south route for Native Americans. The route was used by early Europeans. The Spaniards, in 1789, used it to travel from New Madrid through Cape Girardeau and Ste. Genevieve, to St. Louis, some 180 miles. They called it El Camino Real, "The King's Highway."

Sikeston Ridge is actually an old river terrace, with deposits contributed both by the Ohio, then the Mississippi, rivers. Since this alluvium was deposited, the Mississippi River has eroded much of the original terrace, both west and east of the present ridge. The Sikeston Ridge, then, is an erosion remnant of old Ohio River and Mississippi River deposits that later actions of the Mississippi River have not yet completely removed.

Sand Dunes and Erosional Remnants of Sikeston Ridge

Between mile 58 and 78 are hundreds of low, gentle hills. These hills have a complex history. At one time, the Sikeston Ridge was considerably wider, both to the west and to the east, than it is today. What we see today between mile 58 and 78 are some of the remains of the east edge of this ancient river terrace. The Mississippi River, when it flowed southward on the west side of Sikeston through what we now call the Morehouse Lowland, eroded some of the western part of the "Ridge". During times of high water, it "jumped" over the ridge from west to east at its north end. This helped erode some of the east side of the ridge. Later, when the Mississippi changed course to its present position through Thebes Gap, (See Figure 15, p. 30.) it from time to time eroded even more of the eastern parts of the Sikeston Ridge, but not completely wearing it away. Channels formed during these periods of overflow can still be seen. Include the effects of wind to this scene. Sand was moved around and redeposited as dunes. Then add some "new" braided channels from recent Mississippi River overflow. Finally, historic Lake St. John was drained, its waters flowing just east of the Sikeston Ridge. Scars from these drainages are superimposed over the braided Mississippi River deposits.

I-55 Road Log

The following features are keyed to the mile markers along I–55:

Mile Marker 82.4 Coming from the north, **"Earthquake Alley"** starts here at the crest of this abrupt hill rising out of the Mississippi-Ohio flood plain below. Called **"Benton Hills"** today, it was called **"Tywappity Hill"** in 1811-12. Thousands of refugees from the earthquakes streamed northward over this hill at this spot, fleeing from the terror to the south. This is the northern end of the stretch of I-55 along which earthquake features from 1811-12 may be seen from the highway.

If you are southbound you are now entering the **New Madrid Seismic Zone.** If you are northbound, you are leaving it. There is at least a 30% chance there will be at least one small earthquake recorded on any day you pass through this zone.

East side of Interstate 55. This is the **Proctor Landslide**. It is an old landslide area on the Benton Hills escarpment. The area from 300 feet to 1100 feet east of the Interstate, and from the large grey barn almost to the valley floor, is landslide material. This feature is quite typical of scores of similar landforms along the south and southeast-facing escarpments of Crowley's Ridge, and along the west-facing escarpments overlooking the floodplain in Kentucky and Tennessee. We believe most of these were at least partially triggered by the great earthquakes. You may wish to check with the owners of this property, Roy and Elaine Proctor, for permission to examine their slide close-up. To get to their farm, you need to exit I-55 at the Benton exit (called exit 80 even though it is at mile marker 81), drive to Benton, and take blacktop "E", which hooks back 1.7 miles to the northeast. This road crosses over I-55. The Proctor farm is the first one east of the overpass.

82.0 Both sides, especially East. This **"sunk" land** is in the middle of the former channel of the Ohio River. The area has since been invaded by some more recent Mississippi River overflow, by migrating sand dunes, and, toward the west, by ponding of Lake St. John. (Fault-finders on Side Trip B will see this earthquake lake site close-up) If conditions are right, you might be able to see an extra-large **7-acre sand boil** 1000 feet to the east. Notice how plant growth is stunted. This is because the sand, a coarse textured material, has a low water-holding capacity that results in plants rooted in it not getting their share of water or nutrients. This sand boil is the northernmost seismically-induced liquefaction feature we have found near the interstate highway. For persons looking north, the Proctor landslide can be seen just east of I-55 on the Benton Hills escarpment. The Proctor's large grey barn marks the head of the slide.

81.5 Notice how the highway northward from this point actually dips lower before it climbs the Benton Hills escarpment. This dip is an **earthquake subsidence feature** from 1811-12. The town of Benton is to the west. The Proctor landslide can be seen a mile away to the north on the east side of the Interstate.

80.9 East. Several round, light-colored areas can be seen in the field northeast of the overpass. These are typical sand boils.

80.8 Exit 80. Benton via highway 77. Side Trip B exits here.

80.2 East. Low linear zone in field appears to be a former channel of a former braided stream. It has almost certainly been altered by earthquakes. In addition, the lowest part has been dug for a farm pond and stocked with bass, according to Mr. Hutson, owner. We think that all natural drainages in the New Madrid Seismic Zone have been altered by some degree of differential subsidence, ranging from very slight to very intense. Many have been altered to the extent that they are classified as "discontinuous channels." See the discussion of discontinuous channels in Chapter Three.

78.7-79.3 Both Sides. These small hills are erosion remnants of Sikeston Ridge. The land through here was once all at the elevation of the tops of the highest of these hills. See more detailed discussion above.

78.3 West. Borrow pit. Material was removed for construction materials for I-55. The most common use was in building up the ramps for overpasses.

77.5-77.9 East. The north-south feature in the field is probably a discontinuous channel of a former natural drainage channel at least partially caused by seismically-induced ground motion. Farmers often have been successful in partially filling in and farming the least-subsided of these features, but, in some places, must "farm around" the most-subsided portions.

77.55 Overpass. Blacktop C crosses over I-55.

76.8-77.1 West. Several large sand boils can be seen, some next to the fence line.

76.0-76.7 West. This is a major man-made drainage canal paralleling the highway. "Town Ditch" was rerouted due to I-55 construction.

76.0-76.2 East. A large low-lying feature, approximately 1200 feet by 100 to 200 feet, can be seen. It is probably a **lateral spread sag.** The sag area is flanked by low seismic sand ridges. The orientation is near north-south. Farmers hate these things, because clay layers of the sediment keep water standing on the surface too much of the time.

75.4 I-55 crosses over Hwy U. A good high-angle view of the terrain.

75.0-75.3 West. Sandy areas at the edge of the field are probably large sand boils. Notice how the farmer avoids the worst of these.

74.5 Drainage canal under I-55. Town ditch.

73.7-73.9 East. The low, wet area is probably a discontinuous channel. It was caused by differential subsidence of a former natural drainage channel. Notice the water grass here, which tells us that this low area gets wet sooner and stays wet longer than the area around it.

73.4 East. Erosion remnant of Sikeston Ridge

73.0 East. I-55 right-of-way cuts through a portion of an erosion remnant of Sikeston Ridge. Wind has modified most of these hills, reworking some of the sand into dunes.

72.0 The Benton Hills can be seen to the north, ten miles away. The base of the escarpment marks the northern boundary of seismically-induced liquefaction features, although landslides and slumps are present in these hills. We think many of them were triggered by earthquakes in 1811-12, 1895 and some as recently as 1990. We know of at least three seismically induced landslides between Benton and New Hamburg and another near Oran, Missori, that were initiated by the New Hamburg earthquake of September 26, 1990—magnitude 4.7. This same earthquake caused another landslide on Crowley's Ridge near Piggott, Arkansas—causing serious damage to two houses 67 miles from the epicenter. If a light earthquake like this can cause six significant landslides up to 67 miles away, how many landslides did the New Madrid earthquakes cause? At least 200 of the New Madrid quakes had Richter magnitudes of 4.7 or greater. The energy released by the largest of these seismic events was more than a million times greater than a 4.7.

71.8 Overpass. County Road H.

71.7 East. The house sets on a sand dune.

71.0 East. Two large sandy areas can be seen some 300 feet from the highway. These features are sand blows (as contrasted with sand boils).

Carbonized wood (locally called "lignite") can be found, as can pieces of Indian pottery.

70.4-70.7 East. Elongated, wind-reworked erosion remnant of Sikeston Ridge parallels the highway.

70.1 East. The hill is a sand dune.

68.9-69.4 West. Sand "mines" can be seen in some of these dunes.

68.3-68.4 East. These dunes were deposited by wind action. Wind has modified material from erosion remnants of Sikeston Ridge.

68.0 East. The sandy area 100 feet from the highway is probably a sand boil.

67.4 Exit 67. **Sikeston** via highway 62. Hungry? Want to experience a unique restaurant? Consider stopping at **Lambert's Cafe**, a few blocks west of this exit. Notice how sandy it is in the southeast quadrant of this interchange at the site of the Coach House Inn. A projection of the **Bootheel Fault** (see glossary) may pass through here crossing I-55 obliquely between Exits 66 & 67. (See Fig. 36, p. 98.)

66.6 West. The round feature near the fence and just south of the Lambert's Cafe billboard appears to be a filled sand blow explosion crater measuring 35 ft by 45 ft with the long axis oriented nearly north-south. The soil is too sandy to hold water for long, making its use as a farm pond intermittent and short-lived. This feature could be related to the Bootheel Fault which may pass through this area. See Fig. 36, p. 98.

66.5 West. The barn sets on a sand dune

66.2 East. Sand boils can be seen in the field northeast of the I-55 —US-60 cloverleaf.

66.1 Exit 66 To Sikeston via Hwy 60 and to Charleston via I-57. A projection of the **Bootheel Fault** may pass through the western portion of this interchange. Note numerous willow trees on the west side—an indication of groundwater less than 10 feet below surface.

65.3 Sikeston city limits.

65.1 West. Semi-circular pattern of weeds next to the fence probably covers a sand boil that has been half-removed by I-55 construction.

64.85 Overpass. County Rd. AA.

64.4-64.9 East. These very large, tree-covered hills are erosion remnants of Sikeston Ridge. Quite a bit of this sand and silt, originally deposited by the Ohio river, has been reworked by wind into sand dunes.

64.7 Drainage canal overpass.

64.1-64.25 West. These hills are sand dunes. Some of the sand has been "mined".

63.9 East. Notice the dune with the sand quarry behind the house.

63.7 East. A nice dune can be seen close to the fence line.

63.45 West. House on a dune.

63.2-63.3 East. Several dunes 100 feet or so from the fence.

63.0 West. Sikeston power plant smokestack can be seen six miles to the northwest. It sets directly on a large sand fissure!

63.1-63.2 West. Borrow pit.

62.65 North Cut Drainage Ditch.

62.45-62.6 East. This low, poorly-drained area between I-55 and the Sikeston Ridge remnant-sand dune hill farther east and southeast probably has a complex origin. We call features "polygenetic" when we think several factors controlled their origin and development. Regarding this area, we think it was once a braided stream channel that carried Mississippi River overflow, that migrating sand partially filled parts of this channel, that the New Madrid earthquakes caused subsidence of parts of the channel, that construction of drainage canals altered both surface and subsurface flows, and that farmers were successful is converting some of the former channel to agriculture, but unsuccessful in other places.

62.2 East. Part of this dune has been "borrowed".

62.1 East. The hill near the tower is a wind-reworked erosion remnant of the Sikeston Ridge.

61.8 West. A prominent sand fissure can be seen paralleling I-55 about 500 feet distant. The owner reports that he avoids this feature when cultivating his field.

61.3 East. Here, the I-55 right-of-way cuts directly through a **dune.** This is a good place to examine the material which makes up the dunes. The sand was derived from the nearby erosion remnants of Sikeston Ridge or possibly blown from the Sikeston Ridge itself. Sikeston Ridge is only one mile west of this site.

61.0 East. Sand dune and borrow pit.

60.7-61.2 East. These are good examples of erosional remnants of Sikeston Ridge which have been modified and reshaped by wind transportation of sand.

60.25 Overpass. County Road 820 crosses over I-55.

60.05-60.1 East. Two excellent **explosion sand blow craters** can be seen just inside the fence. The diameters are 80 and 100 feet. Their concave profiles indicate an explosional expulsion of sand and water, as opposed to the less violent upwelling of sand and water causing sand boils. These sand blows apparently intruded a dune sand that happened to overlie the liquefaction zone below them. Carbonized wood can be found in these blows, and this is not unusual in blows and boils. Two more sand blows can be seen west of I-55 when condition are favorable. A large 700-foot-tall wireless cable TV transmitting tower has been constructed directly upon them. A major earthquake could cause liquefaction here again, causing the tower to sink and tilt. We call this our "Richter Dip Stick." See the book, *The Earthquake that Never Went Away,* by Stewart and Knox for aerial photos and additional discussion of this tower and set of explosion craters.

58.6-59.7 "Sunk land". Several factors have led to this polygenetic feature. A portion of the Mississippi drainage ran through here during at least two periods of geomorphic history. The historic Lake St. John's drainage outlet was through here. Differential subsidence due to liquefaction during the great earthquakes played a part as well. Notice the small levee along the west side of the Interstate designed to prevent occasional flooding during intense rain fall. Sometimes even this is not adequate and the levee must be sandbagged to keep water off the highway.

59.05 St. John's Ditch. This canal consolidates the drainages of the east side of Sikeston Ridge.

58.15-58.4 Here, I-55 crosses the **Sikeston Ridge escarpment**. The elevation of Sikeston Ridge is about 15 feet higher than the sunk land immediately east of the escarpment. From this point to New Madrid, I-55 will be atop this old river terrace. The large smokestack seen ten miles to the northwest is part of the Sikeston power plant.

58.15 Exit 58. Matthews via highway 80.

56.4-56.8 West. Borrow pits.

55.6 Farm road overpass.

55.4-55.6 East. Borrow pit.

54.6-55.0 East. This large, gentle sand ridge is probably a **"braided bar island"** produced in a braided channel of the ancient Mississippi river when it was depositing the materials now left standing "high" as Sikeston Ridge. Wind has undoubtedly reworked some of this sandy sediment also. This linear feature trends just west of north and crosses I-55 at about the 55 mile mark.

53.45-53.6 West. Borrow pit.

53.1-53.3 West. Borrow pit.

53.0 West. **Sand blow explosion crater.** This 60-100-foot-diameter feature has now been filled, but it is still distinct. Notice its effect on crops.

52.4-52.6 West. Horseshoe-shaped pond with large tree. It appears that this feature has been modified by man. We are not sure just how much is natural and how much is man-made, but we suspect this pond connects with permanent groundwater, and is at least partially seismic in origin.

52.1 Exit 52. Kewanee via route P. Exit here to visit the "witness tree". (See Side Trip A, New Madrid loop, in Chapter Seven).

51.7-51.9 West. Two large borrow pits.

51.7 East. A large sand boil can be seen, 400 feet or so from highway.

51.2-51.5 East. Very large borrow pit.

51.1 Overpass. I-55 crosses over abandoned railroad.

50.2-50.5 East. **Large linear graben fissure.** Grabens are fault blocks that drop down relative to the ground on either side. We think that this and similar features were formed when earthquake ground motion liquified a lower layer of saturated sediment, causing the upper layer of non-saturated soil and sediment to pull apart and drop or sag down. In this case, the upper part dropped deeply enough to intersect the water table creating an intermittent pond. The graben fissure tapers on both ends, but becomes over 100 feet wide in the middle. It is approximately 1500 feet long. The location of this feature probably necessitated the change in direction of I-55 here. (See Figures 21 & 22, pp. 48 & 54.)

49.85-50.0 East. Borrow pit.

49.6 Exit 49. Interchange with U.S. highways 61 and 62. Southbound travellers exit here to visit the **New Madrid Historical Museum**. Hungry fault-finders might check out some of the great restaurants here. See recommendations in Side Trip A .

49.3-49.6 West of Exit 49 are sand blow explosion craters and at least a dozen huge oaks that predate 1811—"living witnesses to the earthquakes." More on this in Side Trip A.

48.3-48.4 West. Borrow pits.

47.75 **Des Cyprie** ("place of

cypress trees", was also known as "St. Martin's des Cyprie" before 1811). This is a morphoseismic feature. A canal now channels the old drainage feature. One mile northwest of this point, Des Cyprie is up to 500 feet wide, and for well over a mile, is a permanent, arcuate shaped lake. Its drainage direction is toward the west and disappears into the ground! Its surface outlet to the Little River was destroyed by the quakes.

East of I-55, this drainage feature passes through the western part of New Madrid. Drainage in this section is toward the southeast. Here, too, except during periods of high run-off, it seems to disappear into the ground before reaching the Mississippi. What was once a navigable boat channel between the Mississippi and Little Rivers is now broken up and discontinuous flowing in two directions—a victim of the earthquakes.

The large lake at the west end of Des Cyprie is at the western flank of Sikeston Ridge. Locals call it "the washout". Excess water from high flooding of the Mississippi in 1912 and 1913 flowed northwestward, scouring the channel of Des Cyprie and producing a fan-shaped deposit of sand at its west end. The Des Cyprie washout can be seen here from I-55 as a grove of cypress trees in the distance one mile to the west.

Pre-1811 Des Cyprie was a tributary of Little River that was one of at least four connections for riverboat traffic between the Mississippi and Little rivers. Des Cyprie probably handled overflow floodwater from floods of the Mississippi (when it would drain westward), and possibly also overflow floodwater from Little River (when it could have drained eastward). The feature undoubtedly was greatly modified by the great earthquakes. We know that at least part of New Madrid was lowered as much as 10-12 feet during the earthquakes. This would have reduced or reversed the gradient of the stream. In addition, New Madrid Bend has been steadily eroding toward the north, cutting into Des Cyprie even more. Much research needs to be done to fully understand Des Cyprie.

47.7 Notice a slight "dip" in I-55 and a patch of repaired surface. At 65 miles per hour it is quite noticeable! We think this marks the **original course of Des Cyprie**. When it was channelized the drainage was moved about 250 feet to the north where it passes under I-55.. The dip is the result of subsidence probably caused by traffic-induced liquefaction (MIL) ongoing today! As your car speeds over this "wump" you are passing over an earthquake feature, a portion of a discontinuous channel broken up by the earthquakes of 1811-12.

47.0 You have just left or have just entered the epicentral region of the 8.8 magnitude earthquake of February 7, 1812. This was the largest quake of the New Madrid series. The epicentral zone of this "New Madrid Megaquake" extends beneath I-55 from at least Milepost 35.0 to 47.0—which includes the New Madrid-Marston Visitors Center.

46.8 Overpass. Highway "U" crosses over I-55. A good place to climb up and see sand boils from a better high-angle perspective.

46.25-46.5 West. Large triangu-

lar dry borrow pit.

45.85 Overpass. I-55 crosses over railroad. New Madrid city limits.

45.2 East. Large substation.

45.1-45.4 West. Large, mostly dry borrow pit.

44.85 Exit 44. Interchange with U.S. highways 61 and 62. Northbound travellers exit here to visit the New Madrid Historical Museum, or to investigate one of the great restaurants here. (See Side Trip A, next chapter, for our recommendations). The New Madrid school buildings to the west are not seismically designed. The school was built on the site of a large Native American village, which was desecrated. The mounds west of the school are Indian mounds—called "The Lilbourn Site."

44.3-44.8 West. **Lake St. Anne** sunk land. The area south of New Madrid school and west of I-55 was part of the land which subsided ("sunk") during the big New Madrid earthquakes. Notice the low area full of vines, willows, and other hydrophytic plants.

Sir Charles Lyell, the great English geologist, visited the area in 1846. He described a great area of sunk lands extending along the course of Little River "between 70 and 80 miles north and south and 30 miles or more east and west". He went on to say, "throughout this area innumerable submerged trees, some standing leafless, others prostrate, are seen; and so great is the extent of the lake and marsh that an active trade in the skins of muskrats, minks, otters, and other wild animals are now carried on there."

43.8   West, then east. A large 200-foot-wide sandy area, marked by the position of some willows and a cottonwood tree on the west, angles under I-55, traverses the field on the east, passes under the railroad, and the levee. It trends directly toward the Associated Electric smokestack visible three miles from here. This sandy ribbon is part of the remains of a pre-1811 bayou called **Gut Ste. Anne (now a discontinuous channel)** which connected boat traffic between the Mississippi and Little River prior to its disruption by the great earthquakes. This sandy deposit is highly liquefiable. When the river is high tractors tilling this field do not cross over the sand to avoid mechanically induced liquefaction (MIL) that can cause their machinery to sink. A good example of transportation induced liquefaction (a form of MIL) is active here. Vibrations of passing vehicles cause partial liquefaction that slowly breaks up the pavement of I-55 and makes the shoulders mushy. Note damaged shoulders and recent repair slabs to the concrete. Imagine! Continuing highway damage today from an earthquake that happened 200 years ago! (See Fig. 35, Photo #2.) Water that soaks into the ground at Lake Ste. Anne flows through here and under the levee as groundwater flow—causing perennial seep-springs on the riverside base of the levee. This also creates an MIL hazard to passing trains. A major quake could liquefy this morphoseismic feature again—taking out I-55, the railroad and the levee all at once.

43.7 New Madrid city limits.

43.45-43.55   East. Large piles of rice hulls are overfilling the borrow pit. Numerous birds are usually seen picking over the piles for food.

43.15   East. Sand boils in field.

42.5-42.8   West. Borrow pit.

42.2   Rest area. You may now consider yourself to be at the very center of **Epicentral Ground Zero** for the largest earthquake in the history of the conterminous United States. Consider this to be the "Bulls Eye," Felt from the Rockies to the Eastern seaboard, from Canada to Mexico, from Yellowstone to Cuba—this was the quake that caused waterfalls on the river and made the Mississippi run backwards on February 7, 1812. This quake was felt by every man, woman and child living in the United States at the time. For a detailed account of the far-reaching effects of this "megaquake," see *The Earthquake America Forgot.*

Sand boils can be seen just east of the rest area of the northbound lane. This area is a gentle topographic high or "raised land" (Tiptonville Dome) which may have been uplifted during the February 7 event. (See Figure 23, p. 55.)

Some day we hope to see a large billboard along the Interstate informing travelers of the highly historic significance, both geologic and political, of this particular portion of planet earth. Few earthquakes, if any, have been felt so far by so many in the history of the world as the monster quake that originated here in 1812.

41.9 West. Sand boils in field.

41.5-41.7 West. Large, dry borrow pit.

41.3-41.4 Sand boils both sides.

40.9 Exit 40, **Marston**. This is within the source zone of the largest of the New Madrid earthquakes,— February 7, 1812. Sand boils can be seen in all directions from this overpass. On the east side, in St. Jude Industrial Park, you can see a grove of tall cypress trees about half-a-mile away. This is a fragment of the channel of Bayou Portage which used to be a navigable stream carrying commercial boat traffic between the Mississippi and Little Rivers before 1812. The channel was destroyed by the earthquakes in 1811-12. If you are hungry when you come by here, **Jerry's Cafe** has a great plate lunch at a great price.

40.25 & 40.35 A pair of Associated Electric power lines.

40.0 West. Sand boils in field.

39.8-39.9 East. Borrow pit.

39.4 West. Sand boils and fissures are numerous in the field.

39.0 East. Sand boils and fissures can be seen in the field.

38.7 West. Sand boils and fissures can be seen in the field.

38.3 West. Sand boils and fissures can be seen in the field.

38.1 West. Sand boils and fissures can be seen in the field.

37.9 Overpass. Highway M crosses over I-55.

37.7-37.9 East. Borrow pit.

37.6 East. Numerous earthquake features can be seen throughout this area.

37.0 West. Several sand boils are visible in the field.

36.8-37.0 East. These fields are filled with earthquake features. Among the features that can be seen are at least five filled sand blow explosion craters 25-50 feet in diameter, and two parallel filled crevasses, several hundred feet long, trending east-west.

36.0-37.0 "Devastation Acres" There are probably more earthquake features in this segment than in any other one-mile stretch of I-55. Notice the Associated Electric smokestack only 5 miles to the northeast.

36.7 East. Notice the grove of willows south of the drainage ditch. They outline a probable earthquake pond. This pond has a diameter of 150-200 feet. Trees leaning at various angles, perhaps indicate that hydrologically-induced liquefaction (HIL) is still occurring.

36.5-36.6 West. Borrow pit.

36.4 West. The small grove of willows some 1000 feet from the highway is **Swilley Pond**. It was modified by farmers years ago to make it more useable as a local swimming hole. It is a natural feature, communicating with groundwater. Ninety-six-year-old Mr. J. K. Swilley recalls the trauma and sadness of an event that occurred over 45 years ago, when two young boys tragically drowned here. He also recalled that two or three other nearby ponds were natural, but have been filled in recent years. These "ponds" are at least partly due to liquefaction which occurred during large earthquakes.

36.1 East. Sand boils. These are good examples of boils that, when investigated in the field, do not have the characteristic sandy soil of most sand boils. In fact, the soil over them appears to be the same kind of soil as between them. After consulting with Dr. Mike Aide, soil scientist at Southeast Missouri State, we think we have an explanation. Farmers, when "grading" their fields to make them very level, plane off the slightly convex boils, then move over them many times with their heavy equipment, thoroughly mixing the upper two or three feet of soil. For a number of years, the boils below this upper layer are hidden, but, sooner or later, the differing permeabilities of the sandy soil of the boils below make their presence noticed. The crops above are the first to show this. They are usually stunted. Finally, the soil above the boils becomes leached and turns a lighter color. Thus, the lighter colored, circular features, even if they are not sandy, indicate sand below. At least, this is our best hypothesis at the present time!

35.9 West. Sand boils in field.

35.5-35.6 West. Water-filled borrow pit.

35.0 You have just entered (or have just left) the epicentral region of the 8.8 magnitude earthquake on February 7, 1812. The epicentral zone of this Megaquake extends beneath I-55 from at least Milepost 35.0 to 47.0—which includes the New Madrid-Marston Rest Stop.

34.15 This drainage ditch is all that remains of former Bayou Portage, which, prior to 1811-12, carried keelboat traffic between the Mississippi and Little rivers. The big earthquakes caused its banks to cave in, sands from its bed to be blasted into the air in places, and its gradient to be disrupted. See discussion of stream alterations in Chapter Three.

33.0-33.2 Large borrow pits on both sides.

32.85 Exit 32. **Portageville** via highway 162. The town gets its name from the days predating the big quakes when keelboats would sometimes need to be carried or dragged across low places in the channel of Bayou Portage or Portage Open Bay at the site of the present town, where the two bayous joined. Portageville (formerly a trading post called Shinbone) was founded by Edward and Modest Meatte, and partner Charles Davis. Modest's mother was Teceikeapease, sister of the great Shawnee chief Tecumseh! A more detailed version of the romance between Teceikeapease and a New Madrid Frenchman is told in the book, *The Earthquake America Forgot*.

32.1-32.35 West. Borrow pit.

31.8 Portage Open Bay. New Madrid/Pemiscot county line. Notice the mature Cypress trees. Early reports state that before the big earthquakes, Indian canoes and keelboats regularly came up the St. Francis River, entered the Little River drainage, and on into the Mississippi River (and vice versa) at least four points south of New Madrid. One of these passages was through here! More about the distributaries crisscrossing the Bootheel connecting the Mississippi, the St. Francis and the Little Rivers prior to the earthquakes is described in the book, *The Earthquake America Forgot.*

31.0 West. Numerous sand boils.

30.6 Overpass. Highway T crosses over I-55.

30.15-30.55 West. Large, water-filled borrow pit.

29.35 Borrow pits both sides.

28.6-28.85 Substation (west) and transmission lines (east).

27.8 Drainage ditch.

27.55 Exit 27. Wardell via blacktop Highway "A".

27.3-27.5 West. Water-filled borrow pit.

26.5-26.6 West. Sand boils. A few miles east, between I-55 and the River, is the best estimate of the probable epicenter of the magnitude 8.4, January 23, 1812 earthquake.

25.7 Drainage canal with high spoil banks. Notice that the drainage direction is to the west, not toward the Mississippi river as one might expect. This is due to both the natural and artificial levees of the Mississippi. The lowest land on flood plains of most large rivers is not near the rivers, but back in the "backswamps". Most small drainages must empty into larger ones before the combined water can find access to the major rivers.

24.6 East. Hayti/Portageville **KOA** Campground. This campground is nicely located for fault-finders, and the proprietors, Dan and Joyce Webb, are knowledgeble about the area and can give you some good advice. You may also purchase copies of several of the earthquake books mentioned in this text, including this one. The Webbs are from California and moved away from there to get away from earthquakes. They did not know until they arrived and settled in Missouri that the property and campground they had purchased is situated in the very center of the most seismically active earthquake zone east of the Rocky Mountains!

A Civil War Cemetery and a large, picturesque graben fissure lies to the east and within sight of this campground. The fissure lies along the west side of Dry Bayou Baptist Church. See Side Trip D for directions to this scenic earthquake feature. A great place to get pictures of yourself standing in an earthquake crevasse.

From the Interstate you will notice that the Mississippi River levee is visible over three miles to the east.

24.5 West. Borrow pit.

24.45 East. Deep borrow pit.

24.25 East. Gravel road 335, off outer road, leads to **Dry Bayou,** 0.4 miles to the east. Dr. Stewart thinks Dry Bayou is a linear graben feature, which he believes was caused by earthquake-induced ground motion or lateral spreading. Dr. Knox thinks a large channel explosion is more likely. Either way, it is considered to be a bona fide earthquake feature from 1811-12. The beautiful cypress trees here all postdate 1811-12, the oldest ones having sprouted shortly after the earthquakes—that is, after the bayou was formed that supports them. See our discussion of this feature in the **Side Trip D** log.

24.0 Exit 24. Highway "K" crosses over I-55. The Mississippi River levee is quite close, less than a half-mile. Exit here to visit Dry Bayou.

22.6-23.2 East. Sand boils.

22.3 **East**. Borrow pit.

22.1-22.3 West. Pecan grove.

21.5-21.6 East. Borrow pit.

21.45 Drainage ditch. West of I-55 the ditch has a conspicuous 150-foot diameter circular depression which sometimes contains water. This is man-made and not a seismic feature.

21.1-21.2 Borrow pits on both sides of Interstate.

19.4-19.7 East. Enormous borrow pit.

19.05 Exit 19. Hayti via highway 84. Light colored patches can be seen in the field to the west.

18.4-18.8 West. Enormous borrow pits.

18.35 Overpass. Blacktop crosses over I-55.

17.65 Interchange 1 and 17. I-55/I-155. South exit to Hayti.

16.8-17.2 East. Pierce catfish farm.

16.7 West. The circular, light-colored features in field are clay, not sand. See our comments at mile 36.1.

16.0 West. The relatively high area some 400 feet from the highway is probably a remnant of a natural levee of a former stream that meandered through here before drainage canals were constructed. Old topographic maps show that a prominent meander loop existed there.

15.85 Drainage ditch.

14.8-15.75 East. Catfish farms.

15.25 I-55 crosses over abandoned railroad. This overpass affords an excellent opportunity to see numerous sand boils in the fields to the west.

14.5-14.6 Borrow pits on both sides of highway.

14.45 Exit 14. Caruthersville and Braggadocio.

13.3 Drainage ditch.

12.35 Borrow pits on both sides.

12.25 Overpass. Blacktop crosses over I-55.

11.4-11.6 East. These large, water-filled borrow pits are lined with willows.

9.9 Both sides. Weigh stations.

9.6 East. In the field just south of the weigh station a zone of light-colored soil can be seen. The diameter is about 70 feet, containing a wet spot of about 20 feet diameter in the center. Though farming practices have spread clay over this area, this feature probably communicates with the groundwater table and is quite possibly seismic in origin.

9.35 West. Willow grove in old borrow pit.

8.95 Drainage ditch.

8.75 East. Old borrow pit and willow grove.

8.6-8.7 East. Linear low area. This is probably a seismically-induced sag area. A possible sand boil can be seen in the field.

8.2-8.4 Both sides. Large, triangular borrow pits.

8.0 Exit 8. **Steele** via highway 164. **Duckies** gas station, snack bar, and gift shop is here, a good place to take a break and visit with the local owners, Tony and Pat Holmes. This book, as well as several of the other earthquake books mentioned can be purchased at Duckies. Southbound traffic can exit here to see the German earthquake crevasse along the east outer road two miles south at milepost 6.0 (See Figure 26, p. 61)

6.25 Overpass.

6.0 East. **Large linear crevasse.** This 100 foot by 2000 foot feature has the appearance of a man-made drainage ditch, but it is not. The white house you see facing the ditch to the east of I-55 has been there for more than 100 years. Ruby German, who lives there today, assures us that this feature was there before her family settled there. The local name for this feature is "The Race Track." It holds some water intermittently, but apparently does not intersect the water table. It was probably formed when wet, sandy sediment a few feet below the surface became liquefied, allowing the unliquefied sediment above to spread both north and south, opening up the crevasse. This feature actually passes under I-55 where it ends in the vicinity of a brick house visible from the highway. The owner of the west portion of the feature has partially filled it in.

This large lateral spreading feature is only a few miles west of where Cagle Lake formed on December 16, 1811. (See *The Earthquake America Forgot* for more details on Cagle Lake and its history.)

Northbound fault finders can get a better look at this earthquake feature by exiting I-55 at Exit 8 and doubling back on the side road paralleling the interstate. Southbound fault finders can do the same from Exit 4. (See Figure 26, p. 61.)

4.6 West. Borrow pit.

4.45 Exit 4. Cooter and Holland via highway E.

4.4 East. Large, water-filled borrow pit.

4.2 Drainage ditch.

4.0 West. A north-south oriented linear feature, at least 500 feet in length, can be traced through the field. It crosses areas of different grasses through a gap in the trumpet vines, possibly crossing I-55 to the east side. Our best guess is that this is a sand fissure that has been modified by farming practices.

3.6 East. Light colored areas in field. The soil over them appears to contain just as much clay as the areas between them. We suspect that sand lies just below the surface zone which has been mixed by agricultural practices, and that they are actually sand boils that have been leveled.

2.7 Both sides. Rest areas.

1.9 Belle Fountain ditch, a major drainage canal.

1.1 Exit 1 to highway O.

0.85 West. The circular moist area may be seismic. At least the top 32 inches is clay, not sand. It is probably a sand boil that has defied attempts to farm it.

0.6 East. Notice the round, wet spot in field 175 feet east of highway. The water here is clearly above the water level in the ditch.

0.0 (Missouri) or 72.3 (Arkansas) Arkansas-Missouri state line. Drivers going north will use Missouri mileages. Drivers going south use Arkansas mileages.

71.6 Pemiscot Bayou, a major drainage canal.

71.25 Exit 71 to highway 150.

69.4 West. Square borrow pit.

69.35 Drainage ditch.

68.2 West. Visitor center and rest area.

67.9 Drainage ditch.

67.3 Interchange 67. North (or east) exit to Blytheville via highways 18 and 151.

66.8 Overpass. I-55 crosses over railroad and blacktop.

66.5-66.7 West. Large, water-filled borrow pit.

66.25 Overpass. Highway 312 passes over I-55.

65.2 Overpass. Blacktop passes over I-55.

64.7 West. Lake in old borrow pit.

64.2 Overpass. I-55 crosses over railroad.

65 to 59 Along this segment, numerous circular areas of light coloration can be seen. On close inspection, these areas are no more sandy than the areas between them. See our discussion of these features at Missouri mile **36.1**.

63.25 Exit 63. South exit to Blytheville via highway 61.

62.5 Drainage ditch.

61.95 Overpass. Arkansas highway 312 crosses over I-55.

61.4 Drainage ditch.

61.0 Drainage ditch.

60.3 Drainage ditch.

59.7 Overpass. Blacktop crosses over I-55.

59.1 Drainage ditch.

59.0 East. Light-colored area is not sandy. It may be a sand boil that has been covered by land-leveling practices.

58.0 Drainage ditch.

57.8 West. Linear depression some 300 feet from the highway, probable linear crevasse or graben of seismic origin. It is about 400 by 100 feet, oriented ENE-WSW. It "pinches out" at both ends, making it canoe-shaped.

57.65 East. Cotton Boll Vocational Technical School

57.4 Exit 57. Overpass. Highway 148 crosses over I-55.

56.85 Drainage ditch.

55.7 Drainage ditch.

55.15 East. Two prominent sand fissures meeting in a giant "V" can be seen in the field.

55.1 Overpass. Farm road 565 crosses over I-55.

55.05 East & West. **Classic sand boil** 300 feet west of I-55. Dimensions 140 feet (north-south) by 110 feet (east-west). Sandy area has stunted crop growth. Carbonized wood and black shale fragments on the surface. Several hundred feet to the east are at least five large sand boils. These are best seen from a vantage point above I-55 on Farm Road 565 Overpass. These are the southernmost seismic feature we have found along I-55. However, the country to the west (to Jonesboro) and to the south (to Marked Tree) contains thousands of additional seismic landforms beyond the view of I-55. (See Figure 18, p. 34.)

54.5 Drainage ditch.

52.95 Overpass and exit 53. South end of road log and southern end of **"Earthquake Alley."** From this point northward for approximately one-hundred miles one can see thousands of earthquake features—permanent scars in the landscape from the great earthquakes of 1811-12. If you are northbound, you are now entering the **New Madrid Seismic Zone.** If you are southbound, you are leaving it. There is a 30% chance that at least one small earthquake will be recorded here on any day you pass through this zone.

• **A Suggestion for Serious Fault Finders:** Many roads that overpass I-55 have been built up quite a bit higher than the I-55 roadside itself. It is usually possible (such as at the overpass at mile 55.1) to pull off on the shoulder near the overpass and climb up to the road passing over. A better, higher view of all four quadrants is your reward for the effort.

CAUTION: Please don't try this at I-55 exits or other places with a lot of traffic on the overpass.

FIGURE 34. Photos of Morphoseismic Features Visible from Interstate 55. Photo #1 is taken just north of Exit 80 looking north toward Benton Hills. On the right is the Proctor Landslide with a barn at the top of the headscarp. The dip just before you get to the base of the hills is an old Ohio River channel. Photo #2: Large sand boil at Mile 75.2 taken from Hwy U Overpass. The farmer continues to plant and irrigate the boil, but the crop never does well. Stunted crops are a key to discovering seismic sand features. Photo #3: Filled sand blow explosion crater at Mile 66.6. Photo #4: 700 ft Cable TV Tower on an explosion crater at Mile 60.0 seen from County Road 820 overpass. This tower will sink into the ground with a major earthquake. We call it our "Richter Dip Stick." Photo #5: Large Graben Fissure 100 ft wide, 1500 ft long, Mile 50.2-50.5, seen looking south from I-55 where the Interstate bends westward to avoid this major feature. It looks like a patch of willow trees from the highway, but when you walk down into the crevasse, you see the view in Photo #6.

FIGURE 35. More Photos of Morphoseismic Features Visible from Interstate 55. Photo #1: Filled Explosion Crater at Mile 53.0. Photo #2. Mile 43.8, View from shoulder of southbound lane, a 200 foot wide band of sand on the east side of I-55 (barely visible in this photo as lighter soil on the upper left) marks the old channel of Gut Ste. Anne—a navigable stream that used to link the Mississippi and Little Rivers. Prior to the quakes keelboats and Indian canoes passed through here. Destroyed by the quakes, the channel carries boats no more, but is now traversed by a major highway, a railroad and a levee. Traffic-induced liquefaction (a form of MIL) over this feature causes I-55 to crack, sink, and break up. Note light patches of repaired pavement and dark portions of damaged shoulder. (The book, *The Earthquake that Never Went Away*, has photos and discussion of this feature on pp. 79-81.) Photo #3: This huge earthquake crevasse at Mile 6.0 is 2000 feet long, 100 feet wide, and passes under I-55. It could easily be mistaken for a drainage ditch. The white house owned by Ruby German is more than 100 years old. The large cypress tree in front of the house is 170-180 years old. It sprouted soon after the quakes and helps to date this feature as originating in 1811-12. Photo #4: Mile 55.1, Arkansas, southern end of "Earthquake Alley." We are standing on the east slope of the overpass of Road 565 looking toward I-55. A string of sand boils or a discontinuous sand fissure can be seen running across the field parallel to the Interstate. Photos #5 and #6 are of a classic sand boil at Mile 55.05 (Arkansas). Photo #5 was taken from the shoulder of I-55 looking west showing how the boil would appear from your car just south of the overpass. This is the southernmost earthquake feature we have seen along I-55 and the starting point for the Earthquake Alley Field Trip for northbound Fault Finders. By climbing up onto the Farm Road 565 overpass, one can get a much better view of this sand boil as shown in Photo #6 where I-55 is seen in the background. The 12 photos of Figures 34 & 35 are only a sample of the dozens of earthquake photo possibilities along this route. As a serious Fault Finder, you will make your own collection of pictures. *The Earthquake that Never Went Away* contains many other photos of seismic features along I-55 not included in this book.

98

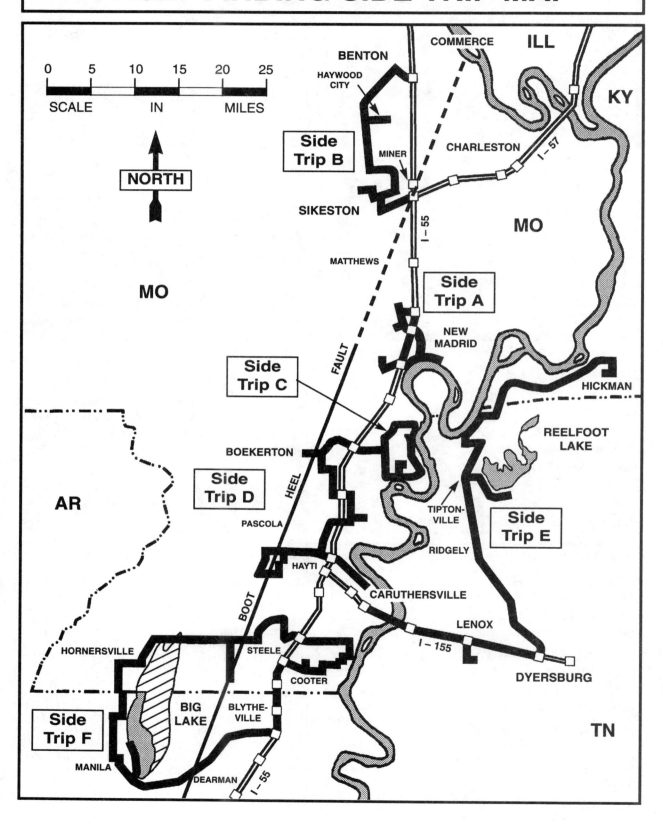

FIGURE 36
FAULT FINDING SIDE TRIP MAP

CHAPTER SIX

OVERVIEW OF FAULT FINDING SIDE TRIPS

The chapters following this one consist of six road logs designed to direct fault finders to many outstanding seismic features not seen from Interstate 55. These features can all be observed from a vehicle or from the roadside.

Please remember that these features are on private property.

The side trips range from 21 to 96 miles in length. Four of the six form loops with a segment of I-55, and may be traversed in either clockwise or counterclockwise directions, returning, if you wish, to the starting point.

You can plan any number of combinations to enrich your tours. Travel at your own pace, enjoy the laid-back hospitality of the area, and have some nice adventures!

To help with your planning, a brief summary of the side trips follows:

CH 7: SIDE TRIP A.
THE NEW MADRID LOOP

The **New Madrid** loop consists of 21 miles of road log. This is a good "get started" trip, especially for fault finders who begin their adventures at the **New Madrid Historical Museum**. Places to visit include the museum and **Mississippi River observation deck,** a **giant sand boil**, an **Indian mound,** an **earthquake lake** and several **"witness trees"**. There are also two seismically **retrofitted buildings**—one reinforced from inside, the other from the outside.

FIGURE 37. Snapshot from Side Trip A.
This is David Stewart holding up granite monument marking El Camino Real (gravel road in background). You'll drive by this at mile 18.5 on Side Trip A.

CH 8: SIDE TRIP B.
THE BENTON—SIKESTON LOOP

Benton exit to **Sikeston** exit or vice versa. 37 miles of road log. Add 14 miles of I-55 if you wish to "close" the loop back to where you started. Landforms to see and photograph include the **Benton Hills** escarpment, **Sikeston Ridge**, former site of large seismic **Lake St. John,** some washouts, **sunk lands,** active **sand dunes,** and **seismic sand fissures.**

FIGURE 38. Snapshot from Side Trip B.
Sikeston Power Plant has been built astride a major seismic fissure. At the time it was built, no one knew how to recognize these features. Here's a place where the ground split open during the quakes and quicksand flowed in. You'll see this at Mile 30.1 on Trip B.

CH 9: SIDE TRIP C.
PORTAGEVILLE—POINT PLEASANT LOOP

Portageville to **Point Pleasant** and Return. A 25 mile loop that visits the sites of pre-earthquake **Cushion Lake,** the present-day Point Pleasant, near the site where original Point Pleasant fell victim to the earthquake and the river, and back to Portageville. An excellent trip for history buffs.

FIGURE 39. Snapshot from Side Trip C.
Portage Open Bay from Hwy TT bridge, Mile 4.9 on Trip C. Looking up stream toward outlet from Cushion Lake. Once a major artery of boat traffic, the quakes changed that forever. Near the clump of trees on the left in the distance was an Indian Village. Many Native American villages used to line this stream which they used for fishing, transporation and commerce.

CH 10: SIDE TRIP D.
BOEKERTON-HAYTI-CARUTHERSVILLE

In this 48 mile trip you will visit **Boekerton, Hayti,** and **Caruthersville.** You'll see linear sand fissures galore, a channel blowout or possible graben fissure at **Dry Bayou,** sites of the former towns of **Spanish Mill** and **Little Prairie** and the escape route of its terrified citizens. You'll also see the **Bootheel Lineament,** a possible surface trace of the New Madrid Rift Complex, and **an enormous compound sand boil**—the world's largest!

FIGURE 40. Snapshot from Side Trip D.
This sign on the Mississippi is the last stop on Trip D to see where Little Prairie used to be—a town wiped off the map by the earthquakes. The boat marks the exact spot, now under the river, where the town used to be. This is steamboat *Casino Aztar*—a gambling vessel.

CH 11: SIDE TRIP E.
CARUTHERSVILLE-REELFOOT-HICKMAN LOOP

This trip may be taken from **Caruthersville**, Missouri, to **Hickman**, Kentucky, or vice versa. 79 miles of road log. Features to explore include an **enormous earthflow landslide** near Lenox, Tennessee, the famous and beautiful **Reelfoot Lake,** the **Reelfoot Scarp**, the place where the **Mississippi River "ran backwards"**, and a Kentucky **town built on creeping landslide blocks** from the earthquakes of 1811-12.

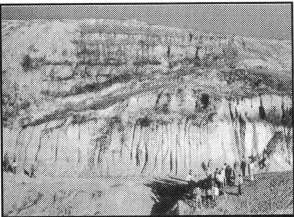

FIGURE 42. Snapshot from Side Trip E.
This enormous landslide, the first stop on Trip E, is a mile wide. Originally caused by the quakes of 1811-12, it eventually stabilized with the growth of trees. When it was deforested to mine gravel a few years ago, it became reactivated to a rapid creep. The slumping blocks of loess can be clearly seen above like giant stair-steps marching up the scarp.

CH 12: SIDE TRIP F.
Steele-Blytheville-Big Lake Loop

Steele to **Blytheville** or vice versa. 96 miles of road log. Visits **Big Lake** (an earthquake lake), **the epicentral area** of the December 16, 1811 earthquakes, and large numbers of **sand boils, sand ridges, and sand fissures**. Also tours the site of old **Cottonwood Point**, another town claimed by the earthquakes.

Detailed logs and commentary on these six trips are to be found in the next six chapters. There are hundreds of thousands of morphoseismic features in the New Madrid Fault Zone, more, perhaps, than anywhere else on earth. If it could ever be said that "Nature was generous to a fault," that statement would have to apply to the New Madrid Seismic Zone.

May your fault-finding field trips be fun and fruitful.

FIGURE 42. Snapshot from Side Trip F.
This large Indian Mound with a house built upon it is 2.5 miles north of Hornersville, Missouri, on highway 164. The line of tall cypress and cottonwood trees in the background is the Big Lake sunk land—a huge subsided area from the first of the New Madrid earthquakes—the 8.6 event of December 16, 1811.

What to do if a Big Quake Happens During Your Visit

Chances of a major earthquake occurring while you visit are extremely remote—probably less than your chances of winning the lottery or being struck by lightening. However, a major earthquake along the New Madrid Fault is highly probable during your lifetime. You may not be there when it happens, but a lot of people will be—including a few fault finders searching for earthquake features in the field.

Should it occur while you are driving through, you will find steering difficult and may think you have a flat tire. Pull over. Turn on your radio and wait for a news bulletin. Proceed slowly and with caution, particularly when passing over or driving under an overpass. Watch out for fallen power lines. They may still be hot. There may also be damage to the highway, itself, such as cracked concrete, shifted slabs, or gaps in the pavement. Strong earthquakes are always followed by aftershocks. Some may be powerful and destructive. Some can be as strong or stronger than the initial shock. Use common sense and you will be fine.

If you should be standing on a sand boil or other liquefaction feature during a strong earthquake, you will be safe. You are not going to sink into a quagmire of quicksand. Seismically induced liquefaction does not manifest itself at ground surface until a few minutes after the shocks have ceased. Sometimes the delay can be twenty minutes or more. In the unlikely event you are caught on a liquefiable feature during a major shock, simply ride out the ground motion. You are safer here, out of doors, than inside a building. Then walk to your vehicle and drive to solid pavement if you aren't parked on it already.

If you happen to be in the New Madrid area inside of a building during an earthquake, duck and cover. Don't try to run out during the shaking. Bricks, power lines, and broken glass may be falling just outside the door. While the shaking lasts, get under a table or chair or doorway to protect yourself from falling objects and collapsing ceilings. The quake shouldn't last more than 30 seconds. Then leave the building carefully and get into an open area away from buildings and power lines.

The New Madrid Historical Museum has free earthquake safety literature available. You may also obtain a free brochure from Gutenberg-Richter Publications. It is called *Earthquake Guide for Home and Office*. See the end of this book for details.

Again, we emphasize that for any specific individual such an experience is extremely unlikely, but some day it will happen to someone. Hopefully this will not be you when you visit the fault zone, unless, of course, you like earthquakes and want to be there for the experience.

As far as we are concerned, whether you would consider the experience of a large earthquake an excellent adventure or your misfortune is your business. We don't recommend it. We want your excursion into the Fault Zone to be exciting, but not that exciting. We just hope that this book and this set of self-guided field tours brings you some pleasure and, perhaps, a better understanding and appreciation of the power and awesome forces of nature.

The authors of this work have often felt humbled by the the majesty and magnitude of what we have seen in this unique region. Once your sensitivies are sharpened and you acquire the "eyes of a true fault finder," you will find this to be one of the most fascinating areas on the suface of planet earth.

Have fun.

Enjoy.

FIGURE 43. Aerial View of NMSZ Over the Bootheel Fault West of Steele, MO. This photo shows the portion of Side Trip F described on page 143, (miles 8.0-16.0 shown with arrows). Hwy 164 crosses east-west in the upper portion of the picture passing through Denton just west of Pemiscot Bayou. The Bootheel Fault is noted by arrows. Notice how much larger and more prevalent the sand boils are on the east side of this strike-slip fault than on the west. This is true throughout most of the fault's 90 mile length. Nobody knows why. Photo U.S. Geol. Survey, 1974. Scale: 2.125 in = 1 mi or 1 in = approx .5 mi.

104

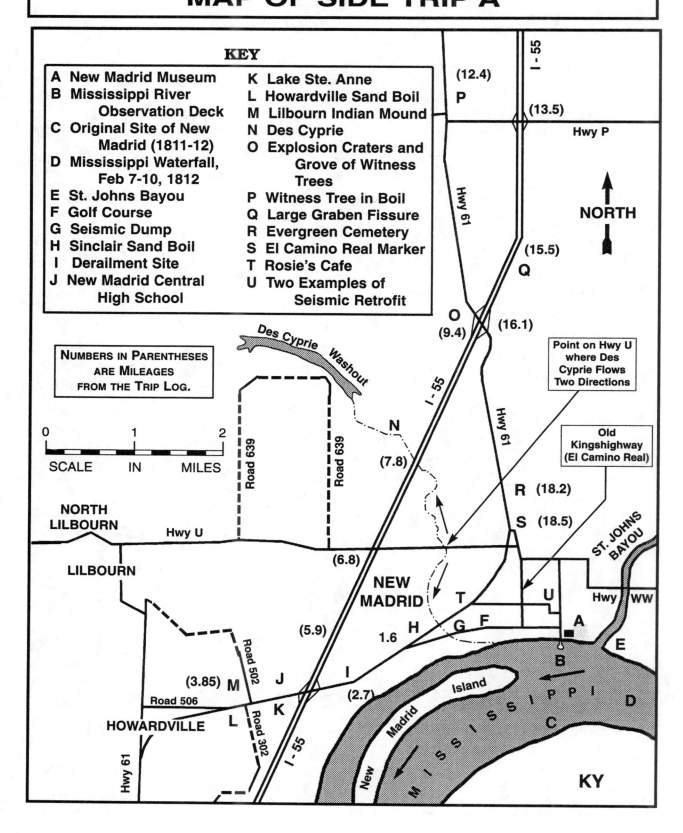

FIGURE 44.
MAP OF SIDE TRIP A

CHAPTER SEVEN

FAULT FINDING SIDE TRIP A: THE NEW MADRID LOOP

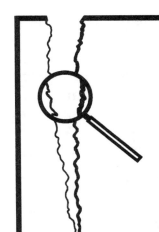

This side trip of 21 miles explores the immediate New Madrid vicinity. Almost all of this tour is within the epicentral region of the largest of the New Madrid earthquakes—the jumbo 8.8 event of February 7, 1812. The tour begins and ends at the **New Madrid Historical Museum** and scenic **Mississippi River Observation Platform**. The first stop after the museum is a visit to a **Seismic Dump**, where people have been filling a sand blow explosion crater. Next is a visit to a huge **sand boil** where you can walk on the sand blanket. Following this is an example of **mechanically-induced liquefaction (MIL)**, where railroad traffic is turning wet, unconsolidated sediment into "patty-cake" terrain. Next, visitors can view the site of former **Lake St. Anne**, created when the big earthquakes caused an area to subside a few feet. A view of a seismically unprotected high school and a white man's cemetery built on the site of a large **Native American village** is next. A view of the **Howardville Sand Boil** (25 acres in extent—the second largest in the NMSZ) is afforded from the top of the

Indian Mound. From here, the tour crosses **Des Cyprie**, an enigmatic morphoseismic drainage feature.

Next, we visit a grove of trees at the historic Chartreau Estate that includes several huge pre-earthquake oaks and several filled explosion craters. Then we visit the famous **"Witness Tree,"** where visitors can see a giant Red Oak that survived the great earthquakes—even though it got caught in a large mounded sand boil. The tour continues to a "text book example" of a **graben fissure**. Then we pass **Evergreen Cemetery** where descendants of Thomas Jefferson's family are buried. We then drive by a granite monument marking **El Camino Real**—the original 18th century Spanish highway from New Madrid to St. Louis.

Finally, we come to a possible refreshment stop or meal at **Rosie's Colonial Restaurant** after which the tour continues past a school and a telephone equipment building **retrofitted to withstand earthquakes** and then—back to the New Madrid Museum. (Unless you want to stop for a **"Quake Burger"** at **Tom's Grill**.)

0.0 The **New Madrid Historical Museum**. Open the year round from 9 A.M. - 4 P.M. Monday through Saturday, and 1 P.M. - 4 P.M. Sundays except in the summer months (June, July, August) when hours are extended to 5:00 P.M. every day.

Earthquakes, Civil War, Native American culture, Mississippi River folklore, steamboats, Colonial and early U.S. history—it's all there. Inside the museum are thousands of items that greatly enrich visitors understanding of the New Madrid area. Old photographs, maps, and antiques galore portray the rich heritage of this town and vicinity.

Create your own shock waves at the **liquefaction model**. See for yourselves what happens when shock waves clobber loose, wet sand. Check the **seismograph** to see if tremors are occurring. There's about one chance in three that an earthquake will be recorded on the day you visit New Madrid--or on any other day in the New Madrid Seismic Zone.

Look at maps and photos of the physical setting of this town. At the south end of Sikeston Ridge, it sets several feet higher and dryer than sites off the ridge. It had excellent harbors, both upstream and downstream from town. Keelboats could connect with interior trading sites on Little River and St. Francis River. There was an established trail to the north—El Camino Real. What a promising future! Prior to 1811, it must have seemed that this town was destined to become the largest and most prosperous city between St. Louis and New Orleans. But oh, those earthquakes! Plan on at least a couple of hours here! The museum also has a good selection of T-shirts,

earthquake books, and other gift items for sale.

Visitors will also want to walk up to the **Observation Platform**, a few hundred feet south of the museum up on the levee, which overlooks the Mississippi River. From here, the site of old **pre-earthquake New Madrid** can be seen, now under the river a half-mile south. The land you see looking straight across the river here is Kentucky. Looking eastward (left) the site of one of the **temporary waterfalls** that appeared during and shortly after the February, 1812 earthquake, can be seen.

Just upstream from the observation deck is the mouth of **St. John's Bayou**, just behind the trees. Here is where boats were thrown upon to the bank during the great shock of February 7, 1812.

Ten to Twenty miles upstream from here is the site where the **Mississippi actually "ran backwards"** for a few hours. A few miles upstream from that area is the site where a large cypress forest was leveled.

Accounts of the waterfalls, river running backwards, boats being thrown up on land, and the destruction of forestland by the earthquakes are detailed in the books, *The Earthquake America Forgot* and *The Earthquake that Never Went Away*, both available in the New Madrid Museum.

The large smokestacks to the south-southwest mark the Associated Electric Company and Noranda Aluminum Company plants in St. Jude Industrial Park at Marston, Missouri. They make a convenient reference point for **Earthquake Epicentral Ground Zero for the February 7, 1812, Magnitude 8.8**. On a clear day, the tallest stack (812 feet) can be seen from as far as 30 miles away. It can be seen from almost any point described in this book, including Reelfoot Lake, Tennessee, and Hickman, Kentucky.

When your visit to the museum and observation platform is completed, drive one block **north** on **Main Street** to the first intersection.

0.05 Turn **left** (west) on Mott.

0.5 Mott Street crosses **Old Kingshighway**.

0.7 Golf course on right. This is one of the few golf courses in the world where some of its natural sand traps were produced courtesy of the earthquakes via some of its sand boils! Somewhere along golf course, Mott changes to Kingshighway.

1.1 A Seismic Dump. Turn right into the parking area of the First General Baptist Church. The depression directly ahead is over a sand blow explosion crater that is full of junk. Attempts have been made for years to fill it, with varying degrees of success. Several loads of soil were hauled in to cover the site in 1991, which seems to have finished the job, but . . . During some future earthquake all the old bed frames, refrigerators, used brick, broken radios, wringer washing machines, and other buried items will be blown back to the surface. Notice the low area running to the north and northwest, lined by cypress trees past the golf course. This sand blow is actually located at the south end of the **Des Cyprie** drainage, which finds its way into the Mississippi River near here.

A more detailed description of Des Cyprie can be found in Chapter 5 (Interstate 55 Fault Finders Guide) at mile 47.75. A photograph of this seismic dump taken in 1990 before it was covered with dirt can be seen on page 64 of *The Earthquake that Never Went Away*. (Available at the Museum.) When finished here, continue **west** on Old Kingshighway.

1.5 Notice how the elevation of the Mississippi River levee along here is closer to the elevation of the street. Because the elevation of this portion of the **Sikeston Ridge** is relatively high here, the levee does not need to be built up above it as much

1.6 Turn **right** into the parking area at the Sinclair station/deli. Across the blacktop (highway 61) to the north is the **Sinclair Sand Boil.** This boil is very large, almost perfectly circular, and occupies an area of perhaps 10 acres. The highway runs over one edge of the circle. After having a bowl of stew and a piece of cornbread at the deli (scrumptious), walk across the blacktop and observe this huge boil close-up. The owner, Mr. Robert Riley, generously invites you to enter his property and walk around on this feature at your leisure. (You can thank the Rileys by helping to keep this area clean). An aerial view and discussion of the Sinclair sand boil can be found on pages 66-67 of *The Earthquake that Never Went Away*. When finished, turn **left** (west) out of the parking area onto highway **61.**

2.7 Right. Notice the railroad bed to the right. Obviously, the railroad maintenance people are having problems here. The railroad crosses an earthquake liquefaction feature. Because this morphoseismic feature is under the tracks, ground vibrations from railroad trains sometimes cause traffic-induced liquefaction here. When a train is too long, too heavy or too fast, the vibrations can induce temporary quicksand conditions—causing the track to give way and derail the train. The last time a train was derailed here was in 1993. This is an example of "mechanically-induced" liquefaction (MIL). Imagine! A train derailed today because of an earthquake that happened 200 years ago! That's why we wrote a book entitled, *"The Earthquake that Never Went Away . . . The Shaking Stopped in 1812, but the Impact Goes On"*.

3.15 Continue west on Hwy 61. As you overpass I-55 look for sand boils, especially to the south near the levee. Look ahead and note the jungle of willows and vines south and along side of Hwy 61. This is a seismically-caused sunk land which flooded as a result of the New Madrid earthquakes. It holds water intermittently and is called **Lake St. Anne**.

3.75 Junction of highway 61 with blacktop 502. Turn **right** on **502** and pull off to the right side of the road. **New Madrid Central High School** is **not** seismically designed. It was constructed on the site of a large native American (Indian) village which was desecrated. To the left (west) of 502 are two Indian mounds.

3.85 These are called "**The Lilbourn Mounds.**" The lifestyle of the Indians who lived here is well told in the New Madrid Museum. Feel free

to get out and climb the mounds. Before the quakes a navigable stream called **Gut Ste. Anne** flowed through the site of Lake Ste. Anne and through the **Mound Cemetery** connecting the Mississippi and Little Rivers. Until January of 1812 a ferry operated here at the base of the mound. Over the centuries, hundreds of boats and canoes have cruised by here, but never again after 1812. The earthquakes destroyed the channel. From the top of the large mound, look to the southwest across Hwy 61. Between Lake Ste. Anne and the houses in the distance is the huge 25 acre **Howardville Sand Boil** just west of Farm Road **302.**

3.95 To continue Side Trip A, **turn around** at the road leading into the school grounds and **return to highway 61.** However, for an added adventure, you may continue north, then west, into the village of Lilbourn where you can drive through the town and, if you wish, continue on to explore the morphoseismic area of Des Cyprie Washout by County Road 639. Lilbourn was named after Lilbourn Anexamander Lewis, grandson of Lilbourn Lewis who was a nephew of Thomas Jefferson. Many descendants of Jefferson's sisters—Lucy and Mary—live in the area and many are buried in Evergreen Cemetery (Mile 18.2 of this loop). For a spellbinding account of "The Jefferson Connection" with the New Madrid earthquakes, get a copy of the book, *The Earthquake America Forgot.*

4.2 Back at junction of 502 and 61. Turn **left** (east) on 61.

4.8 Prepare to enter I-55 north.

4.9 Turn **left** (north) onto I-55.

5.9 Railroad overpasses I-55.

6.8 Blacktop U overpasses I-55.

7.8 Slight "dip" in road. This marks the original course of the morphoseismic drainage feature called **Des Cyprie.** Traffic-induced liquefaction, a form of MIL, is causing it to subside, creating a headache for highway maintenance people.

7.85 Present man-modified course of Des Cyprie. Read a more detailed description of this feature in Chapter Five. (*Interstate 55 Fault Finders Guide)* at mile 47.75, pp. 86-87.

9.4 Exit 49. **Exit** I-55 here.

9.65 Turn **left** (north) on highway 61 overpassing I-55..

9.8 Left. (west) Pull off the highway to the right or onto one of the two field roads to the left and stop. To the west and southwest on the historic **Chartreau Estate** notice a grove of trees that include several massive oaks. At least 12 of these predate 1811-12—**living witnesses to the giant earthquakes**. Several filled or partially filled explosion craters are out there. Two can still be seen just west of the highway to the north. One of these classical conical craters was adjacent to Highway 61 and a few feet south of the northern field road— in the front yard of the Chartreau home. The Chartreau house and barn were torn down and the crater filled in in 1994. (Figure 27, p. 65.) On the east side of Highway 61 is an excellent sand blow explosion crater partially

filled in by farming but which still contains a healthy crop of water-loving grasses that nicely outline the circular feature as a bright green spot much of the year. Wouldn't this area make a great county or state park? It could be called "**Witness Tree State Park**" or "Craters of the Earthquake Park" or, perhaps, "Witnesses to the Craters of the Earthquake Park." What do you think? Maybe you can come up with a good name.

10.5 Notice the long, massive sand hill in the field to the right (east). Its size can be judged by comparing it with I-55 traffic passing behind it. This is a "braided-bar island", a remnant from the braided rivers that deposited, then reworked this sandy sediment, flowing around it in the later stages. It has also been extensively modified by wind, giving it many dune-like characteristics.

12.3 Junction of highway 61 and blacktop P. Continue north on 61. Notice the large, solitary tree in the field some 400 or 500 feet to the east. It is the **"Witness Tree"**.

12.4 Pull off the highway to the right. This is a good spot from which to observe and photograph the **Witness Tree**. The owner, Mr. William B. Fowler, asks that you **do not enter his property**. Please observe and photograph the tree from the roadside. This 300-year-old Southern Red Oak is called the "Witness Tree" because it not only predated the earthquakes of the winter of 1811-12, but got caught in a huge sand boil. Its twisted limbs as seen from the ground seem to be gesturing as if to say, "Look at what the earthquake did to me!". Here is an excellent chance to study a **mounded sand boil** that has had little alteration by people. Notice the change in soil color around the boil.

12.5 **Turn around** and **drive south** on highway 61.

12.75 Junction 61 and blacktop P. This time, turn **east** (left) on **P.**

13.0 Left. Dune with small cemetery. It is quite common to find old cemeteries on sand features. They are often a little higher, dryer, and are less desirable for crops.

13.55 Entrance to I-55. Turn **right** (south) onto **I-55.**

13.7 Merge with I-55 traffic.

15.45-15.65 Left (east). **Large linear graben**. This down-dropped secondary fault block is a "textbook" example of these features. A more complete description of it can be found in Chapter Five (I-55 Fault Finders Guide) at mile 50.2.

15.8 Exit 49. Turn **right** off I-55. Turn **left** (southeast) on highway **61.**

16.1 Overpass over I-55.

16.6 A good view of the smokestacks of the Associated Electric Company and the Noranda Aluminum Company plants. They make excellent orientation references from almost any location described in this book since they mark the approximate epicenter of the largest of the New Madrid earthquakes—the Richter 8.8 that struck in February 1812.

18.2 Left. **Evergreen Cemetery.** Many of the pioneers of the area are buried here. Among them are descendants of the Lilbourn Lewis clan, which traces back to Thomas Jefferson's sister, Lucy Jefferson Lewis, and the Dabney Carr clan, which traces back to another of Jefferson's sisters—Mary Jefferson Carr. Many fascinating details of this lineage, the relationship of Thomas Jefferson to New Madrid and the earthquakes, as well as other aspects of the rich history and folklore of the area, can be found in the book *The Earthquake America Forgot.*

18.5 Left. Granite monument to El Camino Real—"The King's Highway." This road was first marked out by the Spanish in 1789 to connect New Madrid, Cape Girardeau, Ste. Genevieve and St. Louis—a distance of about 180 miles. The "highway" incorporated many Native American trails used by the Indians for centuries before the coming of European and African Americans. Hundreds of refugees from the earthquakes fled from the terror of the temblors along this route in 1811-12.

19.65 Rosie's Colonial Restaurant at right. Take a break for a piece of peach pie and coffee, or if it is meal time, order some catfish fillets with hushpuppies, and then have the peach pie. They don't get any better than this! When leaving Rosies, drive **east** (directly across the road) on Scott Street into downtown New Madrid.

20.6 Intersection. As you turn **right** (south) onto Powell Street here, two notable examples of **seismic**

retrofitting can be seen from this corner. Looking straight ahead (east), across the block and over to Main Street you can see the back side of a brick building strangely encased in a box of steel beams on the top and all four sides. You can drive over later to getter a better look, but that is the **Southwestern Bell switching building.** When engineers were assigned to retrofit it, the telephone company required that they stay outside of the building so as not to disturb any of the expensive equipment inside. Hence, an external bracing approach was used. This building will resist collapse so that, hopefully, the telephones of the area will still be operational in the event of a large earthquake. Southwestern Bell has retrofitted all of their buildings in southeast Missouri and northeast Arkansas. Now look to your right and notice the **Immaculate Conception Elementary School** at the corner of Scott and Powell. Unlike the New Madrid High School, this one has been retrofitted to withstand a moderate earthquake. Unlike the Southwestern Bell building, Immaculate Conception has been retrofitted from the inside. The diagonal braces are

quite visible from the outside as seen through the windows. Although this building could still be seriously damaged in a strong earthquake, because of the retrofitting it won't collapse and hurt anyone. The cost was about $500 per student—a wise investment, indeed! Some day it will pay back a priceless dividend. Continue south on Powell to Mott Street.

20.7 Intersection of Powell and Mott Street. Turn **left** (east) on **Mott**. On left side of the street (across from City Hall) is **River Bend Cafe,** (locally **Jack's**), which has the best bowl of chicken creole this side of New Orleans. Only Jack knows the secret that make his cooking so special.

20.75 Turn **right** (south) on Main Street and return to the New Madrid Historical Museum **(21.0)** or, if you wish, turn left (north) where two blocks down Main Street (across from the courthouse) you will find **Tom's Grill**. There you can get the one and only **New Madrid "Quake Burger."** The Southwestern Bell Building is one block north of Tom's Grill on the left.

End of Side Trip A.

FIGURE 45. **Photos from Side Trip A.** Southwestern Bell switching facility at New Madrid, seismically retrofitted. View looking east from Hwy 61 in New Madrid showing a ground view of some of the same sand boils seen from the air on the cover of this book. The New Madrid Nursing Home is behind us. The houses whose backs we see across the field are facing Old Kingshighway (El Camino Real).

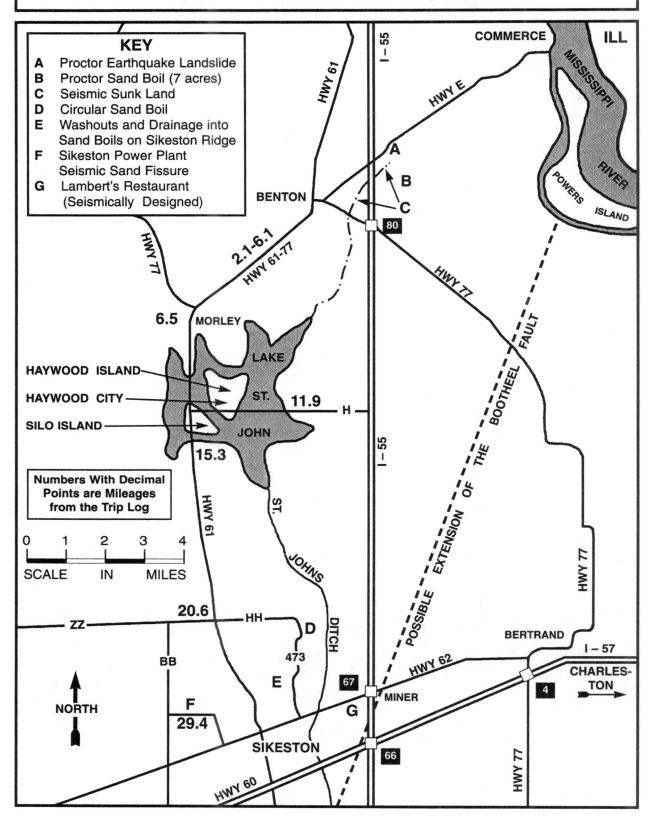

FIGURE 46
MAP OF SIDE TRIP B

KEY

A Proctor Earthquake Landslide
B Proctor Sand Boil (7 acres)
C Seismic Sunk Land
D Circular Sand Boil
E Washouts and Drainage into
  Sand Boils on Sikeston Ridge
F Sikeston Power Plant
  Seismic Sand Fissure
G Lambert's Restaurant
  (Seismically Designed)

Numbers With Decimal
Points are Mileages
from the Trip Log

SCALE   IN   MILES

NORTH

CHAPTER EIGHT

FAULT FINDING SIDE TRIP B: THE BENTON–SIKESTON LOOP

This side trip of 37 miles looks over the **Benton Hills Escarpment** and its apron of **colluvial fans**, explores the north end of **Sikeston Ridge,** the former site of **Lake St. John, Silo Island** and **Haywood Island.** Next, we observe some "**washouts**" and some **houses at risk** in the next big earthquake. Following this we visit the **Sikeston power plant fissure,** a **sunk land** adjacent to the Sikeston Ridge, and finally a possible crossing of the **Bootheel Fault.**

0.0 Exit 80. Exit I-55 here and turn **west** on Hwy **77** toward Benton. Set your odometer at the junction of the offramp with Hwy 77. The lowland between I-55 and the Benton Hills to the west is a former course of the Ohio River. (See Fig. 15, p. 30.)

0.45 The small drainage crossed here is a headwater of St. Johns Bayou that drains all the way to the Mississippi at New Madrid. It was also a major feeder to Lake St. John.

1.0 Lambert city limit sign.

1.3 Benton city limit sign.

1.4 Junction Hwy 77 and Hwy E. Continue on 77. (Turn right here to get to the Proctor farm and landslide area discussed in Chapter Five at mile 82.4 of the I-55 Trip.)

1.6 Turn **left** (south) on **Hwy 61** and 77.

1.9 Highway 61 descends the Benton Hills Escarpment.

2.1-6.1 This segment of Hwy 61 runs along the escarpment of the Benton Hills. The high areas to the right (northwest) are actually portions of the Ozark Highlands that have escaped erosion by the big rivers. (See Fig. 15, p. 30.). The low areas to the left (southeast) are portions of the Mississippi Alluvial Valley. Gravel, sand, silt, and clay eroded from the highlands are being deposited as an "apron" of coalescing fan-shaped **colluvium** on top of the alluvium all along the base of the escarpment. The extra-large fan between mile 5.3 and 6.0 probably choked off a drainage through the northernmost part of Sikeston Ridge. The gentle rises and depressions of the highway are caused by these alluvial-colluvial fans. The configuration of some of these fans, as we see them today, were also shaped by earthquake-induced landslides. Farther to the left is a "sunk area" more depressed than the average terrain out there that marks the location of a portion of former **Lake St. John**.

6.1-6.2 Junction. Highway 77 leaves 61. **Continue south** on 61.

6.5 Left. Community of **Morley**.

6.7 Hwy 61 drops down several feet. About here was the shoreline of an arm of former **Lake St. John**— one of at least a dozen lakes created by the New Madrid earthquakes. Prior to 1811 this area was the largest of several dispersal channels at the north end of Sikeston Ridge. These old drainages used to carry flood waters when the Mississippi River ran west of Sikeston Ridge. (See Fig. 15, p. 30.) During times of major flooding these dispersal channels handled the overflow—transferring some to the east side of the ridge. Lake St. John used some of these channels for bays and coves while some of the easterly and southeasterly channels became spillways for this earthquake lake.

8.0 Lake deepens. Your car would have been in at least 10-15 feet of water here when the lake was full.

8.4 Road 428 to left (east). From this deep part of the lake, you can see Haywood Island to the southeast about a mile away and Silo Island straight ahead 0.8 mile away.

8.7 Road 432 to right (west). Look 0.5 mile to the west across the field and you can see the western bank of old Lake St. John.

9.1 Drive up out of the lake floor and onto Silo Island.

9.2 Junction Hwy 61 and Hwy U. Turn **left** (east) on **U**. The farm house, barn and silos you see near this intersection would have been lakefront property had the water not been drained for agriculture in 1924.

9.7 Note black soils—old lake bed deposits. This point is near the center of the largest of the dispersal channels of the ancestral Mississippi River. Lake St. John was more than 20 feet deep here. Looking ahead and to the left, notice the island-like hill. This hill actually was an island in Lake St. John. It is actually an isolated piece of Sikeston Ridge—a former braided bar island cut off on all sides by dispersal channels. When these channels became flooded during the quakes, creating Lake St. John, this high place became an island again. We call it "Haywood Island" after the town there now.

10.0 Western limits of **Haywood City**. The community is located on a compound braided bar island covered with active sand dunes. Present-day land use practices make the sand more available to wind erosion than it would be in the natural state.

10.7 East city limits of Haywood City, descending downhill into former bed of Lake St. John.

10.8 St. Johns Ditch. This partially man-made canal channels present day runoff from the Lake St. John basin all the way to the Mississippi River at New Madrid. Note black lake bed deposits here in contrast to light colored soils on shore at Haywood City.

11.5 Back on high ground, out of the lake again.

11.9 Turn around at intersection of blacktop U with blacktop 425 and **retrace route** back to highway **61.** On return trip notice when you drive into and out of the Lake level.

14.5 Back on Silo Island. Hwy U and U.S. 61. Turn **left** (south) on 61.

15.3 Deep channel of Lake St. John between Silo Island & Sikeston Ridge. 61 climbs **Sikeston Ridge.**

18.2 Junction of Hwy 61 with Hwy 450. **Continue south** on 61. Some road log followers may wish to follow 450 to the east where it passes several prominent sand dunes that have "blown off" Sikeston Ridge.

19.9 Red and white smokestack ahead marks Sikeston power plant.

20.6 Junction Hwy 61 with Hwy **HH** and ZZ. Turn **left** (east) on HH.

22.7 Blacktop HH descends the eastern edge of Sikeston Ridge.

22.8 Turn **right** (south) on **473.** This road parallels the east escarpment of the Sikeston Ridge.

23.0 Large circular sand boil in field to left (east).

24.0 Sikeston City limits, 473 becomes **North Ingram Road.** Rodeo Grounds to left (east). There are lots of seismic sand features between Sikeston Ridge and I-55 2 miles to the east here. (See aerial photo of this area on p. 133 of *The Earthquake that Never Went Away.*)

24.6 Intersection of Ingram Road and **Campanella Street** to left. For next mile, Ingram Road runs along base of Sikeston Ridge escarpment. Notice how the streams are eroding into the ridge. Instead of sharp, "V"-shaped valleys, many of the streams have produced wide fan-shaped landforms that give the appearance of having been ejected from the ridge toward the lowland beside it. At this point (mile 24.6) drainage atop the ridge (west) soaks underground into a pair of seismic sand boils, reappearing just east of Ingram Road. We are interested in these features because they might be small versions of "Des Cyprie", which some locals call a "washout", and indeed, the term might be appropriate for these small ones also. See discussion of Des Cyprie on page 86.

Houses to the right (on flank of Sikeston Ridge) and to the left (along base of Sikeston Ridge) are at risk of landslide damage in the next major earthquake.

25.6 Intersection with **Linn Street.** Turn **right**

25.75 Stop sign at Linn and **South Ingram.** Turn **left** (south), crossing railroad tracks.

25.8 Junction of South Ingram and U.S. 60 (East Malone Avenue).

Turn **right** (west) on East Malone, and climb back up Sikeston Ridge. If all these ups and downs on the ridge are causing your ears to hurt from the drastic elevation changes, we suggest that you chew some gum.

26.35   Intersection of East Malone with Hwys 61 & 62. Continue west on East Malone (city Hwy 60).

27.45   Intersection of West Malone and North West Street. Turn **right** (north) on North West Street. (This is correct! The street is West Street and we are on the north half of it, hence, North West street.) Notice 410-foot-tall Sikeston power plant stack, bright red and white, visible to the west (left).

28.3 Intersection of North West Street and Wakefield Street. Turn **left** (west) on Wakefield.

28.9   West edge of Sikeston Ridge. For the next half mile, notice sand boils in the fields to the right (north). They reveal themselves by the light-colored patches of sandy soil, and the stunted vegetation. Sikeston power plant is to the left.

29.4   Pull off to the right and stop at a prominent sand feature in the field to the right. It has a distinct north-south lineation. Notice that the south extension of the fissure heads directly toward the power plant! We call this the **Sikeston Power Plant Fissure**. Considerable discussion and several photos of this fissure are in, *The Earthquake that Never Went Away.* **Turn around** and retrace route back east along Wakefield to North West Street.

29.9 Climbing back up on Sikeston Ridge again.

30.5 Turn **right** (south) on North West Street.

31.35   Turn **left** (east) on West Malone.

32.45 Turn **right** (south) on **61** (South Main Street). An **alternate route** to I-55 would be to continue east on Malone past **Lambert's Restaurant**. We have brought scientists, teachers, and engineers there from all over the world. Allow some extra time. This is not a fast-food place. There is often a line of people waiting. But the wait is well worth it. Norman Lambert is a personal friend of ours and tells us the place is built with seismic design, so you'll be safe. Your greatest risk would be getting hit with a flying hot roll.

34.15   Intersection of Hwy 61 and Hwy 60. Turn **left** (east) on 60 past Hampton Inn.

35.5 East edge of Sikeston Ridge. The entire low area immediately east of the ridge is a **sunk land and seismic high risk area**—subject to seismic liquefaction and landslides.

37.1   I-55 Exit 66. As you approach from the west, you are probably crossing an extension of the **Bootheel Fault**. This interchange seems to be built on unstable soil and would be at high risk of collapse during a major earthquake.

End of Side Trip B.

FIGURE 47. Photos from Side Trip B. The upper left photo is a view of Haywood Island from mile 8.4, standing on the floor of old Lake St. John along highway 61. Upper right, Silo Island visible 0.5 miles ahead from shoulder of highway 61, so named because of the prominent silo there today. Haywood and Silo Islands were both surrounded by water for more than 100 years after the earthquakes of 1811-12. The middle left photo is a view of Haywood Island from Silo Island at about mile 9.3. A "lake" of corn is seen growing where water used to be. This soil is extra rich because it collected the nutrients of a lake bottom for more than 100 years following the earthquakes. Earthquakes are not all bad. They can create lakes, which are good for recreation (like Big Lake and Reelfoot Lake) and, if eventually drained, they create fertile soils. The next photo at Mile 10.8 is looking west toward the east side of Haywood City from St. John's Ditch standing in a deep branch of old Lake St. John. Here you see the road going up hill onto the old shore of Haywood Island. Bottom left is a sunk land crossed by highway 61 at mile 15.3 seen as a dark streak with some water standing on it. This was a deep channel of Lake St. John between Silo Island and the north end of Sikeston Ridge (dark trees in photo). The last photo shows the west side of Sikeston Ridge in the distance with the Sikeston Power Plant Fissure across the center of the photo seen as a lighter soil. This is at mile 29.4 of the log. The Sikeston Power Plant, itself, is behind the photographer in this picture.

118

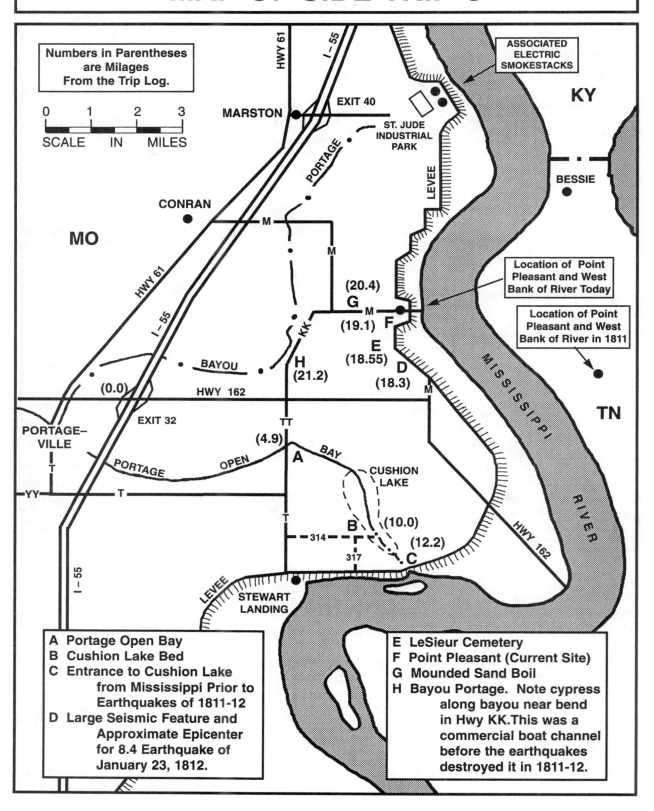

FIGURE 48
MAP OF SIDE TRIP C

A Portage Open Bay
B Cushion Lake Bed
C Entrance to Cushion Lake from Mississippi Prior to Earthquakes of 1811-12
D Large Seismic Feature and Approximate Epicenter for 8.4 Earthquake of January 23, 1812.

E LeSieur Cemetery
F Point Pleasant (Current Site)
G Mounded Sand Boil
H Bayou Portage. Note cypress along bayou near bend in Hwy KK. This was a commercial boat channel before the earthquakes destroyed it in 1811-12.

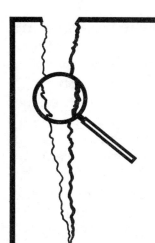

CHAPTER NINE

FAULT FINDERS SIDE TRIP C: PORTAGEVILLE– PT. PLEASANT

This loop of 27 miles takes you to sites occupied by Indians and once busy with boat traffic. **Portage Open Bay** and **Cushion Lake** connected the Mississippi to points west and south, but these connections were destroyed by the quakes. A drive along a levee road will provide a good view of the landscape from which you may see sand boils and a huge **circular morphoseismic feature** one mile south of **Point Pleasant.** You'll drive through present-day Point Pleasant. The original town was literally "wiped off the map" by the quakes. Then we will return you to Portageville.

0.0 Leave Interstate 55 at the **Portageville Exit**. Drive **east** on blacktop **162**. Look for sand boils in the field along the way.

3.8 Junction of 162 and blacktop **TT**. Turn **right** (south) on **TT**.

4.9 Portage Open Bay. If you thought the Mississippi River carried nearly all the river traffic in this part of the world before 1811, forget it! Prior to 1811, this bayou was a major route of commerce between the Mississippi and the Little River (and St. Francis River via Little River). Indian, Spanish, French, and American settlers' canoes and keelboats traversed these waters. As you stand on the bridge over this small channel today, visualize the sight of boatmen, trappers, traders, hunters, and Native Americans gliding by, carrying loads of furs, game, lumber, housewares, and produce. Imagine the sounds of their poles and paddles dipping in the water, and the muffled conversations of passers-by uttering the syllables of many languages. Imagine the waters flowing gently and teeming with fish. And see the banks lined with majestic trees—giant cypress, sycamore, cottonwood and oak. For centuries Indians also lived along there. Several villages lined the south bank along here. One was on the north bank about 500 feet from here within sight of this bridge.

5.9 Junction of TT and T. Continue south on TT. The road is built on a subtle "ridge", which probably controlled the west bank of the pre-earthquake **Cushion Lake** which can be seen 1.5 miles in the distance on the left (east) as a line of willow trees.

6.0 TT and T merge. Continue south.

7.4 Bridge. Pavement ends just ahead. Continue, veering to **left** (east) to climb to levee road ahead. Stewart landing was here until early 1900's.

7.6 Levee Road. Drive east along levee. Notice the Associated Electric smokestack 10 miles to the north— epicenter of 8.8 quake, Feb. 7, 1812.

8.0 The road to the right goes to a large borrow pit, stocked with fish.

8.5 Yellow House and "Levee Road Bargain Center." Cushion Lake seen 1.5 mi north as grove of willows.

9.0 Twin Borrow Pits. (A good place to try your luck with some of the catfish!) Go down levee on left to lower levee road **322**. Turn **left**

9.1 Gravel Road **317**. Turn **right** (north). This road probably passes near the western edge of the pre-earthquake **Cushion Lake**.

9.6 Right (east) on Road 314.

9.9-10.1 Trailer, houses, and Dead End in **Old Cushion Lake Bed**. The pre-earthquake lake was 1-2 miles wide and 2-3 miles long. You are well within the old bed now. Parts of this low, wet basin still hold water permanently. The deepest channel is just beyond in the willows. The name dates back to pre-earthquake times because of the mossy

growth that covered the banks, giving the ground the soft feel of a cushion. **Buried** somewhere in the willows is a **Spanish boat**, which sank in the lake in the 1790's. Cushion Lake survived the great quakes, but was modified. Its connections with Portage Open Bay and the Mississippi were destroyed so it could no longer serve as a passage for boat traffic. Most of the lake was permanently drained for agriculture early in the 20th century. More about Cushion Lake can be found in *The Earthquake America Forgot*. **Turn around & head back.**

10.4 County Road **314-317** junction. (Hwy T is 1.5 miles west of here.) Turn **left** (south) on 317.

10.9 Lower levee road **322**. Turn left then angle right back onto levee where you'll turn left continuing east.

12.2 This is about where boats entered **Cushion Lake** from the Mississippi, and vice versa.

14.5 Junction of levee road with blacktop 162. Turn **left** (northwest) on **162. CAUTION: There is no stop sign here for cross traffic. Look both ways before entering highway.**

17.2 Junction of 162 and blacktop M. 162 turns left. **Go north on M** as it approaches the levee.

17.6 Climb up onto levee and turn **left** (northwest). Look to left for sand boils—patches of bare sand or distressed crop growth.

18.3 Large Circular Earthquake Feature on left, clump of willows in center. 600-700 feet in diameter.

Approximate Epicenter of the 8.4 Quake of January 23, 1812. If the December quakes had not destroyed the connections between the Mississippi, Cushion Lake, and Portage Open Bay connection, this one certainly finished the job.

18.55 Levee bends north. Clump of trees 0.5 mi to west is **LeSieur Cemetery**—dating to early 1800's.

19.1 Point Pleasant. This community lies about five miles northwest of the original Point Pleasant. The Mississippi River has migrated to the west so much in 180 years that the original site now lies on the other side—two miles within the state of Tennessee! **The original town was thrown into the river during the January 23, 1812, earthquake**. Details of the unpleasant fate of Point Pleasant can be read in the book, *The Earthquake America Forgot*. Current residents experience small tremors on a regular basis as a fact of life.

19.2 Bend to the right and circle the town on the levee.

19.45 Take ramp off levee to left and drive through town.

19.6 Hwy M. Head **straight ahead** from here (west).

20.4 Mounded sand boil to right near road. Another boil in the field further out. There is a field access to Hwy M here with scattered gravel.

20.9 Junction M and KK. Continue west on **KK**.

21.2 KK turns southwest, paralleling **Bayou Portage**, another route of access between the Mississippi and Little rivers destroyed by the quakes. Bayou Portage joins Portage Open Bay at present-day Portageville (formerly Shinbone), where traffic from both passageways entered Little River at Spanish Mill (now Boekerton). (More on Boekerton on Side Trip D).

23.5 Junction of KK and 162. Turn **right** (west) on **162.**

27.3 Back at I-55/162 junction at Portageville exit. If you wish to do Side Trip D, continue west on 162.

End of Side Trip C.

FIGURE 49. Photos from Side Trip C. View of old Cushion Lake bed from levee as seen from Mile 8.5 of trip log. View of large liquefaction earthquake feature at Mile 18.3 of trip log—approximate epicenter of 8.4 magnitude quake, January 23, 1812. This feature boiled in 1811-12 (SIL) and could boil any time even today when the river is high (HIL) or with any future large earthquake.

122

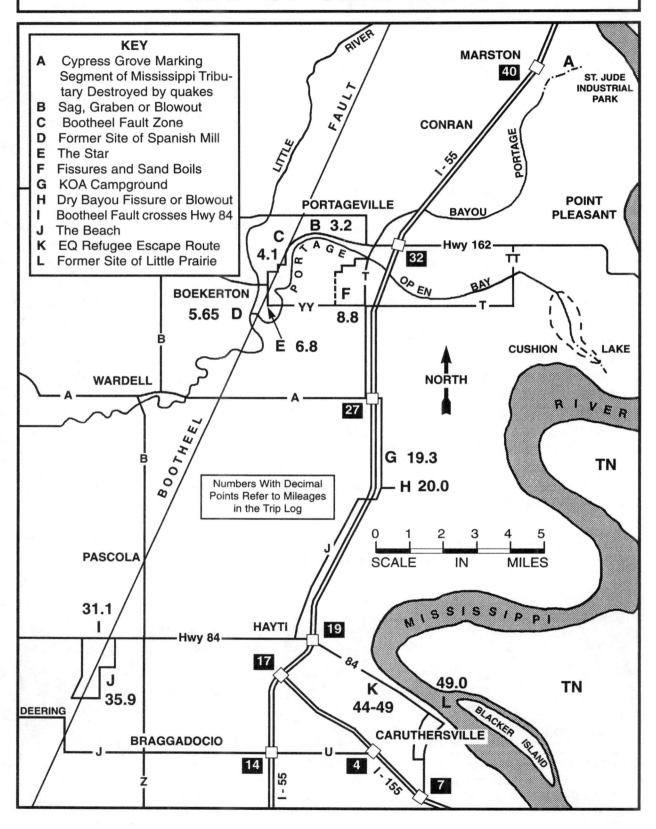

FIGURE 50
MAP OF SIDE TRIP D

CHAPTER TEN

FAULT FINDERS SIDE TRIP D: BOEKERTON-HAYTI CARUTHERSVILLE

This side trip of 48 miles takes fault-finders through **Portage-ville**, a town whose early history sounds like a plot for a Hollywood movie as told in the book, *The Earthquake America Forgot*. Next it parallels **Portage Open Bay** a seismically altered stream, and visits an impressive morphoseismic feature that may be a **channel blowout** or a **graben fissure**. From there, **Boekerton** is explored—a site destined to become a major center of commerce till the earthquakes hit. Following that, our trip pauses at the hub of **"The Star"**. Next, our route traverses an area of **criss-crossing linear sand fissures**. We then visit a beautiful churchyard from which a **graben fissure,** or perhaps a large **curvilinear channel blowout**, can be studied. From here we visit the largest **compound sand boil** described anywhere in the world. The tour crosses across the **Bootheel Fault** several times. Finally, we visit the site of **Little Prairie** and drive the earthquake refugees' escape route.

0.0 Interstate I-55 Exit 32 at Portageville. Turn **west** into town.

0.6 Junction of blacktop T, highway 61, and highway 162 at east side of Portageville. **Continue west through town on Main Street**.

1.45 Junction of Main and McCrate. Main street becomes road 355. Continue **west** on gravel road **355.** The drainage feature to the left is **Portage Open Bay**. Prior to the great earthquakes, it was the major passageway between the Mississippi and Little rivers. Today it is a major drainage canal.

3.2 To the left is a morphoseismic feature that is probably either a **sag**, a **graben fissure** or a **channel blowout**. The larger trees are "witness trees", over 200 years old, here when the great earthquakes occurred. We think the former course of Portage Open Bay went through the low, linear depressed area. The present course was probably created by humans to make the drainage more efficient. The deepest part of the linear depression was almost certainly created by the earthquakes. See a more complete discussion of the possible origins of these things at Dry Bayou, later in this side trip. When finished here, continue west on 355.

3.3 Junction of gravel roads 355 and 353. Continue southwest, then south, on 355.

3.65 Bridge over drainage canal.

4.1–5.1 For the next mile 355 zigzags back and forth directly over the **Bootheel Fault Zone.**

5.25 Junction 355 and blacktop YY. Continue **west** on **YY.**

5.4 Boekerton. The street to the left (south) with the sign, "Boekerton Beauty Shed..." is actually across the old channel of the mouth of Portage Open Bay which used to enter the Little River here. After the earthquakes, its mouth was moved to a point about a mile south. Look one block down this street and you will see a trailer up on the south bank of the former channel that was here.

5.5 Bridge over what is left of Little River—a stream flowing free, clear and full of fish before the earthquakes. The first bridge built here was by a private individual, John Weaver, who charged for its use. He was shot and killed by a stranger who refused to pay the five cent toll.

5.65 The school to the left is setting at the site of **Spanish Mill**, a settlement that dated back to the 1780's that was destroyed by the earthquakes of 1811-12 This site, where Portage Open Bay entered Little River, according to pre-1811 geography, seemed to be a very promising

place to set up a business. Boats carrying valuable goods could pass north and south along the Little River as well as east and west from the Mississippi to the St. Francis River and back. The future all seemed rosy for Spanish Mill--but that was before the big earthquakes. The quakes destroyed the mill, moved the mouth of Portage Open Bay and broke up the channels that made commerce possible. After the quakes, boats could never again pass between the two rivers. A more complete account of the saga of Spanish Mill can be found in *The Earthquake America Forgot*. When finished here, **turn around** and drive **east** on **YY**.

5.8 Crossing Little River

6.0 YY turns south at 355 junction. **Bear right and stay on YY** and you will cross the pre-earthquake channel of Portage Open Bay.

6.8 YY turns left (east). The **Bootheel Lineament** passes through here—plus or minus half a mile.

   In 1993, Kim Myers, a graduate student at SEMO State University, discovered a feature on landsat satellite imagery which she calls **The Star**. The hub of this radial feature appears to be about here. It appears to be the intersection of three or more lineaments, the largest of which is the Bootheel Lineament. We can only speculate at the present time, but one intriguing possibility is that the star is "ground zero" (the epicenter) of the greatest of the New Madrid earthquakes, the 8.8, of Feb. 7, 1812. See Fig. 51, p. 130.

7.1 Portage Open Bay bridge.

7.8 Junction of YY and 209. Continue east on YY.

8.8 Junction of YY and 204. Turn **left** (north) on **204**. Several sand fissures and sand boils can be seen left and right when moisture and crop conditions are favorable.

10.2-10.8 204 zigzags east and north several times.

11.2 204 turns northeast, passing cemetery.

11.4 Cross railroad tracks, turn **right** (south).

11.5 Junction 204 and Hwy T. Continue **south** on **T**. For the next two miles or so, linear sand fissures are quite numerous, especially in the fields to the left. When moisture and crop conditions are favorable, they are quite spectacular—both on ground and in air photos. They appear to have two preferred orientations which could be the result of more than one earthquake or from some kind of seismic wave harmonics. The search for an answer looks like an interesting research project!

13.0 Junction of T and YY. Continue south on T.

13.1 Junction of Hwy T with outer road paralleling I-55. Continue **south** on **outer road**.

13.2 Large borrow pit on left.

16.1 Junction of outer road with blacktop A. Notice the unreinforced masonry school to the right (west). Turn **left** on **A,** cross over I-55, and turn **right** on blacktop **BB** paralleling I-55 on east side. Drive south.

17.3 **Continue south** at junction of outer road and BB. Stay on **outer road.**

18.2 Drainage ditch with modern spoil banks. Notice that the Mississippi River levee is getting much closer, due to a big meander loop that swings westward.

19.3 **KOA Campground**. See pp. 91-92 for information on this campground. It's an ideal place for Fault Finders to stay—and within walking distance of several earthquake features.

19.4 Borrow pit to left (east).

19.7 Junction of outer road with gravel road 332 at Dry Bayou Church sign. Turn **left** (east) on gravel road **332.**

20.0 **Possible Graben Fissure** or the remains of a massive, curvilinear **Channel Blowout** at rustic and beautiful **Dry Bayou Baptist Church.** Dr. Stewart believes this feature is a graben fissure. The shape and orientation suggests a seismic connection resulting in a classic linear graben fissure. Old maps show the Mississippi River running through here in the mid-1800's. If it is a graben fissure, it had to survive this river course. It could not have survived a "direct hit" of the Mississippi, but it is quite possible that it was once a nearby bayou off the main channel. Dr. Knox thinks another explanation is more likely. He believes it may have been formed by a massive sand blow, possibly directly out of the channel of the Mississippi or, more likely, out of an adjacent slough near the main channel. Notice how vertical the big cypress trees are. Best estimates, from coring the trees and counting rings, date the largest of these trees right at 180 years of age, which puts their birthdays very close to 1812. Thus, they were probably not there during the earthquakes, but took root right after them. Probably the earthquake created conditions that favored the rapid growth of these cypress trees. Post-1812 differential subsidence and (HIL) hydrologically-induced liquefaction probably continues today. Most likely, hydraulically-induced liquefaction, operating when the river level is high, has helped keep the Dry Bayou open. (The levee is only 1500 feet from Dry Bayou) Whenever the Mississippi River level is 20 feet or more over flood stage, a hydrostatic head of pressure is exerted on the water system of which Dry Bayou is a part. This forces ground water up, keeping the feature "open". **Turn around** and drive gravel road 332 westward.

20.4   Junction of gravel road 332 with **outer road**. Turn **left** on **outer road.**

20.6   Turn **right** on blacktop **K** over I-55. From this junction before crossing I-55, the entire Dry Bayou area can be seen. It is a good place to get a broader perspective, and a few snapshots!

20.7   Immediately after crossing over I-55, turn **left** (south) on blacktop **J**. For the next three or four miles many boils and fissures can be seen in the fields to the right. This area is close to the epicenter of the January 23, 1812 magnitude 8.4 earthquake. Note that Reelfoot lake is only 16 miles east-northeast of here.

25.7   Junction of blacktop J, blacktop 412, and highway 84 at **Hayti**. If you're hungry, you might enjoy some of Hayti's local cuisine. **Chubby's Bar-B-Que** is one good choice.   If you like genuine cajun cooking, then try **Boudreaux's Cafe.** Crawfish, shrimp creole, and the best bowl of cajun gumbo you ever had is waiting for you here. You'll also enjoy talking with Mr. & Mrs. Richard (pronounced "Ree-<u>shard</u>") who moved up here from Louisiana. The **Curtis Cafe** is also a good place with down-home cooking, a great western omelet, and the only place in the fault zone where you can get **Fried Dill Pickles**. All three of these restaurants are at or within sight of the junction of 412 and 84. To continue trip, turn **right** (west) on **84**. Drive through Hayti.

27.2   **Hayti Heights** city limit.

27.4   Junction of Hwy 84 and Hwy 264 on right (Pascola Rd.) and Hwy 405 on left (Braggadocio Rd.). Continue west on Hwy 84.

29.3   Bridge over main ditch #8 drainage canal. Notice spoil banks.

30.4   Junction of highway 84 with blacktop Z (south) and blacktop B (north). Continue west on 84. The town of **Pascola** is seen 2 miles to the north. The Bootheel Fault runs squarely through Pascola.

31.4 Road 411 left (south) with cluster of houses. Road 221 to right (north). Notice Pascola water tower 2 miles to north. Bootheel Fault runs under tower and across road just ahead.

31.5-31.6 The Bootheel Fault runs through here. To line up with the strike of the fault, imagine a line from where you are to the Pascola water tower 2.3 miles to the north-northeast. Note the sand boils and stressed vegetation on the southside of Hwy 84. These seismic features are in the fault zone.

31.3 County road 415. Turn **left** (south) and drive by row of houses on the east side.

32.25 The world's largest sand boil is only .25 miles straight ahead, but the road here veers right (southwest) to avoid it.

32.7 Notice the lone walnut tree .25 miles due east (left). It is squarely within "The Beach" but you probably can't tell it from here. Continue.

33.5 Dirt road 412. Make a **sharp left turn** (east). Note the dark clay soils for the next 0.2 miles.

33.7 Dirt road to right leading to farm house. You are now driving into the **Bootheel Fault Zone.** Note the sandy soils right and left. To get the trend of the fault, line up with the Pascola Water Town visible 3 miles to the north-northeast.

33.9 Soil changes from sand to black clay. You are driving back out of the fault zone.

33.95 Dirt road 413. Turn **left** (north). The fault zone is to your left as you head north on 413.

34.3 Note change of soil back into almost pure sand. You are now back over the fault line and are driving onto "**The Beach,**" so named by students from SEMO State U.

34.4 Park here and explore. Note the walnut tree 250 feet ahead you saw from across the fault at mile 32.7 coming in. This portion of sandy road is built directly over part of this feature. The gravel found here was imported by the truck-load to strengthen the soft sand. **The Beach** is a huge, compound sand boil. It is the world's largest—1.4 miles long, 136 acres in extent. We have personally brought earthquake liquefaction experts from many countries to inspect this site and they all agree that no sand boil is known to be larger anywhere in the world. This feature is discussed in some detail in the book, *The Earthquake that Never Went Away*, along with several photographs from both ground and air on pages 144-149.

The Beach lies directly along the **Bootheel Fault (or Lineament)** which trends to the north-northeast toward the Pascola water tower 3 miles north and south-southwest toward a point to the left (east) of the Deering water tower visible 2 miles south. The name refers to a long, narrow feature that can be traced from near Marked Tree, Arkansas to just west of New Madrid—and which may extend northward to Matthews, Sikeston and beyond. Landsat satellite images show it distinctly. It can also be followed on airphotos—especially old airphotos. (See "Bootheel Fault" in glossary for further information.)

Visitors can search for clues that help explain some of the history of the Beach. With luck, one can find fragments of carbonized wood, lignite, coal or even black shale. These materials are found in sand boils and sand blows because they are light and easily float upwards with the extruded sand. They originally come (by way of streams) as part of the sediment eroded from older rocks in the Benton Hills and Crowleys Ridge. It is ejected with the sand as water is set free during seismically-induced liquefaction.

The searcher might also find fragments of pottery, flint chips, or other artifacts from the Native Americans who liked to use sandy areas for village and camp sites. Although this feature undoubtedly boiled during the 1811-12 sequence of seismic events, the presence of Indian artifacts suggests that it predates 1811—a sand boil from previous major earthquakes reactivated in 1811-12. In fact, whenever we find Indian artifacts in seismic sand features, we generally conclude that these landforms, while active in 1811-12, were there before—the work of former great earthquakes.

You may also find some "petroliferous nodules" or "seismic tar balls," as we call them. These appear at first to be hardened pieces of asphalt of human origin. If you scratch them with a knife and sniff them, they smell like petroleum. We believe them to be natural. We have seen them in a variety of locations in sand boils throughout the New Madrid Fault Zone. For a more thorough discussion of these enigmatic entities, see *The Earthquake America Forgot.*

Along the roadside you will find pebbles of gravel brought there by the highway department to strengthen the bed of the road. Do not mistake these as indigenous to the area. They are not. Some materials dropped by steam-driven locomotives can also be found in this feature. Old maps show a railroad running through this site. We are told that there also used to be some houses in the vicinity.

We think the cause of the lineament is the New Madrid fault. While the actual fault is buried beneath the river deposits making up the present-day surface, large earthquakes originating along this fault have disrupted the poorly consolidated, saturated sediments above. There may well be an actual fissure, a secondary fault, through which much of this sand has been ejected. Another hypothesis is that a discontinuous line of sand boils and sand blows form a linear pattern when viewed from above. Land use practices, ranging from selection of sites for roads and railroads to different farming practices based on different soil compositions, help accentuate the linear pattern. We think the lineament is a secondary fault and an expression of the primary New Madrid fault below from where earthquakes originate.

When through exploring, continue on 411, rounding the 90 degree corner at the telephone pole and head east.

34.5 The soil changes abruptly from sand to black clay again. You are now driving out of the fault zone.

34.9 Junction of gravel road 412

and gravel road 411. Turn **left** (north) on **411.**

35.9 Junction of gravel road 411 and blacktop 84. Pascola water tower visible due north 2.25 miles away. Turn **right** (east) on blacktop **84.**

40.15 **Hayti** city limit. Continue east on 84 through town to I-55.

42.2 **I-55** Overpass. Continue east 84. We are approaching the Mississippi River levee on the left. The river runs east-west here. Notice the 10-story elevator 5 miles ahead in Caruthersville which marks the site of **Little Prairie**—destroyed by the New Madrid earthquakes. About 100 refugees of the New Madrid earthquakes camped near hear on the night of December 16, 1811.

43 to 48 It is along this stretch of Hwy 84 that a group of 100 terrified souls waded in water up to 2 or 3 feet deep—escaping what remained of **Little Prairie** after the earthquake of December 16, 1811. These folks struggled northward, arriving in New Madrid on Christmas Eve. They had heard hat "the upper country was not damaged!" Flint, who visited the site of Little Prairie seven years after the earthquake, described the "whole region" as covered with sand to depths of 2 or 3 feet. The water that engulfed their houses and through which these folks had to wade to find safety came from liquefaction-induced sand extrusion and the groundwater flooding that accompanies such extrusions. As you drive the distance from Hayti to Caruthersville, visualize those frightened, wet, cold refugees trudging through murky waters with small children on their shoulders, stumbling into unseen fissures, tripping over hidden stumps, and all the while trying to avoid the other critters swimming for their own lives—possums, wolves, raccoons and snakes. A chilling and more detailed account of "Escape from Little Prairie" is told in *The Earthquake America Forgot.*

44.9 Caruthersville city limits.

46.6 Blacktop 84 veers to the right. **Stay straight ahead** past the **Roundhouse Restaurant** (try their outstanding liver and onions!) on **Third** street.

47.3 Intersection of Third Street and Ward Street. Turn **left** on **Ward Street** through the levee wall at the large bell. Turn right before you get to the river and you will see a parking area with a raised concrete slab where you can view the river and look through a metal sign that says "Welcome to Caruthersville."

47.5 From this position on the banks of the present Mississippi River, one can view the site of Little Prairie beneath the swirling waters. The river flows from west to east here. The former town site was about half way across the channel opposite the ten-story-tall Bunge elevator. The other side here is Tennessee. A gambling boat is docked nearby—*The City of Caruthersville—Casino Aztar.* The boat travels up the river and back several times a day, passing directly over the spot now under water where Little Prairie used to be.

End of Side Trip D.

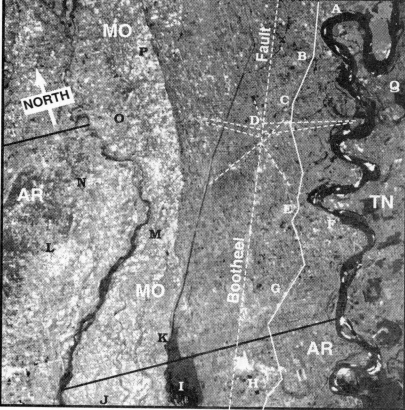

FIGURE 51. Satellite Image of the Boekerton Star.

Kim Meyers, a graduate student working with Dr. Knox, was the first to notice a faint star pattern centered on the Bootheel Fault at Boekerton, Missouri, on a Landsat Imagery Photograph.

The picture on the top left is a half-tone reproduction of the photo. Of course, the quality is not as good as the original photograph and fine details are not resolved, Nevertheless, you can still make out "The Star." There seems to be a convergence of lineaments here. Whether they are natural, cultural, neither or both and whether they have geologic, tectonic, seismological, (or extraterrestrial) significance remains to be determined. Your hypothesis is as good as anyone's.

The reproduction on the bottom left has added state lines and other cultural items as well as a set of dashed white lines delineating "The Star." The solid white line zig zagging from top to bottom is Interstate 55. The letters A thru Q designate the following:

A	New Madrid
B	Marston
C	Portageville
D	Boekerton
E	Hayti
F	Caruthersville
G	Steele
H	Blytheville
I	Big Lake
J	Leachville
K	Hornersville
L	Rector
M	Kennett
N	Piggott
O	Campbell
P	Malden
Q	Reelfoot Lake

FIGURE 52. Photos from Side Trip D. The upper left morphoseismic feature is a small body of water at mile 3.2. Note the 200-year-old overcup oak and the bald cypress next to it. Dr. Knox standing at the base of these trees is dwarfed by their size. At upper right is mile 5.4 at Boekerton. The Little River bridge is off camera to the right. The sign says "Boekerton Beauty Shed" and "Willard's Woodshop." This simple lane crosses the former channel of Portage Open Bay where it entered the Little River prior to the earthquakes of 1811-12. At the end of the lane on the left the former south bank of Portage Open Bay can be seen. This picturesque country church at mile 20.0 is situated next to a major earthquake feature created in 1811-12. It holds water some of the time and is called "Dry Bayou." The stand of large cypress are just the right age to have sprouted within a decade or two after the quakes. Right center view is behind Dry Bayou Baptist Church looking northwest. Dr. Knox is seen standing in the crevasse. The grove of trees in the distance is the Portageville-Hayti KOA Campground. Bottom left is at mile 33.2 from highway 84 looking south at one of several sand boils on the Bootheel Fault which crosses the highway here. The last photo is from the I-55 overpass, Exit 19, Hayti-Caruthersville (mile 42.2 in your road log). We are looking east along Hwy 84 toward Caruthersville 5 miles away on the horizon. Barely visible in the distance is the ten-story-tall Bunge elevator which marks the location of Little Prairie—a town totally destroyed by the earthquakes. The refugees from Little Prairie fled on foot along the route now traversed by Hwy 84. These pioneers lived in a natural environment. They would never have dreamed that today their escape route would be lined with gas stations and fast food restaurants. The main danger they faced then was exposure to the elements. Today that danger has been replaced by highway traffic.

FIGURE 53
MAP OF SIDE TRIP E

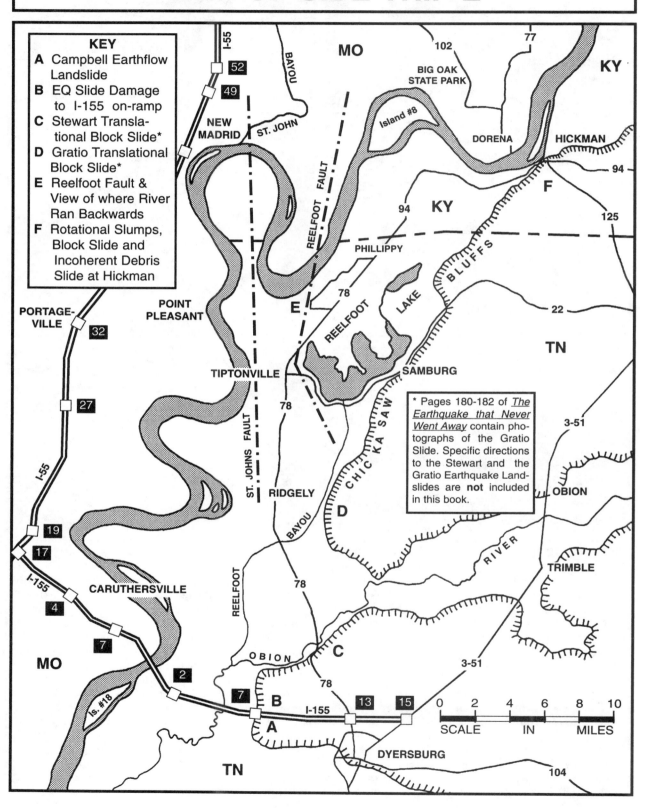

KEY

A Campbell Earthflow Landslide

B EQ Slide Damage to I-155 on-ramp

C Stewart Translational Block Slide*

D Gratio Translational Block Slide*

E Reelfoot Fault & View of where River Ran Backwards

F Rotational Slumps, Block Slide and Incoherent Debris Slide at Hickman

* Pages 180-182 of *The Earthquake that Never Went Away* contain photographs of the Gratio Slide. Specific directions to the Stewart and the Gratio Earthquake Landslides are **not** included in this book.

SCALE IN MILES

CHAPTER ELEVEN

FAULT FINDERS SIDE TRIP E: CARUTHERSVILLE-REELFOOT-HICKMAN

This side trip of 79 miles crosses the Mississippi River and investigates some seismically-induced landforms in Tennessee and Kentucky. One of the enormous landslides can be seen. The **Campbell Landslide** is plainly visible from I-155. Next, the area in the center of the **Tiptonville Dome** is traversed. Following this is a visit to famous **Reelfoot Lake**. Then the trip continues to impressive views of the **Reelfoot Scarp** and the site of one of the major **waterfalls** that were created on February 7, 1812, and where the **river ran backwards**. Finally, the town of Hickman, Kentucky, is visited. **Hickman** is constructed on and among several old landslide blocks, and is awaiting more landslides in the future.

0.0 I-155 Exit #7 at Caruthersville. Drive **eas**t toward Tennessee.

3.4 Bridge over Mississippi.

4.0 Tennessee State Line near east end of bridge.

6.1 Exit 2. Hwy 181 overpass.

7.0 Mile marker 3. For a mile or so through here sand boils can be seen on both sides. Notice the patches of distressed crop growth. These liquefaction features are not seen closer to the river. This suggests that some critical distance is needed to allow enough depth to the water table to provide a non-liquefiable "cap" over saturated sand to meet the conditions necessary for these features.

9.3 Obion River bridge.

10.4-10.5 Excellent view of **Campbell Earthquake Landslide** about a mile from here straight ahead. The slide is a mile wide and extends to the right (south) from the eastbound on-ramp of I-155 and includes the part of the Chickasaw Bluffs where the trees have been removed. This is a good place to stop and take a photo.

11.2 Exit 7. Turn **right** (south) on Hwy **182**. Hwy 182 runs along the base of the Campbell Landslide here with the escarpment to the left and toes of the slide to the right.

11.7 This spot is directly below the most unstable portion of the **Campbell Landslide.** You may wish to turn into the gravel driveway and staging area for the gravel quarrying operation and get permission to look around and take some photographs. The Campbell family living there has been most cordial to visitors wishing to see this feature. This landslide is best described as a **Seismically Induced Earth Flow Slope Failure.** It is one of some 200 identified landslide features attributed to earthquake shaking between Memphis, Tennessee and Wickliffe, Kentucky.

The geologic circumstances along this line of bluffs make an ideal situation for slope failures to occur. (see Fig. 24, p. 57.) The escarpment averages 100 feet high, reaching 200 feet in places. The material on top is loess, a poorly-consolidated wind-blown silt up to 80 feet thick. Under this is a highly permeable zone of glacial outwash gravel which sits over an impermeable clay zone. Rainwater pipes down through the loess and into the gravel, but must then flow out horizontally because it cannot get through the clay. This creates a perfect zone for slippage along the wet, slick clay. All that is needed is a little ground shaking from an earthquake!

There is a spectacular view from the top. On a clear day you can see the Bunge elevator at Caruthersville, 15 miles away, where Little Prairie used to be. On a really clear day you can see the Associated Electric smokestack near New Madrid 30 miles away where the epicenter of the 8.8 quake occurred. Return to Exit 7.

12.2 Exit 7 of I-155. Turn **right** (east) to **enter I-155,** but drive slowly and look. Above the right side of the on-ramp are numerous cracks and bulges of an active slope failure—the north end of Campbell Slide. Part of the concrete aqueduct has been buried and part of the pavement has been heaved up and cracked. That's what happens when you build over old earthquake landslides. Once a slide, always a slide. The ground is never quite stable again. The best course is to let the trees grow and keep off. When deforested and built upon, old landslides reactivate, creep, and fail indefinitely. By choosing a morphoseismic site for the interchange, the highway department created a problem that will never go away. That's why we call it *"The Earthquake that Never Went Away."*

17.9 Exit 13. Turn **right to exit** I-155. **Dyersburg** is to the **right** (south) if you need gas, refreshments, a good meal or a place to spend the night. To continue Side Trip E, turn **left** (north) on blacktop **78.**

21.8 Passing Spring Hill Baptist Church and Navoo Water Tower.

22.7 Junction of Hwy 78 & Harness Road. Continue on 78. Notice the problems the highway department has been having as highway 78 descends the bluff line. Two places in the pavement here failed in December, 1990, in response to heavy rains. The hole was so big one pickup truck dropped in out of sight. How will the soils here respond to an earthquake?

23.5 Junction Hwy 78 & Burntmill Road. Continue north on 78.

25.2 Obion River bridge. The

area here and Tiptonville contains many seismically-induced liquefaction features. The **Chickasaw Bluffs** can be seen to the far right (east). Many earthquake landslides tumbled down these bluffs in 1811-12.

30.8 Obion County Line.

31.9 Lake County Line. How can we have two county lines within 1.1 miles? A thin piece of Obion County sticks out between Dyer and Lake Counties. Lake County gives the name to **"Lake County Uplift"**— another name for the Tiptonville Dome.

33.0 Highway 78 is now atop a subtle uplifted feature called the **Ridgley Ridge.** Notice that the roadbed is not nearly so "built up" as it was further south.

34.2 Ridgley City Limit

37.8 Notice the "waves" on the railroad tracks to the left. It is a pretty safe bet that at least some of this is due to a kind of liquefaction induced by vibrations of heavy rail equipment. This is an example of mechanically-induced liquefaction (MIL). Keeping these tracks level and true is a never-ending task because the very use of them by heavy trains is probably the cause of the problem. Periodic derailments occur along here—all because of a series of earthquakes that happened two centuries ago. This stretch of track is unstable for about a 70-mile stretch here—all the way into Kentucky to the north.

38.0 This area is on the **Tiptonville Dome,** the largest and most conspicuous raised land in the New Madrid Seismic Zone. Most researchers believe this raised area is older than the 1811-12 quakes and that uplifting during these events was only the latest in a much longer history. (See Figure 23, p. 55.)

41.8 Tiptonville City Limit.

42.4 Intersection of highway 78 with blacktops **21** and **22.** A gas station and quick-stop at this intersection used to sell fried baloney sandwiches. Maybe they still do. If this brings up memories of your childhood, you may wish to check this rumor out! Turn **right** (east) at red light. This road runs along the edge of the **Tiptonville Horst**, at the zone of most intense uplift of the Tiptonville Dome. The numerous sand boils seen in the fields along here have created a "horst of a different color," wouldn't you say.

43.7 Blacktop 21 descends the east escarpment of the horst block, the **Reelfoot Scarp**. The escarpment can be seen to the right (south). Reelfoot Lake is to the left (north).

45.1 Visitor Center, **Reelfoot Lake State Park.** Turn **left** into the visitor parking lot. Reelfoot Lake is probably the landform most associated with the New Madrid earthquakes. It seems to have attracted more attention and stirred more imagination than any other seismic feature in the New Madrid Seismic Zone. Take advantage of the attractive visitor center. A wealth of information can be acquired from a tour of this facility. Walkways take you directly to the lake itself. You might consider taking the **Auto Tour** or the **Pontoon Boat Cruise.**

Reelfoot Lake occupies the center of a very large earthquake-induced subsided area. This area was a low, swampy area even before the earthquakes. Oxbow lakes, bordered by walnut, ash, oak, mulberry and other species, occupied the lowland. Additional subsidence associated with the big earthquakes, allowed the Mississippi River waters to spill into the basin, creating the lake. (See our discussion of its origin and how it ties into other earthquake-induced phenomena in Chapter Four.)

The lake was apparently much larger immediately after the earthquakes than it is today. One account has it up to 100 miles long. Another has its depth up to 100 feet. The facts don't support these figures. Most likely, the original lake was on the order of 20 miles long, five miles wide, and five to twenty feet deep—an area of 64,000 acres. Today, because of natural siltation and sedimentation processes, the lake occupies only 41,000 acres.

During your visit to Reelfoot Lake, you might wish to sample some outstanding catfish at **Boyette's Restaurant**, across the blacktop from the State Park Visitor Center. Another class restaurant is the **Blue Bank Restaurant**, a little farther east off highway 22.

After your visit, **return to Tiptonville** on blacktop 21 and 22.

46.4 The east escarpment of the Tiptonville Horst block.

46.7 Tiptonville City Limit, atop the horst block.

47.8 Intersection of blacktop 21 with highway 78 in Tiptonville. Turn **right** (north) on **78. Check your odometer carefully** at this point. The next turnoff of highway 78 is an unmarked blacktop **5.3** miles from this intersection. It is easy to miss.

48.1 Notice the Associated Electric Power Plant at New Madrid to the northwest. We are less than 11 miles from the plant and less than 15 miles from the epicenter of the 8.8 magnitude earthquake.

50.6 Tennessee Prison facility to left. Let's hope it is earthquake proof. We don't need any felonious escapees during a seismic disaster.

50.9 Highway 78 traverses down the Reelfoot Scarp, a fault scarp that experienced a recurrent uplift in the same event that lowered the sunk land to the east. Reelfoot Lake can be seen to the right (east).

52.0 Reelfoot Scarp can be seen to the left (west).

53.1 Junction of highway 78 and unmarked blacktop to left. Turn **left** on the **unmarked blacktop**. Cross the railroad tracks. Notice unevenness of the rails in response to MIL. Reelfoot Scarp can be seen in the distance ahead to the west.

54.2 Blacktop turns to right (north). This location is probably the best view of the **Reelfoot Scarp**. On the scarp near the house to the west is the site of a trench investigated by David Russ of the United States Geological Survey in the late 1970's.

54.8 Junction of unmarked blacktops. Look for gravel road across the junction that leads to the top of the levee. Drive to the top and park.

54.9 This location is atop the Mississippi River Levee at its intersection with the Reelfoot Scarp. During the February 7, 1812, earthquake, renewed uplift of the Tiptonville Horst occurred. The normal fault that marks the Reelfoot Scarp was one of the planes of movement. This fault extends across the channel of the Mississippi. The uplifted block raised the channel of the river at the same time as the downthrown block (east) was lowered. This set off a chain of events.

We think this is what happened, in quick succession: The fault created a waterfall in the channel under the section of river directly in view. The gradient (slope) of the river was reversed, causing a great tumult of raging water moving upriver. For a few hours, the river actually ran backwards, starting here and for about ten miles upstream to Island #8. Great quantities of water simultaneously spilled into the depression that was to become Reelfoot Lake. It also spilled over like a tsunami into the Missouri side along the east side of Donaldson Point—overwhelming and destroying thousands of acres of mature forest.

When finished, **drive back down the levee,** turn left (northeast) on the blacktop which parallels the levee.

(For an added adventure, fault finders may wish to turn right (west) off the levee and drive to **Bessie** and **Kentucky Point**. If so, follow the unmarked blacktop east to its junction with Tennessee highway 22, then stay on 22. Explore the Bessie community area. This is the site of a business that existed in the late 1700's and early 1800's involving riverboat passengers who were journeying downriver to New Orleans. Boats would leave passengers at **Bessie's Neck** while they traveled the 18 miles around the loop back to the west side of the neck. Meanwhile, the passengers could spend some time on land, even getting a night's sleep in a real bed. They would then catch the boat on the west side of the neck! The neck is less than one mile across! Adventurers may wish to drive highway 22 northward past the Tennessee/Kentucky state line, to Kentucky Point, only two miles from New Madrid!)

56.7 Junction of blacktop paralleling levee with yet another unmarked blacktop. Turn **right** (southeast) **on road away from levee**.

57.8 Junction of unmarked blacktop with highway 78. Turn **left** (northeast) on highway **78**. Reelfoot Lake can be seen to the right (east), and the Chickasaw Bluffs beyond to the east.

60.0 Town of Phillipy.

61.8 Tennessee/Kentucky State Line. The highway number in Kentucky now becomes 94. Continue north on 94.

63.3 Historical marker at junction of highway 94 and blacktop 1282. Continue north on 94.

72.8 Junction of highway 94 and blacktop 1099. Continue on 94. Hickman, Kentucky, is seen ahead.

73.4 Hickman levee.

73.7 Hickman ferry landing. Entering **Hickman**. Notice the huge earth flow slope failure in bluff ahead.

74.1 The stone steps are in the earth flow material!

74.4 Intersection of 94 with business 94. Veer to the **right** on **94,** which is **Carrol Street**. Notice the wavy street, the bulging retaining walls, the leaning poles, porch pillars, trees, etc. The entire slope to the right is active. An old adage regarding slope failures says "once a landslide — always a landslide." This area of town was built over an old earthquake landslide of 1811-12. You are driving on it. Figure 25, p. 58 shows three varieties of landslides. This one is a rotational block slide. You'll pass the **Bait Shop** on Carrol Street. See caption for Figure 4, page 17.

75.1 Intersection of 94 with Alleghany Street. Turn **left** on **Alleghany Street,** and follow it to the right where it becomes Magnolia Street. Park someplace along here and grab your cameras! The view west from the curve is spectacular! Notice especially the blocklike profile of the slopes above highway 94 (Carrol Street). You can plainly see where two coherent blocks have broken and dropped downward. The streets and businesses in this part of town have used these stair-steps to

build on! After getting your photos to the west, walk to the east toward the barricaded end of Magnolia Street. You will come abruptly to a very large, very scary, noncoherent debris slide, still very much active! Use extreme caution. Magnolia Street once ran through here. In fact, a scenic overlook once existed. An unwise decision to eliminate some trees on the slope to allow a better view was the trigger that started this particular slope failure. It has steadily gotten worse, and now threatens the huge water tanks, the public buildings, and several homes.

A discussion of Hickman and its slides along with nine photographs can be found in *The Earthquake that Never Went Away*. Certainly, it has never gone away for Hickman. Imagine, a town still suffering ongoing damages from an earthquake that happened almost two centuries ago!

75.2 Retrace route back to the Magnolia Street/Route 94 intersection. **Turn right on 94.**

75.3 Intersection of 94 (which turns sharp right) and Wabash Street. **Continue straight (west) on Wabash Street.** Drive a block or two ahead and park. Notice how homeowners have taken countermeasures to prevent or retard slope failure of their homes and lots. Walk down the concrete steps that connect Wabash and Carrol streets. Evidences of past and incipient slope failures are everywhere. An overactive imagination is not necessary to predict what will happen here during the next major earthquake in the New Madrid Seismic Zone.

End of Side Trip E.

For an added adventure, consider

taking the Hickman Ferry across the river to Dorena, Missouri, if it is operating. From there, Big Oak Tree State Park is not far, nor is New Madrid.

FIGURE 54. Photos of Side Trip E. View of Campbell Landslide in Chickasaw Bluffs one mile due east from shoulder of I-155 (mile 10.4). Slide is a mile wide and extends from I-55 on the left to the treeless portion on the right. This is mile 12.2 where the landslide has slumped over the concrete drain by the on-ramp of Exit 7. Here the landslide has pushed from the left under the on-ramp—cracking and heaving it up. The dark grass to the right of the oncoming truck is a groundwater seep from rain runoff infiltrating into the blocks of the slide above and to the left and flowing under the pavement to emerge in the grass. This sidewalk and house in Hickman on Wabash Street are built on an 1811-12 earthquake landslide. Creep has broken up the sidewalk. Lower left is looking east on Carrol Street at Cumberland intersection opposite the Bait Shop—mile 74.4. (See Fig. 4, p. 17.) Note how telephone pole leans to the left and how the sidewalk has dropped down and pulled away from Carrol Street. The last photo is on the corner of Carrol and Cumberland looking west toward where the photographer was standing in the previous shot. Here you can see how the sidewalk has slumped and the curbs are cracking up. The above photos demonstrate the consequences of building on old earthquake landslides.

FIGURE 55
MAP OF SIDE TRIP F

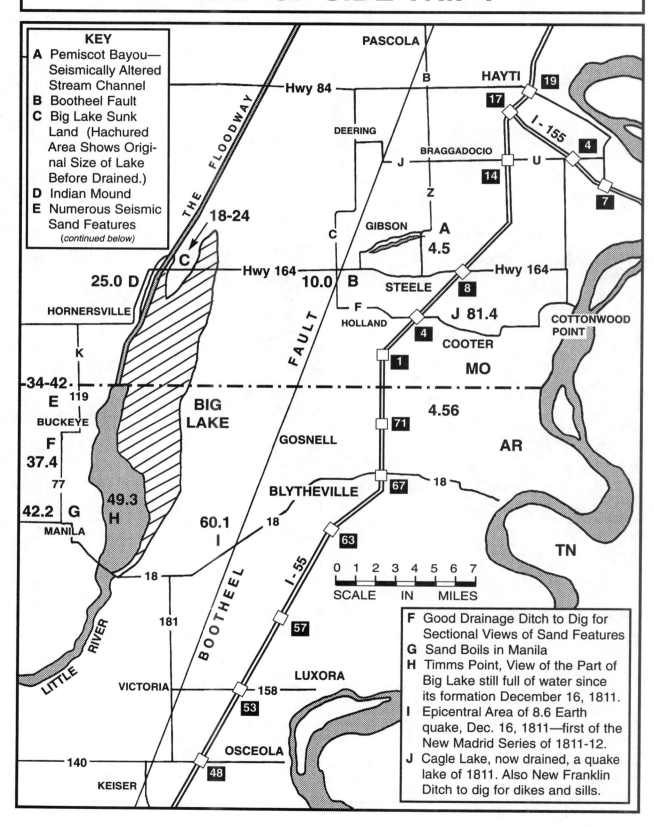

KEY
A Pemiscot Bayou—Seismically Altered Stream Channel
B Bootheel Fault
C Big Lake Sunk Land (Hachured Area Shows Original Size of Lake Before Drained.)
D Indian Mound
E Numerous Seismic Sand Features
(continued below)

PASCOLA

HAYTI

Hwy 84

DEERING

BRAGGADOCIO

GIBSON

18-24

C

25.0 D

Hwy 164

HORNERSVILLE

STEELE

Hwy 164

COTTONWOOD POINT

HOLLAND

COOTER

MO

K

34-42
E   119
BUCKEYE

BIG LAKE

GOSNELL

AR

4.56

F
37.4
77

42.2 G

H 49.3

BLYTHEVILLE

60.1
I

MANILA

18

181

VICTORIA

LUXORA

158

OSCEOLA

KEISER

TN

0 1 2 3 4 5 6 7
SCALE   IN   MILES

F Good Drainage Ditch to Dig for Sectional Views of Sand Features
G Sand Boils in Manila
H Timms Point, View of the Part of Big Lake still full of water since its formation December 16, 1811.
I Epicentral Area of 8.6 Earthquake, Dec. 16, 1811—first of the New Madrid Series of 1811-12.
J Cagle Lake, now drained, a quake lake of 1811. Also New Franklin Ditch to dig for dikes and sills.

CHAPTER TWELVE

FAULT FINDERS SIDE TRIP F: STEELE, BLYTHE-VILLE, BIG LAKE

This side trip of 96 miles makes a loop from **Steele** through **Hornersville, Manila, Big Lake, Blytheville, Cooter, Cottonwood Point**, and back to Steele. It passes the area where a cabin got separated from its well and smokehouse by a seismically-induced drainage change. It visits a portion of **Pemiscot Bayou** that still holds a lot of water, possibly due to several large channel explosions. It then crosses the **Bootheel Fault** three times and visits **Big Lake**—created by the December 16, 1811 earthquake. We also visit the epicenter of the 8:15 A.M.. earthquake, that occurred the same day near the **Cagle Lake** area and the **Campbell Indian site.** You'll have two opportunities (one near **Buckeye** at mile 37.4 and one near Cooter at mile 81.4) to climb into a drainage ditch and look for **seismic dikes and sills.** (You'll need a shovel and some shoes you won't mind getting muddy if you want to do this.) This trip features some stretches of terrain that exhibit the greatest number of **sand boils, sand ridges,** and **sand fissures** in the entire New Madrid Seismic Zone.

This trip can start at Blytheville and loop back to Blytheville just as easily as it loops from Steele.

0.0   Leave I-55 at Exit 8. Set odometer at Hwy 164/61 junction. Turn **west** and drive toward Steele.

1.0   Steele city limit.

1.7   Yum Yum Drive-In on right. Try their Jalapino Burgers! A tasty treat you aren't likely to forget.

2.0 Junction of Hwy 164 and 61. An earthquake knocked groceries off shelves in the Piggly-Wiggly Store to the left on April 27, 1989. The quake was centered at the weight station on I-55 five miles north of here. It registered 4.2 on the Richter Scale. A thorough discussion of significant damages from small earthquakes in and around the New Madrid Seismic Zone is found in Chapter Six of *The Earthquake America Forgot.* Turn **right** (northwest) on blacktop **164** which is also Main Street.

2.3   Junction of blacktop 164

and blacktop Z. Turn **right** (north) on **Z**. Numerous sand boils can be seen in the fields on both sides.

2.7 Crossing former channel of Pemiscot River. "Pemiscot" is a Native American word meaning "liquid mud." Do you suppose they knew about the proneness of this area to liquefaction during earthquakes?

2.8-4.3 Notice the curved sandy patterns in the soil. These were produced by high water taking "short-cuts" during flooding creating curvilinear sand deposits called **chute bars**. Older, buried chute bars or younger ones on the surface can liquefy during earthquakes.

Somewhere in this vicinity is our best guess for the location of the Culbertson family on December 16, 1811. Their home was said to have been located inside a meander bend of the Pemiscot River. They experienced a frightening dark early morning as the 2:30 A.M., then the 8:15 A.M. earthquakes hit. When daylight came and a check of family showed that all had survived, Mrs. Culbertson left the house to draw some water from their well and get some meat from their smokehouse. To her amazement, there was no well and no smokehouse! Instead, a new channel, flowing with water, had established a course. There on the other side, was the well and smokehouse! To get bacon for breakfast, the Culbertson's had to use their canoe!

4.5 Pemiscot Bayou. We will be driving parallel to a 3-mile stretch of the Bayou. This is a strange almost linear body of water that cannot have been formed by the normal stream processes that create meanders, bayous, and oxbow lakes. Pemiscot Bayou, as it is called today, was called Pemiscot River prior to 1811. This piece is the only part of the river left with water in it. It holds water like a long lake, but apparently hasn't flowed like a river since the earthquakes. This channel has been seismically altered, if not seismically created. Its anomalous shape can most easily be seen on a map or aerial photo such as that seen on page 222 of *The Earthquake America Forgot*.

4.55 Junction of blacktop Z and gravel road 454. Turn **left** (west) on **454.** This road parallels the only portion (2.5 miles) of Pemiscot Bayou that presently holds significant water. There may be a seismic reason for this. This part of the channel may have experienced one or more **channel blowouts** when its wet, loose sand and silt became liquefied during one or more major earthquakes. Another possibility is that Native Americans modified and managed this segment of the bayou. They may have long pre-dated the present catfish pond industry!

5.25 Gibson community. Road 431 left (south) which crosses Pemiscot Bayou.

5.5-7.5 Although not visible from road 454, there are many seismic sand features 0.25-0.75 mile north of here not accessible by good roads. See aerial photo on page 222 in *The Earthquake America Forgot*.

6.5 Left, (between road and Bayou) small Indian mound in pecan grove. Large sand deposit on right.

7.0-10.5 In this stretch, several Indian kitchen middens have been mapped by soil survey personnel, indicating that one or more large villages existed here. The terrain here is relatively high and dry, and the Pemiscot River provided abundant fish, waterfowl, and game as well as canoe access to the Mississippi— prior to the earthquakes of 1811-12.

7.3 Road 443 right (north) Pemiscot Bayou turns south here. This is the end of the anomalous channel that started with mile 4.5.

7.8 Junction, gravel road 458. Veer right (west), staying on 454.

8.1 Four-way junction. Turn **left** (south) on **461.**

9.0 Community of Denton. Junction, gravel road 461 and black-top 164. Turn **right** (west) on **164.**

10.0-10.1 The animal shelter and houses on both sides of 164 are directly on the **Bootheel Fault**. (Fig 43, p. 103) Notice sand boils south of 164. Also notice 100-year-old pecan tree in the middle of a large boil south of 164—west of grain bins and white house. There is also a large sand boil just east of the house on the north side of 164. All of these are manifestations of the Bootheel Fault.

10.3 Junction of highway 164, C, and F. Turn **left** (south) on **F.**

10.7 Small sand boils west side.

10.9-11.2 Bootheel Fault angles across Hwy F here from northeast to southwest. The lone sycamore tree to the left (east) marks the center of a large compound sand boil or sand fissure directly along the Bootheel Fault. This feature lines up with "The Beach", 10 miles to the north-northeast. (See Side Trip D.)

200 feet north of the sycamore is the site of a trench dug by scientists from the University of Memphis in 1989. In the fields south and east of this point numerous classical sand boils can be seen. Notice how they stunt plant growth. To the west, two north-south rows of willow trees can be seen. Eighty-year-old Mr. Andrew Jenkins, the owner of this property, tells us that the ditches marked by these tree-lines are not seismic features. They are simply old drainage ditches that the willows "took over". However, the southernmost of these ditches does cut across a sand ridge that trends northwest-southeast. It may be seismic, or may be an old natural levee of a former drainage.

11.1-11.2 Note fine cracks in pavement and at least two places where the pavement has been repaired because of the unstable soil beneath (i.e., the fault). Fault angles to the south-southwest from here through community of Samford, Missouri, seen as a cluster of houses in the distance.

12.3 Junction of blacktop F and gravel road 484. An enormous sand boil can be seen in the northwest, southwest, and southeast quadrants from this corner. The field southwest of the corner contains some 15 or 20 acres of sand. This feature is 0.5 miles east of the Bootheel Lineament. **Retrace route** to the north back to junction of F with highway **164.**

14.3 Junction of blacktop F and highway 164. Turn **left** (west) on **164.** For the next mile or two, numerous sand boils can be seen on both sides of the road.

16.8 Junction of blacktop 164 and blacktop NN. Pemiscot/Dunklin County line. Continue west on 164.

18.3-19.5 Notice how the highway road bed is raised up as we enter the north east branch of the **Big Lake Sunk Land**.

20.1 To the left of the road is a large, sandy area, probably a compound sand boil.

20.6 Deering Ditch, a major drainage canal. Continue on 164

21.6 Elk Chute Ditch, a major drainage canal. Entering northwest branch of Big Lake Sunk Land.

22.0 The bridge over original channel of **Little River.** It has been extensively channelized by the Little River Drainage District since 1924. Continue on 164.

23.3-23.7 **The Floodway.** A series of 5 great canals that drain the former Little River basin. The story of how this was done in the 1920's is remarkable. It ranks as one of the great topographic surveying and engineering feats in history.

24.1 Topography rises out of Big Lake Sunk Land. This would have been the western shore of the lake after 1811, before it was drained.

24.2 Junction Hwy 164, N, and Y. Turn **left** (south) and continue on **164.** We are skirting the west side of the sunk land. Notice that the road bed is now at the field level.

25.0 The mound to the left is an **Indian Mound**. It was a "temple mound", and was once ringed by seven smaller mounds, which have been removed. Fannie E. Langdon, age 92, who lives here, remembers what the great cypress forests looked like before they were removed. She remembers in the old days before the lake was drained when folks loaded cotton bales on flatboats here and floated them to Osceola, Arkansas, to sell and load onto larger boats on the Mississippi. When the canals were being dug, "earthquake logs" of trees downed by the quakes, were encountered. Some of the wood was used for decorative purposes.

25.3 The cemetery to the left is on an Indian mound.

26.5 Cemetery on the right contains some trees that might have witnessed the great earthquakes.

27.4 **Hornersville** city limit.

27.6 Junction of highway 164 and YY. Continue west on 164.

29.8 Hornersville Flying Service left (south) Prepare to slow down and turn left in 0.5 miles.

30.3 Junction of highway 164 and K. Turn **left** (south) on **K**. The trees to the east are in Hornersville Swamp Wildlife Area, a part of the Big Lake Sunk Land.

33.7 Arkansas/Missouri State Line. Missouri Hwy K becomes Arkansas **Hwy 119.**

33.7-33.8 Many seismically induced sand features are apparent almost immediately after crossing into Arkansas on both sides of Hwy 119. They include large sand boils and sand fissures. One huge sand boil several acres in size can be seen to the right behind the berm along the road which was built to keep sand from blowing across Hwy 119.

34.2 Junction of highway 119 and W38. Drainage ditch. With the possible exception of mile 36 to 38 along I-55, this zone has as many SIL features as we have seen anywhere in the NMSZ.

36.3 Buckeye, Arkansas.

37.0 Major drainage ditch. You may have noticed how important the sun angle is when observing sand features. Moisture conditions are almost as important. It is a good idea to drive both directions in a stretch that has lots of features, in order to get more than one sun angle. The best possible situation is about one to two days after rain. The sandy soil dries faster than the clay soil, making the maximum contrast in soil color and brightness.

37.2 Road bends sharply to the south.

37.4 Major drainage ditch with spoil banks (same one as at mile 37.0). This is a good place to get out with a shovel, walk down the ditch to the right and dig around to expose sand boils, dikes and sills in sectional view and collect some large pieces of lignite. Winter, when the weeds are down, is the best time for this.

38.0 Fissures and boils galore can be seen through here. Notice how the vegetation helps mark SIL features. It is easy to see why farmers hate these things. They not only stunt the growth of crops planted across them, but they also sap an endless amount of moisture during dry seasons, or, in some cases, bubble water up as a hydrologically-induced liquefaction feature during wet seasons.

38.25 Drainage ditch.

39.2 Junction of blacktop 119 with 77. **Continue south on 77.**

40.2 Drainage ditch.

41.7 Manila city limit.

42.2 Junction of blacktop 77 with 18B. Turn **left** (east) on **18B.** Field behind Dobbin's Grocery on your left has several sand boils. A good place to stop, chat with Mr. Dobbins, and enjoy a soda from an old fashioned cooler. Drive east on Lake Street.

42.8 Road 18B turns south. Continue on 18B, now Baltimore Street.

43.8 Junction of 18B and 18. Turn **left** (east) **at monument** with Union and Confederate statues. Sand features left and right for the next mile.

46.0 Drainage ditch with levees.

46.1 Big Lake Wildlife Refuge Headquarters. Turn left. This area is part of the sunk land of more than 100,000 acres created by the 8.6 magnitude earthquake of December, 16, 1811, that started the New Madrid series. Turn left onto gravel road leading into refuge.

46.3-46.6 Good view of Big Lake with **submerged cypress trees from 1811-12**. These trees are much older than they look. Their growth has been stunted by the earthquake flooding. The original lake, at the time of the quakes, was much larger than Reelfoot Lake in Tennessee, which was also created by the New Madrid earthquakes.

49.3 Timms Point Lake Access. This is a good place to park and look for eagles. One of the cypress trees out in deep water here has a large eagle's nest (an eyrie) which can be seen from here. Look for eagles, but also watch for cottonmouth water snakes. Turn around and return to entrance.

52.4 Entrance to Big Lake Wildlife Refuge and Hwy 18. Turn left (east).

47.2 Big Lake Bridge.

56.1 Junction. Blacktop 181 joins 18. Continue east on 18.

57.9 West Dell city limit. Be on the lookout for the farmer in the Dell.

60.0-60.2 Bootheel Lineament crosses Hwy 18 through here. Some-

where near here is the epicenter of the first of the great New Madrid earthquakes at 2:30 A.M. on December 16, 1811—magnitude 8.6.

62.4 Some excellent sand boils can be seen in the field to the right.

65.3 Blytheville city limit.

65.5 Junction of blacktop 18 and blacktop 239. Blytheville sets atop a subtle feature called the **Blytheville Dome.** It is a slightly raised area. Some of the movement which raised it may coincide with the sinking of the Big Lake area to the west.

66.2 Junction of blacktop 18 and blacktop 151. Follow highway 18 through Blytheville. Several jogs will test your alertness.

69.3 To the left (north) find **Pancho's Restaurant**. Excellent Tex-Mex food.

69.6 I-55 interchange 67. **Enter the northbound lane of I-55**. For the description of features along the next nine miles, refer to the I-55 road log from Arkansas mileage 67.3 to Missouri mileage 4.45.

79.2 Cooter-Holland Exit #4. Junction of I-55 and blacktop **E. Exit I-55 and turn right** (east). Drive east toward Cooter.

80.7 Cooter city limit. Blacktop E is Main Street.

81.4 New Franklin drainage ditch. This ditch is a good one to dig in for dikes and sills and drains the site of an earthquake lake, **Cagle**

Lake, formed by the December 16, 1911 earthquakes. It was a mile wide and several miles long. Mr. Cagle lived in a house built atop an Indian mound which became an island in the sinking and flooding land even as he watched! The lake was later named Franklin Lake, then Martin Lake, and was successfully drained in the 1920's. The mound and surrounding Indian grounds is known as the "Campbell Site" to archaeologists, who excavated specimens of Mississippian age Indians and artifacts from it. *The Earthquake America Forgot* contains a more complete narrative on Cagle Lake—including photographs of Indian skeletons found on the site with seismic sand fissures slicing through the graves separating the bones of the bodies. Thus, the New Madrid earthquakes disturbed not only the living, but the dead.

83.3 Junction of blacktop E and blacktop H. Continue on E.

83.7 Blacktop E turns left, to the north. Junction with 570. **Stay on E.** The epicenter of the second of the great earthquakes (around 8:30 A.M. on December 16, 1911) is somewhere in this area. It is thought to have been **8.0** on the Richter scale.

85.2 Junction of blacktop E and blacktop DD. Continue east on E.

86.2 Access road to levee continues east. Blacktop E turns north. Continue on blacktop E.

88.7 Junction of Hwy E and 164. This is **Cottonwood Point.** The original community was severely damaged by the 8:30 A.M. December 16, 1811 earthquake. Residents in this area report "feeling" small tremors quite often. At one time, a ferry connected Missouri 164 with Tennessee Hwy 20. **From the E/164 junction, drive north.**

90.4 Junction of Hwy 164 with Hwy D. Turn **left** (west) on **164.** For the next 2-3 miles, many sand boils can be seen both left and right.

94.4 Junction of blacktop 164 and H. Continue west on 164.

95.8 Duckies and I-55.

End of Side Trip F.

FIGURE 56. Photos of Side Trip F. Sand boil south of Hwy 164 on Bootheel Fault with pecan tree on right, mile 10.0-10.1. Lone sycamore tree in large sand boil on Bootheel Fault, trip log mile 10.9.

FIGURE 57. More Photos of Side Trip F. In the upper left photo you can a gigantic sand boil at least 10 acres in size at intersection of Hwy F and Road 484. This is at mile 12.3 in the road log. The sign in the upper right photo says "Welcome to Arkansas, the natural state, Home of President Bill Clinton." Just behind the sign is a berm of soil parallel to Hwy 119. Behind the berm is a large sand boil several acres in size barely visible in the photo. The berm was put there after Clinton became President to keep the wind from blowing sand across the highway. This is at mile 33.7. The next photo is Dobbins Grocery in Manila, Arkansas, at mile 42.2. The whole town of Manila is surrounded and underlain by dozens of sand boils and seismic fissures. (See aerial photo on page 104 of *The Earthquake that Never Went Away.)* Note sand boil in field behind store seen just above the head of boy on bicycle. Looking north from mile 81.4, the New Franklin drainage ditch spoil bank is seen to the left. To the right is the basin of Cagle Lake, created by the December 16, 1811, earthquakes. The site of the Campbell Indian Mound, now buried in spoil, was probably near the drag line and crane in the distance, where the road disappears. The two bottom photos are views of Big Lake also created by the December 16th earthquakes. The photo on the left is at mile 46.3 while the photo on the right is at Timms Point, mile 49.3. The lake is several miles wide here.

How You Can Become A CERTIFIED NEW MADRID FAULT FINDER

There are seven self-guided field trips in this book: The Interstate 55 "Earthquake Alley" trip and six side trips:

- A.   The New Madrid Loop
- B.   The Benton-Sikeston Loop
- C.   The Portageville-Point Pleasant Loop
- D.   The Boekerton-Hayti–Caruthersville Loop
- E.   The Caruthersville-Reelfoot Lake-Hickman Loop
- F.   The Steele-Blytheville-Big Lake Loop

Complete any one or more of these seven trips and you can qualify to become a *CERTIFIED NEW MADRID FAULT FINDER* at any one of seven levels of achievement. • For just one trip, you would be classified as a "Certified Amateur Fault Finder" and would be entitled to place the initials after your name "AMAFF." • For two completed trips, you would qualify as a "Certified Assistant Fault FInder" and would be entitled to use the initials, "ASSIFF." • For three trips, your title would be "Certified Associate Fault Finder," or "ASSOFF." • Four trips and you would become a "Certified Advanced Fault Finder," or an "ADVAFF." • Five trips and you would "Certified Master Fault Finder," or a "MAFF." • Six trips and you become a "Certified Full Fledged Fault Finder," or "FUFFF." • Complete them all and you will have climbed to the highest level of achievement in New Madrid fault finding—earning the most coveted title of "Certified Totally Awesome Fault Finder," or "TOAFF."

After completing a fault finding trip you may vaidate your certificate at the New Madrid Historical Museum—Official Fault Finding Headquarters. Most of the year, Museum hours are 9-4 Monday thru Saturday and Noon-4 on Sunday. During summer months (June, July, August) hours are extended to 5 P.M. every day. Tell any Musem staff member which trip or trips you have taken and ask them to sign your certificate for you. The certificate has seven boxes and seven places to be signed—one for each trip and level achieved. If you complete one or two trips on your first visit, you can check off them off and become certified right away.

Remember to bring your certificate and your *Fault Finders Guide* on your next visit to the New Madrid Fault Zone so you can complete another trip or two— thus working yourself up the ladder to the pinnacle of Fault Finding success. You will need to return to the New Madrid Museum to have a staff member sign your certificate, or if you happen to see Dr. Knox or Dr. Stewart, they can furnish you with a certifying signature, too. While you're at the Museum, buy youself an "Official Fault Finders" T-Shirt.

The program works entirely by the honor system. We know that no self- respecting *Fault Finder* would be dishonest. If you tell any of the New Madrid Museum personnel that you have completed one or more of these trips, they won't question you. Your word will be considered your bond. But you do need signatures to validate your certification. The names and addresses of all certified fault finders will be kept on file at the Museum and by the publisher, Gutenberg-Richter.

You will find your certificate at the very end of this book. (On page 181) Carefully remove it. Print or type your name in the blank. Obtain the appropriate signatures. Then take it home and frame it. It will make a proud addition to your wall of plaques in your living room or office. And, of course, don't forget to include it in future editions of your resume. If you already have initials to place after your name like BS, RN, MS, MBA, PhD or MD, etc., just think what an impression you can make by adding ASSOFF, MAFF, FUFFF, or TOAFF. No doubt the respect you already receive from friends and colleagues will only increase with such epithets appended to your title.

Don't underestimate the educational value of this program by our toungue-in-cheek humor. Learning should be fun. Reading these books and completing one or more of these trips is truly an education of the highest order in earthquake field science. As a participant you will have acquired hands-on skills and first-hand knowledge in recognizing morphoseismic features—skills that most geologists and seismologists don't even have unless they, too, have participated in the New Madrid Fault Finding Program. For example, most engineers and geoscientists have never seen a real sand boil and don't know how to identify one in the field. After taking one of these trips, you will have seen dozens of them. You will have aquired the "trained eyes of a true fault finder."

Now you may noticed that there is only one certificate in this book. If more than one of you took a *Fault Finding Tour* and all of you want an official certificate, you'll each have to purchase a copy of this book. Every officially *Certified Fault Finder* must have their own copy of *The New Madrid Fault Finders Guide.* After all, if you were a tennis pro, wouldn't you buy your own racket? If you were a priest or a pastor, wouldn't you have your own copy of the Bible? Would a professional repairman work with someone else's tools? Of course not. Such would be unthinkable. And so it is with the honorable profession of earthquake *Fault Finding.* The price of this book is your registration fee by which your name is entered onto the immortal rolls of fault finding history. The New Madrid Museum would be glad to sell you a copy of the required text and appropriately sign your certificate, right on the spot.

So get out your fault finding magnification glass and start looking. It's never too soon or too late to start fault finding. It's an ageless profession and, perhaps, the oldest.

Bibliography
of Recommended References

1. Algermissen, S.T., and Hopper, Margaret, 1984, *Estimated Maximum Regional Seismic Intensities Associated with an Ensemble of Great Earthquakes that Might Occur Along the New Madrid Seismic Zone.* U.S. Geological Survey, Reston, VA, Map MF-1712, (Reprinted 1986)

2. Amick, D., Maurath, G., and Gelinas, R., 1990, *Characteristics of Seismically Induced Liquefaction Sites and Features Located in the Vicinity of the 1886 Charleston, S.C., Earthquake.* Seismological Research Letters, Vol. 61, No. 2, pp. 117-130.

3. Beveridge, T.R. , & Vinyard, J.D. (1990) *Geologic Wonders and Curiosities of Missouri*, MO Dept of Natural Resources, Div of Geology & Land Survey, Educ. Series No. 4, 400 pp.

4. Blythe, E., et al., 1981, *Earthquakes and related features of the Mississippi River Valley:* Proceedings of symposium and field trip, U. Tennessee Martin, 28 pp.

5. Braile, L.W., et al., 1984, *Tectonic development of the New Madrid Seismic Zone: In proceedings of the symposium on the New Madrid Seismic Zone* USGS Open File Report 84-770. p. 204-233.

6. Braile, L.W., et al., 1986, *Tectonic development of the New Madrid Rift Complex, Mississippi Embayment, North America:* Tectonophysics, v. 131, p. 1-21

7. Clendenin, C.W., et al., 1989, *Reinterpretation of faulting in southeast Missouri:* Geology, v. 17, p. 217-220.

8. Fisk, H.N., 1944, *Geological Investigations of the Alluvial Valley of the Mississippi River.* U.S. Army Corps of Engineers, Vicksburg, MS. 78 pp. Many maps and cross sections.

9. Flint, R.F., 1957, *Glacial and Pleistocene Geology*, Chapter 10 on drainage; Eolian Features. Especially Figure 10-2,

p. 170. John Wiley & Sons, 553 pp.

10. Fuller, M., 1912, *The New Madrid Earthquake:* USGS Bulletin 494. 120 pp. Republished in 1990 with forward and cover story by David Stewart. Center for Earthquake Studies, Southeast Missouri State University, Cape Girardeau, MO. 122 pp. The earliest systematic research publication on the New Madrid earthquakes from a geologic point of view. This book is available from Gutenberg-Richter Publications, Rt. 1, Box 646, Marble Hill, MO 63764. $13.95 plus $3 shipping.

11. Gori, P., Hays, W., et al., 1984, *Proceedings of Symposium on New Madrd Seismic Zone:* USGS Open File Report 84-770, 468 pp. With map.

12. Grohskopf, J.G., 1955, *Subsurface geology of the Mississippi Embayment of southeast Missouri:* Missouri Geological Survey and Water Resources,v. 37, Structure maps and cross sections.

13. Hamilton, R., and Johnson, A., 1990, *Tecumseh's prophecy: preparing for the next New Madrid Earthquake:* USGS Circular 1066, 30 pp.

14. Hildenbrand, T.G., 1984, *Rift structure of the northern Mississippi Embayment from the analysis of gravity and magnetic data:* In proceedings of the symposium on New Madrid seismic zone. USGS Open File Report 84-770 p. 168-203.

15. Hopper, M., et al., 1985, *Estimation of earthquake effects associated with large earthquakes in the New Madrid seismic zone:* USGS Open File Report 85-457. 185 pp. Fold-out map.

16. Jackson, K.C., 1979, *Earthquakes and earthquake history of Arkansas:* Information Circular 26, Arkansas Geological Commission, 70 p.

17. Jibson, R., and Keefer, D., 1988,

Landslides triggered by earthquakes in the central Mississippi Valley, Tennessee and Kentucky: USGS Professional Paper 1336-c, 24 pp. Fold-out map.

18. Johnston, A., 1982, *A major earthquake zone on the Mississippi:* Scientific American, v. 246, p. 60-68.

19. Johnston, A., and Kanter, L.R., 1990, *Earthquakes in Stable Continental Crust:* Scientific American, v. 95, March, pp. 68-75

20. Keefer, D.K., 1984, *Landslides caused by earthquakes:* GSA Bulletin, v. 95, p. 406-421.

21. Knox, Ray, & Stewart, David, 1993, *A Classification of Morphoseismic Features,* Geological Society of America, Abstracts with programs, Rolla, MO, Vol. 25, No. 3, p. 57. Currently in Review with a professional journal.

22. Nishenko, S.P., and Bollinger, G.A., 1990, *Forecasting Damaging Earthquakes in the Central and Eastern United States.* Science, vol. 249, September 21 pp. 1412-1416.

23. Nuttli, O., 1990, *Effects of Earthquakes in the Central United States:* 2nd edition with forward and appendices by David Stewart. Published by Center for Earthquake Studies, Southeast Missouri State University, Cape Girardeau, MO 50 pp. Excellent summary of all of the active earthquake faults in the Midwest. Available from Gutenberg-Richter Publications, Rt. 1, Box 646, Marble Hill, MO 63764. $8.95 plus $3 shipping.

24. Obermeier, S.F., 1984, *Liquefaction potential in the central Mississippi Valley:* USGS Open File Report 84-515.

25. Obermeier, S.F., 1989, *The New Madrid Earthquakes: An Engineering-Geologic Interpretation of Relict Liquefaction Features.* U.S. Geol Survey Professional paper 1336-B. Maps. 114 pp.

26. Obermeier, S.F., et al., 1990, *Earthquake-Induced Liquefaction Features in the Coastal Setting of South Carolina and the Fluvial Setting of the New Madrid Seismic Zone.* U.S. Geol Survey Professional Paper 1504. Maps. 44 pp.

27. Ohasaki, Y., 1970, *Effects of Sand Compaction on Liquefaction During the Tokachioki Earthquake.* Journal of Soils & Foundations, Vol. 10, No. 2, pp. 112-128.

28. Penick, J., 1981, *The New Madrid Earthquakes:* University of Missouri Press, Columbia, MO. 130 pp. A scholarly account of the New Madrid earthquakes from a Historian's point of view. Available from Gutenberg-Richter Publications, Rt. 1, Box 646, Marble Hill, MO 63764. $13.95 plus $3 shipping.

29. Prakash, S., *Soil Dynamics.* SP Foundation, Rolla, Missouri. pp. 274-333.

30. Quinn, J.H., 1961, *Prairie mounds of Arkansas:* Arkansas Archaeological Society Newsletter, v. 2, p. 1-8.

31. Royall, P.D., et al., 1991, *Late Quaternary paleoecology and paleoenvironments of the central Mississippi alluvial valley:* GSA Bulletin, v. 103, p. 157-170.

32. Russ, D.P., 1979, *Late Holocene faulting and earthquake recurrence in the Reelfoot Lake area, northwestern Tennessee:* GSA Bulletin, v. 90, p. 1013-1018.

33. Saucier, R.T., 1974, *Quaternary geology of the lower Mississippi Valley:* Arkansas Archaeological Survey Research Series 6.

34. Saucier, R.T., 1977, *Sand dunes and related eolian features of the lower Mississippi River alluvial valley:* Geoscience and Man, v. 19, p. 23-40.

35. Saucier, R.T., 1991, *Geoarchaeological Evidence of Strong Earthquakes in the New Madrid, Missouri, Seismic Zone:* Geology, vol. 17, April, pp. 296-298.

36. Schweig, Eugene, and Marple, R.T., 1991, *Bootheel Lineament: A Possible Coseismic Fault of the Great New Madrid Earthquakes:* Geology, vol. 19, pp. 1025-1028.

37. Schweig, E., and Jibson, R., 1989, *Surface effects of the 1911-12 New Madrid earthquake sequence and seismotectonics of the New Madrid seismic zone:*

GSA Field Trip Guidebook, pp. 47-67.

38. Seed, H.B., 1968, *Landslides during earthquakes due to soil liquefaction:* American Society of Civil Engineers; Journal of Soil Mechanics and Foundation Division. v. 94 p. 1055-1122.

39. Stahle, D.W., Van Arsdale, R.B., and Cleaveland, M.K., 1992, *Tectonic Signal in Baldcypress Trees at Reelfoot Lake, Tennessee.* Seismological Research Letters. Vol. 63, No. 3, pp. 439-448.

40. Stauder, W., Kramer, M., Fischer, G., Schaeffer, S., and Morrissey, S.T., 1976, *Seismic Characteristics of Southeast Missouri as Indicated by a Regional Telemetered Microearthquake Array.* Bull. Seismological Soc. Am., Vol. 66, pp. 1953-1964.

41. Stewart, David, 1994, (4th Printing) *Damages and Losses from Future New Madrid Earthquakes:* Published by the Federal Emergency Management Agency (FEMA) and the Missouri State Emergency Management Agency (SEMA). 68 pages with charts and foldout maps. Enables user to choose any county in the Midwest, postulate any size earthquake on the New Madrid fault, and calculate numbers of resulting casulties, displaced persons, collapsed buildings, etc. for that county. Technically correct, yet written in simple language, this book is also a good introduction to earthquakes for those without a technical background. Available free from Gutenberg-Richter Publications, Rt. 1, Box 646, Marble Hill, MO 63764. Enclose $3 for shipping and handling.

42. Stewart, David, and Knox, Ray, 1991, *Representative Earthquake Features in the New Madrid Seismic Zone:* Second Printing 1992. Center for Earthquake Studies, Southeast Missouri State University, Cape Girardeau 63701. 62 pp. A two-day technical field guide with seventeen stops for people with a little background in geology or geologic engineering.

43. Stewart, David, and Knox, Ray, 1993, *The Earthquake That Never Went Away:* Gutenberg-Richter Publications, Rt. 1, Box 646, Marble Hill, MO 63764. 240 pp. A photo-tour of the New Madrid Seismic Zone today, emphasizing hundreds of features that still remain, 180 years after the great earthquakes. 150 original photos, maps, and tables of faults, fissures, and historical sites. Available from the publisher at $19.95 plus $ 3 shipping. A set of 150 color slides (same as photos in book) is available for $180. (Includes book).

44. Stewart, David, and Knox, Ray, 1995, *What is the Maximum Depth Liquefaction Can Occur?* Proceedings of 3rd Internat'l Conf. on Recent Advances in Geotechnical Earthquake Engineering and Soil Dynamics, Vol. III, pp. 77-81.

45. Stewart, David, and Knox, Ray, 1995, *The Earthquake America Forgot:* Gutenburg-Richter Publications, Rt. 1, Box 646, Marble Hill, MO 63764. 350 pp. A fascinating mix of history, sociology, and geology. Over a hundred anecdotes that weave heroism, cowardice, religious revival, corruption, murder, family roots, bizarre animal behavior, Indians, and political shenanigans with the geologic upheavals of the times. Available from the publisher at $29.95 plus $3 shipping.

46. Thacker, J.L., & Satterfield, I.R., 1977, *Guidebook to the Geology Along Interstate - 55 in Missouri,* MO Dept Natural Resources, Div of Geology & Land Survey, Rolla, 132 pp.

47. Thompson, John, & Stewart, David, 1992, *Landslides Subsequent to a 4.7 Magnitude earthquake in the Benton Hills of Missouri,* Transactions of Missouri Acad. of Sci., Vol. 26, Illustrated, pp. 91-104.

48. US Department of Agriculture, 1977, *Soil survey of New Madrid County, MO:* US Department of Agriculture and Missouri Agricultural Experiment Station, 71 pp. With maps.

49. Zoback, M.D., 1979, *Recurrent faulting in the vicinity of Reelfoot Lake, northwestern Tennessee:* GSA Bulletin, v. 90, p. 1019-1024.

GLOSSARY

ALLUVIUM A general term for clay, silt, sand, and gravel deposited by a stream. Most of the deposits seen throughout lowland regions of the New Madrid Seismic Zone are alluvium. The term may also be used in its adjective form, such as "alluvial sand".

ALLUVIAL FAN An outspread, gently sloping mass of alluvium deposited by a stream, especially where a stream issues from a high area and spreads into a lower plain or valley floor. Viewed from above, it has the shape of an open fan, the apex being at the valley mouth.

AQUIFER A body of rock or sediment that is sufficiently permeable to conduct ground water and to yield significant quantities of water to wells and/or springs.

ARTIFICIAL LEVEE An embankment along one or both sides of a stream channel constructed by humans for the purpose of controlling the stream, especially to reduce the frequency of floods. See "natural levee".

BOOTHEEL The extreme southeast portion of Missouri that extends south of 36.5 degrees latitude which, on a map, has the shape of a bootheel. It is bounded on the east by the Mississippi River, on the west by the St.Francis River, and on the south by the 36th parallel. The story of how the Bootheel came about is told in *The Earthquake America Forgot* by Stewart & Knox.

BOOTHEEL FAULT See Bootheel Lineament.

BOOTHEEL LINEAMENT A line at least 80 miles long visible in the topography from high resolution satellite imagery extending from an area 10-15 miles east of Marked Tree, Arkansas, (near the intersection of Hwy 63 and interstate 55) to an area west of New Madrid and Lilbourn, Missouri, characterized by differences in sand boil appearances, sizes, and distributions on either side and by intermittently distributed massive sand boils along the lineament. It appears to be a strike-slip surface fault. The northern extent of the feature is still unknown. It may extent northward through Matthews, Miner, and Sikeston, Missouri, to the Mississippi River below Commerce, which would make the length of the feature over 100 miles. It is currently under study to determine if it is an extension from depth of one of the branches of the deeply buried New Madrid fault from which quakes originate.

The reason the term "lineament" has been used for this feature is because scientists have not yet agreed among themselves as to what it truly is. It has only recently been recognized by seismologists. (since 1989) However, geologist Myron Fuller, mapped a "lineament" in 1905 through the Bootheel he referred to as the "epicentral line" which the U.S. Geological Survey published in 1912. Fuller's "epicentral line" is perfectly parallel to the Bootheel Lineament—only displaced a few miles to the west. (See Figure 18, p. 34.) Therefore, Fuller may have recognized the Bootheel Lineament then, but did not have the benefit of aerial photos, satellite imagery, nor accurate maps and surveys, as are available today. In any event, it is a tradition among geologists that when features in the landscape line up, they are to be called "a lineament" until it can be established what they are. Sometimes lineaments turn out to be faults—sometimes not.

Many believe the Bootheel Lineament to be a strike-slip fault caused by the primary New Madrid Fault in the bedrock beneath. Others think it may eventually be proven to be an actual extension to the surface of a branch of the New Madrid Fault below. Either way, it is a fault—a break in the earth with relative displacement on both sides. We think it is a fault. Hence, in this book, we use the terms "Bootheel Lineament" and "Bootheel Fault" interchangeably.

For Fault Finders wishing to track down the Bootheel Fault, Side Trips D, F and possibly B, all include crossings of this fault.

Towns through which the fault (or its extension) passes or nearly passes (within a mile) include (from north to south) Miner, Matthews, Boekerton, Pascola, and Samford Missouri, and Gosnell, Victoria, and possibly Keiser, Arkansas. It or its extension crosses I-55 between Missouri Exits 66 & 67 (Sikeston-Miner-Charleston). In Arkansas it crosses Hwy 63 a few miles west of I-55 at Exit 24 (Terrell & Hwys 63/77)

Portions of the Bootheel Lineament can clearly be seen from small and large aircraft in many places. In fact, this is one of the best ways to see many of the thousands of seismic features in the New Madrid Fault Zone—i.e. by air. See "fault," "New Madrid fault," Fig. 10, p. 24, Fig. 22, p. 54, Fig. 30, p. 98, and Fig. 51, p. 130. You may also wish to obtain a copy of Fuller's book—the availability of which is discussed on page 174.

BORROW Earth material taken from one location to be used for fill at another location.

BORROW PIT An excavated area where borrow has been obtained to build up the level of the highway road bed to avoid flooding or to create fill for approaches to highway overpasses. Construction of Interstate 55 required a lot of these.

BRAIDED BAR ISLAND Islands within the branching channels of a braided stream. They are usually quite temporary as long as the stream is active, shifting as the stream "braids". The term may also be applied to a landform that was formed this way, even though the stream that created it is no longer active in that location.

BRAIDED STREAM A stream that divides into or follows an interlacing network of several branching and reuniting channels. Streams tend to braid when their gradients are steep and when there is plenty of sediment available to the stream. In the Bootheel, these conditions were more likely when climates were dry, because sparse vegetative cover does not protect sediment from erosion as well as during more moist climates.

CATFISH FARM A pond or lake which is being used to grow catfish for market.

These catfish taste so much better than catfish caught from muddy rivers that there is no comparison! To begin your test of this hypothesis, try the catfish, hushpuppies, and peach pie at Rosies Colonial Restaurant in New Madrid.

CARBONIZED WOOD Pieces of what was once wood, now altered by time and burial into lignite or near-lignite. Streams have originally deposited most of this, sometimes later removing it and redepositing it. Of special interest to the bootheel are the black or dark brown fragments often found in sand that has been ejected by seismically-induced liquefaction. Sizes found range from granules less than 1/8 inch diameter to pieces two or more inches in size. One can usually find some of this material when investigating a sand boil or sand blow up close. See "coal," "lignite," and "petroliferous nodules."

CHANNEL BLOWOUTS See Channel Explosions.

CHANNEL EXPLOSIONS Eyewitnesses to the big earthquakes frequently reported violent ejections of sand, air, water, and carbonized wood fragments directly out of channels—including the channel of the Mississippi River. They told of the sights, sounds, and odors produced. Today, places where some of these explosions happened are seen as lens-shaped or arc-shaped features that may still hold water. They are difficult to distinguish from graben fissures, and intermediate categories between these two features may exist.

COAL A combustible rock formed from compaction and hardening of plant remains. This ancient organic material has become hardened and modified into material having a high carbon content. Pieces of coal may be found in the sand boils and other liquefaction features of the New Madrid Seismic Zone, some almost fist size. Some of these came from deposits hundreds of miles away, washed here by streams over long periods of time. The age of much of this coal is Eocene, in geologic terms, which makes them 36 million to 58 million years in age. See "carbonized wood" and "lignite."

COLLUVIAL FAN A fan-shaped deposit of colluvium, usually at the base of a slope. See "colluvium".

COLLUVIUM A general term applied to a loose mass of soil material and/or rock fragments deposited by rainwash or slow downslope movement, usually collecting at the base of gentle slopes or hillsides.

CRATON The oldest, most stable portion of a continental mass, usually in the center of the plate. The craton upon which the North American plate is built is centered in Canada and the central U.S., including the Ozark and Ouachita Mountains of Missouri and Arkansas.

CURVILINEAR Consisting of or bounded or represented by a curved line. We use the term to describe curved landforms. An example is "curvilinear crevasse", to emphasize the non-linearity of this particular species of landforms.

DEEP AREAL LIQUEFACTION (DAL) Liquefaction induced at depth near the focal regions of large earthquakes. We believe that some sunklands and associated raised areas are at least partly caused by lateral and upward migration of great volumes of liquefied sandy sediment at depth, and subsequent adjustments due to volume changes that effect the surface. We have recently published a paper showing that this hypothesis is mathematically sound, even at depths of up to 300 feet, if conditions are right. (See Stewart & Knox, 1995, Reference #44 in the Bibliography.)

DIFFERENTIAL SUBSIDENCE Subsidence produced by unequal settling of earth materials, leaving the ground lower in some places than others. In the New Madrid Seismic Zone, earthquake ground motion may be stronger in some places than others, and certain earth materials may react to it differently in some places than others, causing differential subsidence. Foundations of buildings will crack if underlain by soils that differentially subside during an earthquake, a very common cause of damage.

DISPERSAL CHANNEL A channel that "gets rid of" excess water, as from floods or from drainage of a lake. The dispersal channels in the area of the north end of Sikeston Ridge were created by flood water crossing from the Morehouse Lowland to the Eastern Lowland (west to east) during times of flooding when the Mississippi River occupied the Morehouse Lowland. Water freed from the draining of Lake St. John also used some of the same channels.

EARTHQUAKE The sudden release of strain energy when rocks beneath the earth's surface are stressed to the breaking point and suddenly shift along a deep fault zone. Sometimes the break or fault motion intersects the surface with a visible trace. Most of the time, the earthquake faults do not break the surface, but the seismic vibrations caused by the catastrophic, brittle fracture of the rocks deep below can travel thousands of miles through the earth and along the earth's surface. Relatively few people happen to be directly over a faulted region during an earthquake. What most people experience from a quake are seismic waves traveling to them from the source, which can be many miles away. The New Madrid Fault or Seismic Zone is confined to southeast Missouri, southern Illinois, northeastern Arkansas, and western Kentucky and Tennessee. Two to twenty miles below the surface of this area lies the fault that moves and the brittle bedrock that breaks. However, the ripples from the New Madrid Fault events have been felt for hundreds of miles and in 1811-12 were felt from Canada to Mexico, from the Rockies to the East Coast. See "epicenter" and "focus".

EARTHQUAKE CHRISTIAN The church memberships of most denominations in the New Madrid Seismic Zone increased dramatically during and immediately following the series of great earthquakes. A fascinating account of these quake-related revivals is given in the book, *The Earthquake America Forgot*. Baptists and Methodists both had 50 percent increases. Even the Quakers and Shakers of western Kentucky noted sharp increases (really!). However, many of these new church members "backslid" after the ground shaking eased. These folks were referred to as "Earthquake Christians."

EPICENTER   The point on the surface directly above the focus or actual rupture point in the rocks that caused an earthquake. The epicenter is the closest point on the earth's surface to the source zone, but is not necessarily the location of greatest damage. See "earthquake" and "focus".

ESCARPMENT   A long, more or less continuous steep slope facing in one general direction, breaking the continuity of the land by separating two relatively level surfaces such that one surface lies higher than the other. North and west of Reelfoot Lake is an escarpment called the "Reelfoot Scarp" which is several miles long facing mostly toward the east from the Mississippi River southward to the south side of the lake. The flat land west of Reelfoot Scarp lies 10-20 feet higher than the land to the east. Other notable escarpments in the New Madrid Seismic Zone include the flanks of the Sikeston Ridge, the slopes of the Benton Hills and Crowley's Ridge, as well as the Chickasaw Bluffs on the east side of the Mississippi stretching from Wickliffe, Kentucky, to Memphis, Tennessee.

FAULT   A break in earth materials (rock or soil) with relative displacement on both sides. (A break without displacement is sometimes called a "joint" or a "crack".) In regard to earthquakes, there are two basic kinds of faults: One, those that cause earthquakes when they move: and Two, those that are caused by earthquakes. The causative faults are called "primary" faults, while those that are the consequences of earth ground motion are called "secondary" faults. Faults may be quite small, measured in feet, or very large, measured in miles. The New Madrid Fault is a complex of many faults spanning parts of Arkansas, Illinois, Kentucky, Missouri, and Tennessee. It is a zone thought to be some fifty miles wide and 120-150 miles long along a portion of the Mississippi River valley. See "Bootheel Lineament", "earthquake", "New Madrid Seismic Zone", and Figure 22 on page 54.

FLOOD PLAIN   The nearly flat lowland that borders a stream which may be covered by its waters at flood stages. See "terrace".

FOCUS   The actual source zone or region below land surface where rocks suddenly rupture to create an earthquake. Earthquake foci (plural) may be shallow or deep, the shallowest being 2-20 miles deep, the deepest being more than 350 miles below land surface. The most destructive earthquakes are shallow. The source zone of the New Madrid Fault is 2-20 miles deep and, therefore, shallow. See "earthquake" and "epicenter".

GEOHYDROLOGY   Synonymous with the term, Hydrogeology.

GEOMORPHOLOGY   The branch of geology that specializes in the nature, origin, and development of landforms and their relationships to underlying structures, and the history of geologic changes as recorded by these surface features. See "landform" and "morphoseismology".

GRABEN   An elongate, relatively depressed series of sediment or rock units that is bounded by faults on its long sides. Technically, it is a structural form, which may or may not be expressed as a surface feature. Grabens caused by seismically induced liquefaction from the great New Madrid earthquakes will have surface expression. They will usually be canoe-shaped, banana shaped, or slightly curved, tapering at both ends. At least some have formed where intense ground motion has modified a former drainage channel, an extreme variety of differential subsidence. See Figure 22 on page 54.

GRADIENT   When referring to streams, gradient is the slope of the stream down its valley. A measure of vertical drop in a horizontal distance. Most geologists express gradient in units of feet per mile. Gradients range from more than 200 feet/mile in some mountain streams to less than half-a-foot/mile in lowlands, such as the Bootheel. The gradient of the Mississippi River at New Madrid is slightly less than 0.4 feet/mile.

GROUND WATER TABLE   The top of the saturated zone beneath ground surface. Below this level, all the interconnected spaces between sand and silt grains are full of water. In the bootheel, the ground water table is not far beneath the surface, ranging from maximum depths of 30 feet to areas where it is above the land surface. Saturated sediment and soil allows ground motion to create "liquefaction" during earthquakes. When the ground water table is above land surface, swamps and certain kinds of lakes or ponds result.

GROUND MOTION   A general term for the various kinds of ground movements caused by earthquakes. Movements may be up and down, side to side, torsions, rotations, compressions and expansions, or combinations of all of these during an earthquake. Damage during a quake depends on the maximum amplitudes, durations, and frequencies of ground motion as well as soil conditions. Under certain conditions, clay amplifies and sand liquefies. When saturated with ground water, clay amplifies ground motion as much as 20-40 times the amplitudes experienced in bedrock, while saturated sand can turn quick and liquefy. For minimal earthquake damage, the safest foundation earth material for a building is rock or hard, dry soil well above the water table.

HORST   An elongate, uplifted rock unit or block that is bounded by faults on its long sides. It is a structural form and may or may not be expressed at the surface. In the New Madrid area, the Tiptonville "Dome" is best described as a horst. A horst is sort of the opposite of a graben. See Figure 22 on page 54.

HYDRAULIC HEAD   This is water pressure caused by a water level in one location being higher than at another. Water tries to "seek its own level". Water to a faucet in a city flows under pressure because the water tanks are higher than the faucet. In much the same way, water standing higher in a flooded river will produce upward pressure on water on the "protected" side of a levee which is lower than the river. This produces Hydrologically Induced Liquefaction (HIL) defined below.

HYDROLOGICALLY INDUCED LIQUE-FACTION (HIL).   Liquefaction primarily caused by groundwater movements, especially vertically moving groundwater, such as

water seeking its own level behind levees during times of high stream levels. Towns along the river surrounded by levees, such as Cairo, Illinois, experience hydrologically induced liquefaction almost every year as the Ohio and Mississippi Rivers reach their peaks during winter and spring. Such liquefaction periodically damages streets and foundations in such towns. Areas that liquefy due to hydrologic forces will also liquefy when stimulated by dynamic loads of earthquake forces and vice versa. That is, seismically induced liquefaction (SIL) features will also respond to the static loads of hydrology.

HYDROGEOLOGY   The study of water on, in and above the earth's surface. Subcategories of hydrogeology include groundwater hydrology and surface water hydrology.

HYDROLOGY   The same as "Hydrogeology defined immediately above.

INTENSITY   A measure of an earthquake's ground motion as indicated by damages to human constructions or disturbances to the land by way of liquefaction, landslides, subsidences, etc. The Mercalli scale, from I to XII, is used to gauge earthquake intensity. The Mercalli scale, thus, measures the "effects" of an earthquake, not its "cause". The Richter scale is a measure of energy release at the source, or a measure of "cause". See "Mercalli scale", "magnitude", and "Richter scale".

KEELBOAT   A flat-bottomed riverboat that was common on the big rivers before the days of numerous steamboats. They carried freight and/or passengers and were rowed or poled. They were generally more narrow than the flatboats and usually had a high structure on the bow from which a deck hand with a pole could stand and manuever through small waterways. Later ones even had small steam engines. They were definitely not constructed to withstand even modest rapids or waterfalls.

KITCHEN MIDDEN See Midden.

LANDFORM   A component of Earth's surface. One of the multitudinous features that taken together make up the surface of the earth. It may include broad features, such as mountains or plateaus, or minor features, such as valleys or levees. Seismic landforms, such as found in the New Madrid Seismic Zone, include surface faults, fissures, sand boils, landslides, earthquake lakes, and other features of the landscape partly or wholly formed by earthquake forces. (See Table Two in Chapter Three.)

LIGNITE A low-grade coal, usually brown in color. Some of the lignite found in the seismic liquefaction features of the New Madrid Seismic Zone was carried there by rivers from hundreds of miles north or east, and can be many thousands of years old. See "carbonized wood" and "coal".

LIMONITE A term for a group of brown to rust-colored amorphous hydrous ferric oxides. It is a common secondary mineral formed by weathering of iron-bearing minerals. It may also occur as a precipitate in bogs or lakes. It occurs as coatings, earthy masses, and a variety of other forms. It is the coloring material of yellow clays and soils. Pea-sized limonite nodules aresometimes ejected by extrusive sand features during seismically-induced liquefaction.

LINEAMENT See Bootheel Lineament for definition of "lineament."

LIQUEFACTION The transformation of loosely packed, saturated sand and/or silt into a fluid mass due to ground motion, as by an earthquake. Liquefaction is a temporary quicksand condition and can be induced seismically, hydrologically or mechanically. See "deep areal liquefaction (DAL)", "seismically induced liquefaction (SIL)", hydrologically induced liquefaction (HIL)", and "mechanically induced liquefaction (MIL)".

LOESS Wind deposits, primarily silt-size particles of dust. A lot of this material in the bootheel was derived from glacial outwash to the north or from more local braided streams. This process is more active during arid times.

MAGNITUDE The energy released or "size" of an earthquake. It is expressed in Arabic numerals to one decimal place in terms of the Richter scale. Each unit represents a 32-fold increase in energy release while every two units represents a thousand-fold increase. Each two-tenths of a unit represents a doubling of the energy. Hence a 5.2 is double the size of a 5.0 magnitude, a 6.0 is 32 times larger, while a 7.0 is 1000 times the size of a 5.0. See "intensity", "Richter scale", and "Mercalli scale".

MARINE In this book the term is used as an adjective meaning "of or related to the ocean." For example, "marine rocks" are formed from sediments that were accumulated at the bottoms of seas.

MEANDER A sinuous curve or loop in the course of a stream produced as the stream shifts its course from side to side as it flows across its floodplain.

MEANDER BELT The zone along a floodplain across which a meandering stream shifts its channel from time to time.

MEANDERING STREAM A stream that flows in a meandering pattern, as opposed to a braided pattern. Meandering streams are more likely when their gradients are gentle, and where sediment supplied to the stream does not exceed the ability of the stream to handle it without braiding.

MECHANICALLY INDUCED LIQUEFACTION (MIL). Liquefaction induced by ground motion caused by vibrating vehicles, locomotives, or other heavy machinery. We know of one instance where a farmer very nearly lost a tractor which was parked over a liquefiable area and left running during a lunch break. It almost buried itself before the situation was realized and the tractor rescued! The book, *The Earthquake that Never Went Away*, discusses MIL and gives several recent examples, including train derailments in Missouri and Tennessee because of earthquake features created almost 200 years ago by the New Madrid events. That's why we call it *"The Earthquake that Never Went Away."*

MERCALLI SCALE (Also known as the "Modified Mercalli Intensity Scale or "MMI.") A measure of the intensity or effects of an earthquake at different locations on ground surface. See "intensity" and "magnitude".

MIDDEN Literally "dump." A place where numerous Indian artifacts are found indicating the site of a former sttlement.

MORPHOSEISMIC Refers to landforms that were created by earthquakes or pre-existing landforms that were extensively modified by earthquakes.

MORPHOSEISMOLOGY The study of how earthquakes modify the landscape. Morphoseismology is an interdisciplinary field including geology, seismology, and hydrology. (Also see Geomorphology, Hydrogeology, and Seismohydrology.)

NATURAL LEVEE A ridge or embankment of sand and silt, built by a stream on its flood plain along both banks of its channel, especially in times of flood when water overflowing the normal banks is forced to deposit the coarsest part of its load. The term also applies to a sand and silt deposit that was produced this way in a former time.

NEW MADRID FAULT A complex of faults considered to be approximately 150 miles long by 50 miles wide extending in a northeasterly trend from near Marked Tree, Arkansas; through Blytheville, Arkansas; Steele, Caruthersville, New Madrid, and Charleston, Missouri; to Cairo and Metropolis, Illinois. The zone also includes portions of western Kentucky and Tennessee, including the Tiptonville and Reelfoot Lake, Tennessee, areas. The portion of the New Madrid Fault complex from which more than 200 earthquakes a year originate lies from 2 to 20 miles deep. No direct surface expression of the fault has yet been discovered and proven, although many secondary surface faults can be found throughout the zone. See "fault," "Bootheel Lineament.," Figure 1, p. xii, and Figure 10, p. 24.

NEW MADRID SEISMIC ZONE Synonymous with the term, "New Madrid Fault" or "New Madrid Fault Zone". Abbreviated as "NMSZ." See "New Madrid Fault," Figure 1, page xii, and Figure 10, p. 24.

NMSZ Acronym for "New Madrid Seismic Zone". See "New Madrid Fault".

OXBOW LAKE An oxbow is a closely looping stream meander, having an extreme curvature such that only a neck of land is left between two parts of the stream. If and when this meander is cut off, a horseshoe-shaped lake is formed. Maybe we should call these kinds of lakes "horseshoe lakes", because the younger generations have never seen an oxbow. On the other hand, they probably haven't seen a horseshoe either!

PAPAW (or PAW PAW) A North American tree of the custard-apple family (Asimina triloba) especially prevalent in the south and midwest with brownish purple flowers and yellow fruits with a banana-like flavor. The small trees usually grow in the shade near water. Also the fruit of this tree. Often called "Missouri bananas" (according to Stewart) or "Arkansas bananas" (according to Knox).

PERMEABILITY The property or capacity of earth material for transmitting a fluid, such as ground water. High permeability means that the water can move through the material with ease. Low permeability means that the water can move, but with difficulty. Impermeable, or nonpermeable, means that the water cannot pass through the material at all.

PETROLIFEROUS NODULES These enigmatic deposits appear to be small chunks of asphalt ranging from pea-size to an inch in diameter. They are smooth and rounded. Upon first glance, you would think they were of human origin—droppings from a railroad, the paving operations of a highway department, or pipeline company activities. However, they are found scattered in a number of the larger sand boils throughout the NMSZ where no trains, no trucks and no pipelines have ever been. They were also described by several people during the earthquakes of 1811-12.—long before oil had been discovered and asphalt became available. So we think they are natural. They are light in density and, hence, would naturally float to the top of a sand boil when it is liquid. They appear to have come from depth where (who knows) petroleum deposits may lie in the fault zone—as yet undiscovered by any oil company. If you find one, scratch it with a knife or metal blade and sniff—it will smell just like tar. If the term, "petroliferous nodules" is too technical for you, just call them "seismic tar balls." The will burn brightly if ignited, something noted by the pioneers in 1811-12.

POLYGENETIC Literally means "many geneses" or origins. The term is applied when more than one agent or process has been important in producing a landform

RICHTER SCALE A measure of earthquake magnitude or energy released at the focus or causative source. A seismograph is usually needed in order to measure the numerical value of the scale. Magnitude values for large earthquakes can also be calculated when the amount of movement on the fault is known. Estimates of Richter magnitude can be made by analyzing intensity data and damage levels. The magnitudes of the New Madrid earthquakes of 1811-12 mentioned in this book were estimated from damage reports and liquefaction data.

There is a move among some seismologists to abandon the use of the term "Richter" to express the size of an earthquake. They propose to use the term, "magnitude." They object to using the word, Richter, on the technicality that even though the original idea was that of Charles F. Richter back in 1935, his scale was developed only for local California earthquakes and is not the exact scale used today around the world. In fact, there are several magnitude scales in use and all of them are necessary to measure the spectrum of earthquakes from the tiniest to the greatest. Application of more than one scale to the an earthquake will result in a variety of "magnitudes" calculated for the same quake. However, among the various values determined, one will be the most representative of the size of that particular quake. This value is what is normally reported to the news media and the general public as the "Richter scale."

Therefore, we disagree with some members of the seismological community on the discontinuance of the term. "Richter scale" is firmly entrenched in the vocabulary of the English language and has been for decades. The meaning of the word is understood by both professionals and the public. Besides, Dr. Richter deserves the honor, even if we don't use the scale he devised any more. Just as we use the term, "hertz" for "cycles per second" in honor of the German physicist, Heinrich Hertz (1857-1894) we honor Charles Richter, the famous American seismologist.

Hence, in this book and throughout all of our publications, we use the term "Richter scale." In a 1995 statement published in *Seismological Research Letters*, Vol. 66, No. 1, the U.S. Geological Survey stated the following: "In our opinion, the public would not be well served if we reported the results of every magnitude calculation that we perform for the same earthquake. . . The question of labeling these magnitudes as "Richter scale" is a matter of tradition, semantics, and personal perspective. The USGS has no official scientific position of the use of the term. All the magnitudes reported by the USGS through its earthquake center are extensions of the original Richter scale and are compatible with historic earthquakes reported in the Richter scale."

A thorough, yet simple, explanation of the Richter scale is found in the book, *Damages & Losses from Future New Madrid Earthquakes* by Stewart. The book is free. See page 174 for details on obtaining a copy. See "intensity" and "magnitude".

SAND DUNE A low mound, ridge, bank, or hill of loose, windblown sand. Most of the sand in the bootheel dunes was derived from "reworking" the braided streams in the area during dry swings of climate.

SCARP See "escarpment".

SEDIMENT A general term for material carried by streams or other erosion agents and deposited as loose fragments. In the New Madrid Seismic Area, most sediment has been deposited by streams, but considerable wind-deposited sediments exist.

SEICHE (Pronounced "saysh"). An oscillation of a body of water in an enclosed or semi-enclosed basin. Earthquake induced ground motion may cause one type of seiche. If the natural period of vibration is in harmonic phase with the periodicity of the ground motion, a seiche may form in lakes, bays, or segments of a stream. We suggest this factor as a possible contributor to the destruction of the great forest upstream from New Madrid on February 7, 1812.

SEISMIC   Pertaining to earthquakes.

SEISMICALLY INDUCED LIQUEFACTION (SIL).   Liquefaction which is caused by ground motion during earthquakes. Sand boils or sand fissures which are instances of SIL can also respond to ground water pressures and the vibrations of vehicles, trains, or machinery subsequent to the earthquake that formed them. Thus, a SIL feature can also, from time to time, be a HIL or a MIL. See "hydrologically induced liquefaction (HIL)" and "mechanically induced liquefaction (MIL)". Most of the time, SIL is caused by earthquakes at least 5.0 on the Richter scale. However, SIL has been observed by Dr. Stewart in at least ten locations from earthquakes measuring only 4.6. SIL from great earthquakes, such as those emanating from the New Madrid area in 1811-12, can cause SIL more than 400 miles from the epicenter.

SEISMIC TAR BALLS   See Petroliferous Nodules.

SEISMOHYDROLOGY   The study of how earthquakes affect ground water, surface waters, and atmospheric waters.

For example, liquefaction is actually the response of an unconsolidated aquifer saturated with ground water under the dynamic loading of an earthquake. Quakes can also cause groundwater flooding—the extrusion of large quantities of ground water onto the surface and into streams. Earthquakes can also cause streams and rivers to temporarily flow backwards and, in some cases, to permanently reverse their gradients or stop their flow altogether. Earthquakes can also create lakes and ponds. Seismic sand boils, sand fissures, and explosion sand blow craters once created by an earthquake can serve as permanent points on the earth's surface where surface waters enter the ground or where ground waters are discharged onto the surface. Earthquakes can also afect atmospheric moisture—causing fog or "smog"

which can turn a sunny day into a dark one.

Historical accounts of all of these seismohydrologic phenomena are reported in *The Earthquake America Forgot*. Seismohydrology is an interdisciplinary field including hydrogeology, seismology, atmospheric science, geotechnical and civil engineering (soil mechanics). See morphoseismology, hydrogeology, and geomorphology.

SPOIL BANK   An embankment of earth material dredged from a channel and dumped beside it. The spoil may also serve as an artificial levee in some cases.

STANDARD PENETRATION TEST (SPT)
If you want to know whether or not your house is resting on liquefiable soils, the SPT test is the most reliable indicator. If you live on bed rock, on dry soil overlying bedrock, or in a place where the water table is very deep—more than 100 feet—then you don't need an SPT test. You already know you are not on liquefiable soil. If you live on a flood plain, a beach or a coastal plain, the water table is almost always within 100 feet of the surface. You could be living over liquefiable deposits, either at the surface or at depth. Even if liquefiable sediments are 25-50 feet below the land surface, an earthquake can liquefy them and cause damage to your house.

The SPT test is done by drilling a test hole, usually 50 to 100 feet deep. Every five feet the drilling auger is stopped and a 2-inch diameter tube is lowered to the bottom of the hole. A standard 140 pound weight is then dropped 30 inches hammering the 2-inch tube into the bottom of the hole. The number of standard blows are then counted to see how many it takes to drive the tube one foot. If it takes many blows before the tube penetrates a foot, the soil is hard and strong. If it takes only a few, the soil is soft and could be liquefiable. There are many formulas into which SPT data can be fed, but the simplest calculation to determine if you have a liquefaction potential is this: First, you have to be in saturated sand. Even if you are in saturated sand, so long as the number of SPT blows per foot is greater than twice the depth in meters, there is no liquefaction potential. If the number of blows is less than twice the depth in meters, then liquefaction is possible. If the number of blows per foot is a lot less than twice the depth, then the liquefaction potential is very great.

To have the SPT test done you would have to contact a civil or geotechnical engineering company who has the equipment and expertise to do the test. Details of using STP data with this formula to determine liquefaction potential may be found in Ohasaki (1970) or Prakash (1990). Once you have diagnosed a potential liquefaction problem, you can do something about it. Engineering measures can be taken to prevent damage from seismically induced liquefaction during earthquakes. Those measures are beyond the scope of this book.

STRIKE-SLIP FAULT   A fault on which the movement is parallel to the compass direction (strike) of the fault trend. In other words, it's major movement is, for example, north-south instead of up-down (dip). See "fault" and Figure 22, p. 54.

STRUCTURE   The orientations and relative positions of the rock masses of an area. Structural features result from such processes as faulting, folding, or other deformation. Geologists would call the Tiptonville Dome a "tectonic structure".

TECTONIC   Pertaining to the deformation of the earth's crust, including faulting, folding, uplift, and downwarp. As applied to earthquakes, the term is used to describe shocks not due to volcanic action or to collapse of caverns or to landslides.

TECTONICS   A branch of geology dealing with major structural or deformational features of the earth's crust, and their relations, origins, and historical evolution.

TERRACE   A relatively level surface occurring along the margin and above the level of a body of water. In the New Madrid Seismic Zone, the terraces are river terraces and represent old floodplain or alluvial fan remnants from former river actions.

TSUNAMI   This term is normally applied to seismic sea waves caused by earthquakes beneath the ocean. They travel around 400 miles per hour in the open sea with barely perceptible amplitudes. When they reach the shore and shallower water, they slow down to about 100 miles per hour and grow in heights from 30 to over 100 feet causing enormous damage to the coastline. We sometimes refer to the waves violently thrown out of the Mississippi River during the February 7, 1812, earthquake as an "Inland Tsunami" or a "Fluvial Tsunami." Both marine and fluvial types are caused by sudden faulting beneath bodies of water. Both the oceanic and the riverine versins result in great destruction along the shorelines. We think it is an appropriate descriptor of what happened in 1812 along parts of the Mississippi.

WABASH VALLEY FAULT   An active fault zone roughly paralleling the Wabash River valley in southwestern Indiana and southeastern Illinois. The largest earthquakes in this century have originated from this zone, which may well be an extension of the New Madrid Fault. We need to keep a wary eye on this one, too. See Fig. 10, p. 24.

WASHOUT   The washing-out or away of earth materials as a result of a flood or a sudden and concentrated downpour, often causing extensive scouring and bank caving; also, a place where such an event has occurred. In the New Madrid area, water ejected during SIL events might well have created washouts, especially along the flanks of escarpments. See the discussion of the feature known as Des Cyprie on page 86 of this book

WATER GAP   A relatively narrow gorge through a hilly area through which a stream flows. Thebes Gap is an example. Here, the Mississippi River flows through a seven-mile section that has no flood plain. The flood plain goes one way, the river another!

WATER TABLE   See "ground water table".

WIND GAP   A former water channel through a narrow gap that has been abandoned by the stream that formed it. "Water Gap and "Wind Gap" are terms which came from the Appalachians, where these features are fairly common.

INDEX

A

Acadian Orogeny 20
accidents (see safety in driving)
Advance, MO xii, 10, 30, 37
Advance Lowlands 30
Africa 22, 23
African Americans 110
African slave traffic 12
aftershocks 102
Aide, Mike 90
air liquefaction 40
altered stream gradients 29, 42, 53, 56-57, 72, 86-87, 90, 137, 140, 142
American Journal of Nursing 179
Anchorage, Ak, quake 37
anomalies in plant growth (see distressed vegetation)
Antarctica 22, 23
Appalachian Mountains 22
Arkansas Visitor Center & Rest Center 94
Army Corps of Engineers (see U.S. Army Corps of Engineers)
arrowheads (see Native American artifacts)
artesian springs 41
artifacts (see Native American artifacts)
Ash Hills 30
Asia 22, 23
asphalt 128
Associated Electric Co. 4, 5, 25, 59, 75, 88, 89, 106, 110, 118, 120, 134, 136
Atlantic Ocean 23
atomic bomb 13
Audubon, John James 8
Australia 22, 23
Aztar, Casino 100,129

B

back graben 58
backwards motion of Mississippi (see Mississippi River ran backwards)
bacon 142
Bait Shop 17, 138, 139
baloney sandwich 135
Baptist Church of New Madrid 107
barbeque 126
Bayou Fouche 66
Bayou Portage 66, 76, 90, 118, 121, 122
Beach, The 4, 45,100, 122, 123, 127-129, 143
bed frames 107
Bell City xii, 10, 29, 33, 37
Bell City-Oran Gap 33
Belle Fountain Ditch 94
bells ringing 14
Benton, MO 6, 10, 30, 33, 76, 77, 98, 100, 112, 113
Benton Hills 29, 30, 33, 34, 59, 76, 78, 80, 96, 100, 113, 128
Bentonville, AR 178
Bertrand, MO 112
Bessie, TN 75, 137
Bessie Bend 69 (also see New Madrid Bend)
Bessie's Neck 53, 137
Big Lake 3, 7, 10, 12-13, 30, 50, 98, 101, 117, 130, 140, 141, 144, 146, 148
Big Lake Sunk Land (see Big Lake)
Big Oak State Park 132, 139
Big Prairie, AR 42
billboard 88
birds 88
Blacker Island 122
Black Fault 24
Black River 32
black shale fragments 4, 45, 95, 128
blind thrust fault 31
block slide 101 (also see translational block slide & rotational slump)
Bloomfield, MO 30

Bloomfield Hills 30, 59
blowout (see channel blowout)
blow sand 40
Blue Bank, TN 75
Blue Bank Restaurant 136
Blytheville, AR 6, 10, 12-13, 30, 34, 50, 52, 76, 77, 78, 94, 98, 130, 140, 141
Blytheville Dome 146
boat (see canoe, keelboat, & steamboat)
boats thrown on land 67, 68, 71, 72
Boekerton Beauty Shed 124, 131
Boekerton, MO 13, 53, 98, 100, 121, 122, 123, 124, 130, 131
Boekerton Star (see Star, The)
Bogota, Colombia 179
boils (see sand boils)
Bollinger County 30, 31, 179
Books of the Year Award 179
Boone, Daniel 8
Bootheel Lineament (see Bootheel Fault)
Bootheel Fault 10, 24, 25, 52, 83, 98, 100, 103, 112, 113, 116, 122, 123, 124, 126-129, 130, 131, 140, 141, 143, 146, 147, 154, 155
Bootheel of Missouri 16, 91, 154
borrow pit 42, 64, 81, 85, 90, 120, 155
Boudreaux's Restaurant 126
Boyette's Restaurant 136
boys drowned 90
Braggadocio, MO 10, 25, 76, 92, 122, 140
braided bar islands 62, 85, 109, 114, 155

breakfast 126, 142
brick 102, 107 also (see masonry)
British 12
broken cypress (see cypress, broken)
broken stream channels (see discontinuous channels)
Buckeye, AR (nearby drainage ditch is a good place to dig to see sectional views of seismic sand features) 140,141, 145
buried alive 3
buried rift (see New Madrid Rift Complex)
buried Spanish boat 120
buried thrust fault 31

C

Cache Lowland 30
Cache River 31, 32
Cagle Lake 50, 61, 93, 140, 141, 146-147, 148
Cairo, IL xii, 10, 26, 29, 30, 33
cajun cooking 126
cajun gumbo 126
California 91
Cambrian Period (or rocks) 20, 27, 31
Campbell family 134
Campbell Indian Mound 141, 147, 148
Campbell Landslide 132, 133, 134, 139
campgrounds 3, 76, 91, 125
Canada 16, 22, 88
canoe 16, 91, 97, 107, 142
Cape Girardeau, MO xii, 9, 10, 23, 30, 37, 75, 76, 78, 79, 178, 179
carbonized wood 4, 45, 83, 84, 95, 128, 155
Carr, Dabney 110
Carr, Mary Jefferson 107, 110

Castor River 31, 32
Caruthersville, MO 5, 10, 12, 13, 30, 60, 76, 92, 98, 131, 100, 101, 122, 129, 132, 134
Caruthersville Bend 31
Casino Aztar 100, 129
catfish dinner 110, 136
catfish farm 92, 142, 155
caution (see safety in driving)
Centralia Fault 24
Central Methodist College 178
Central Missouri State University 178
Central U.S. Earthquake Consortium 178
Certified Fault Finder 9, 149-150, 181
chances of an earthquake happening 77, 80, 95-96, 101-102, 106, 121, 147, 160
channel blowout 42, 45, 74, 76, 91, 122, 123, 125, 142, 155
channel explosion (see channel blowout)
Chapel Hill, NC 179
Charleston, MO 10, 30, 76, 83, 98, 112, 155
Chartreau Estate 65, 109
Chartreau explosion craters 65
Cherokee 179
Chickasaw Bluffs 29, 30, 57, 70, 72, 73, 132, 133, 135, 137, 139
chicken creole 111
chiggers 3
Christmas Eve 60, 129
Chubby's Bar-B-Que 126
chute bars 142
circular earthquake feature 120
civil engineering 5-6, 163
Civil War 43, 91, 106, 145
Clark, William 8
Clinton, Bill 148
coal 4, 45, 128, 155
coffee 74, 110
Colombia 179
colluvium 113, 155, 156
Colonial history 106
Comet of 1811, The 11
Commerce, MO 30, 33, 98, 112, 154
complete New Madrid Earthquake Library 9,

176, 180
compound sand boil 45 (see Beach & Howardville Sand Boil)
compressional stress 18
concrete block (see masonry)
Confederate Soldiers 145
continental crust 18, 19
continental drift 19
continental ice sheet 26
Cooter, MO 12, 61, 76, 98, 140, 141, 146
cornbread 107
corn field 117
Corning, AR xii, 10
Corps of Engineers (see U.S. Army Corps of Engineers)
Cottage Grove Fault 24
Cotton Boll Vocational Technical School 95
cottonmouth water moccason 146
Cottonwood Point 101, 140, 141, 147
coyotes 60
Craters of the Earthquake Park 109
crawdads 126
crawfish 126
crayfish 126
creep 17, 101, 134, 139
creole 111, 126
Cretaceous Period (or rocks) 20, 27, 31
crevasse (see earthquake crevasse)
Crowleys Ridge 29, 30, 31, 33, 59, 78, 128
crust (see continental crust)
Crystal City, MO 178
Cuba 16, 88
Culbertson family 142
cup of coffee 74
Current River 32
Curtis Cafe 126
Cushion Lake 100, 118, 119, 120, 121, 122
Cyclone, MO 178
cypress, broken 17, 42, 64, 71

D

DAL (see deep areal liquefaction)
damage to highway 88, 97, 102, 132, 134, 138-139, 143

dangers of highway traffic 131 (also see safety in driving)
Davis, Charles 90
Davis, Jefferson 8
deaths 16
December 16, 1811, earthquakes (magnitudes 8.6 & 8.0) 1, 10, 12, 61, 93, 101, 140, 142, 146, 147, 148 (also see great New Madrid earthquakes)
deep areal liquefaction (DAL) 49, 70, 156
Deering, MO 122, 127, 140
Denton, MO 103, 143
derailments 8, 104, 135
des Cyprie 76, 86, 87, 104, 107, 108, 109, 115
Devastation Acres 76, 89
Dexter, MO 1, 29, 30
differential subsidence features 39, 49-52, 156 (also see subsidence & sunk land)
digging sites for sectional views (see sectional views of seismic sand features)
dike (see sand dike)
dill pickles, fried 126
dinosaurs 22, 27
dip slip fault 54
discontinuous channels 16, 42, 51, 64, 76, 81, 86-87, 88, 97, 104, 142
distressed crop growth (see distressed vegetation)
distressed vegetation 2, 17, 81, 133, 145
Dobbins Grocery 145, 148
Dobbins, Mr. 145
dome 42 (also see Blytheville Dome & Tiptonville Dome)
Donaldson Point 60, 66, 67, 68, 69, 71, 73, 74, 75, 137
Dorena, MO 7, 10, 132
drainage ditch good for digging to get sectional views 140, 146
drift (see continental drift)
driving safety (see safety in driving)
drowning 90
Dry Bayou Baptist Church 7, 17, 125, 131
Dry Bayou Earthquake Feature 7, 17, 92, 100, 122, 125, 126, 131

duck and cover 102
Duckies 93, 147
dump (see seismic dump)
dune (see sand dune)
dune pond 42, 62
Dyersburg, TN xii, 5, 10, 30, 76, 98, 132, 134

E

eagles 146
earth flow 42, 101, 132, 134
earthquake, what to do if one happens 101-102
Earthquake Alley 6, 7, 61, 76, 77, 80, 95, 97
earthquake crevasse 3, 47, 48, 61, 64, 89, 97 (also see graben crevasse, German crevasse & sand fissure)
earthquake Christian v, 156
Earthquake Engineering, Journal of 179
earthquake hazard warranty 9, 177
earthquake-induced flooding 15-16, 67, 687, 71. 108, 129
earthquake intensity 14, 15, 16 (also see Mercalli Scale)
earthquake lakes 3, 4, 7, 10, 42, 50, 76, 99, 117, 132, 140 (also see Big Lake, Cagle Lake, Flag Lake, Lake Ste. Anne, Lake St. John, Lake St. Francis, Lake Nicormy, Lake Tyronza, & Reelfoot Lake)
earthquake landslides (see slope failure features)
earthquake logs 144
Earthquake Park 65, 109
earthquake pond 42, 43, 44, 64, 76, 89
earthquakes (see great New Madrid earthquakes)
Earthquake Spectra 179
eclipse 11
El Camino Real 79, 99, 104, 105, 106, 107, 110, 111
embayment (see Mississippi embayment)
Emergency Management Institute 179
Emmitsburg, MD 179

Eocene Epoch (or deposits) 27, 57
epicenter (def. of) 156
epicenters of the biggest quakes (see epicentral ground zero & great New Madrid earthquakes)
epicentral ground zero 76, 88, 101, 106, 121, 124, 140
epicentral line (Fuller's) 34, 154 (also see Bootheel Fault)
escape route 122, 129, 131
Europe 22, 23
European Americans 110
evangelists 12
Evergreen Cemetery 104, 105, 108, 110
explosion sand blow craters 40, 42, 43, 44, 65, 76, 84, 104, 109
extrusive sand features 39, 42, 43-45
extraterrestrial 130
eyes of a fault finder 9, 102, 150
eyrie (eagle's nest) 146

F

failed rift 22 (see New Madrid Rift Complex)
Falls of the Ohio 53
Fancy Farm, KY xii
fast food restaurants 131
Fault Finders Wine 3
fault (def. of) 157
faults 10, 12, 24, 25, 42, 52-53, 54, 69, 78, 132 (also see Bootheel Fault, Jackson Fault, New Madrid Fault, New Madrid Rift Complex, Reelfoot Fault, Ste. Genevieve Fault, St. Johns Fault & Wabash Valley Fault)
Fayette, MO 178
Fayetteville, AR 178
February 7, 1812, quake (magnitude 8.8) 2, 4-5, 10, 13, 17, 53, 59, 67-74, 76, 87, 88, 90, 106, 110, 124, 133, 134, 136, 137
ferry 7, 108, 138
filled explosion craters 42, 43, 44, 76, 83, 85, 89, 94, 96
First General Baptist Church

of New Madrid 107
fish thrown up on land 71
fishing holes 120 (also see Big Lake & Reelfoot Lake)
fissure (see earthquake crevasse & sand fissure)
Flag Lake 50
flatboats 144
flint chips 128
Flood of 1912-1913 86
Flood of 1927 75
flood plain 78
flooding (see earthquake-induced flooding)
Floodway, The 140, 144
fluvial tsunami 71, 137
flying reptiles 27
food (see restaurants)
forestland, destruction of 13, 16, 17, 57, 60, 67, 68, 71, 72, 106, 137
forward horst 58
four-leaf-clovers 179
Fowler, William B. 109
Franklin Ditch (see New Franklin Ditch)
Franklin Lake 147
free earthquake literature 102, 174, 175
French 12, 119
fried baloney sandwich 135
fried dill pickles 126
Fuller, Myron 34, 41, 49, 60, 154, 155, 174
Fuller's epicentral line (see epicentral line, Fuller's)
Fuller's map 34, 154, 174
Fulton, Robert 8

G

gambling boat (see Casino Aztar)
Garden Grove, CA 179
Garden of the Gods, CO 64
General Baptist Church of New Madrid 107
geologic time 27
German Crevasse 61, 76, 93, 97
German, Ruby 93
Gibson, MO 140, 142
gift shops 93, 106, 147
glacial outwash deposits 134 (also see Lafayette Formation)
glaciers 27, 29 (also see Ice Age)
golf course (see New

Madrid Golf Course)
Gondwana 20
good places to eat (see restaurants)
Gosnell, AR 140, 155
graben 54, 58, 122, 157
graben fissure 42, 47, 64, 76, 86, 92, 95, 96, 104, 105, 110, 122, 123, 125
gradient (def. of) 157
gradient (see altered stream gradients)
Grand Tower, IL 38
gravel mine 101, 134
Gratio block slide 132
great New Madrid earthquakes 1-2, 4, 10, 11, 12, 13, 15 (also see December 16, 1811; January 23, 1812 & February 7, 1812)
Groceries knocked off shelves 141
ground failure damage 37-38
groundwater flooding 129 (see earthquake-induced flooding)
Gulf Coastal Plain 26
Gulf of Mexico 23
gumbo 126
Gutenberg-Richter Publications 9, 102, 150, 173-177, 180
Gut Ste. Anne 66, 76, 88, 97, 108

H

Halliday, AR 10, 38
Hampton Inn 116
harmonics (see wave harmonics & resonance)
Harrison, William Henry 8
Hayti, MO 10, 31, 45, 60, 76, 91, 98, 100, 122, 126, 129, 130, 131, 140
Hayti Heights, MO 126
Haywood City, MO 98, 112, 114, 115
Haywood Island 112, 113, 114, 117
Helena, AR 29
Hickman, KY 5, 7, 120, 17, 30, 59, 63, 98, 101, 107, 132, 133, 138
Hickman landslides 132, 133, 138-139
high speed geology 7
highway damage 88, 97,

102, 132, 134, 138-139, 143
highway safety (see safety in driving)
HIL (see hydrologically induced liquefaction)
historic sites (see seismically historic sites)
Holland, MO 140, 146
Holmes, Pat 93
Holmes, Tony 93
Hornersville, MO 98, 101, 130, 140, 141
Hornersville Swamp Wildlife Area (see Big Lake)
horst 42, 54, 58, 69, 158
horst of a different color 135
Hot Springs, AR 64
houses at risk 113, 115
Howardville, MO 10, 64, 75, 104
Howardville Sand Boil 105, 108
Huckleberry Ridge 178
hush puppies 110
hybreds, morphoseismic 40
hydrologically induced liquefaction (HIL) 36, 41, 42, 63, 89, 121, 126, 145, 158
hydrologically induced liquefaction (def. of) 158
hydrophytic plants 87, 109

I

Ice Age 26, 27, 28, 32, 78
Illmo United Methodist Church 179
Illinois Basin 20
Immaculate Conception School 111
incoherent landslide 42, 132, 138
India 22, 23
Indian artifacts (see Native American artifacts)
Indian mounds 42, 64, 87, 99, 104, 108, 140, 141, 142, 144, 147, 148
Indians (see Native Americans)
intensity (def. of) 158
intensity (see earthquake intensity & Mercalli Scale)
interglacial periods 28, 29
intrusive sand features 39, 46
Iowa City, IA 178
irrigation 8, 14

Island #8 10, 67, 70, 72, 73, 75, 132, 137
Island #9 53, 66, 68, 70, 72, 73
Island #10 53, 66, 67, 68, 70, 71, 72, 73
Island #11 66, 70, 72
Island #18 132
islands (see braided bar islands)

J

Jackson Fault 25, 76, 78
Jackson formation 57
Jackson, MO xii, 10, 30, 76
Jack's Restaurant 111
jalapeno burger 141
January 23, 1812, quake (magnitude 8.4) 10, 13, 91, 118, 121, 126
Jefferson City, MO 178
Jefferson, Lucy (Lewis) 108, 110
Jefferson, Mary (Carr) 108, 110
Jefferson, Thomas 8, 105, 108, 110
Jenkins, Andrew 143
Jerry's Cafe 89
Jonesboro, AR xii, 10, 30, 79
Jurrassic Period 27

K

keelboat 16, 52, 90, 91, 97, 106, 108, 124, 158
Keiser, AR 39, 140
Kennett-Malden Prairie 30 (also see Malden Plain)
Kennett, MO xii, 10, 130
Kentucky Bend 69 (see New Madrid Bend)
Kentucky Point 137
Kewanee, MO 5, 10, 75, 76, 85
Kingshighway (see El Camino Real)
kitchen midden 143 (also see Native Americans)
Knox, Karen (Twell) xi, 178
Knox, Ray 9, 49, 60, 64, 91, 125-126, 130, 131, 150, 178)
KOA campground 76, 91, 122, 125, 131

L

Lafayette formation 31, 57
Lake City, AR 10, 38
Lake County Uplift (see Tiptonville Dome)
Lake Nicormy 10, 50
lakes (see earthquake lakes)
Lake Ste. Anne 50, 76, 87, 88, 104, 105, 108
Lake St. Francis 50
Lake St. John 10, 32, 50, 80, 85, 100, 112, 113, 114, 115, 117
Lake Tyronza 50
Lambert, MO 113
Lambert, Norman 116
Lambert's Cafe 83, 96, 112, 116
landsat image 124, 130
landslides (see slope failure features)
Langdon, Fannie 144
Langdon Mound 101, 140, 144 (also see Indian Mound)
Large New Madrid Source Zone 24 (also see Small New Madrid Source Zone)
largest of the New Madrid earthquakes (see great New Madrid earthquakes)
largest sand boil in the world (see Beach, The)
lateral spread features 39, 46-49 (also see graben fissure, sag, earthquake crevasse, sand fissure, sand ridge & sand slough)
lateral spread sags 46-47
Laurentia 20
lava 41
Lawrenceville, IL, quake 37, 57
Leachville, AR xii, 130
Lenox, TN 10, 98
LeSieur Cemetery 118, 121
levee 88, 91, 97, 120-121, 129, 137, 138
Levee Bargain Center 120
Lewis, Lilbourn 110
Lewis, Lilbourn Anexamander 108
Lewis, Lucy Jefferson 108, 110
Lewis, Meriwether 8
lightening 101
lignite 4, 45, 83, 128, 159
Lilbourn, MO 75, 104, 108, 154

Lilbourn Mound 87, 104, 108 (also see Indian Mound)
Lima, Peru 179
limonite nodules 45, 159
Lincoln, Abraham 8
Lincoln-Douglas Debates 32
liquefaction (def. of) 159
liquefaction 36-39, 88, 102, 107, 128 (also see SIL, MIL, HIL)
liquefaction model 106, 174
liquefaction ring dike 46
liquification 36
Little Prairie, MO 3, 10, 13, 42, 60, 100, 122, 123, 129, 131, 134
Little River 13, 16, 53, 66, 86, 87, 88, 91, 97, 106, 119, 121, 124, 131, 140, 144
local cuisine (see restaurants)
locomotives 128
loess 32, 39, 57, 58, 59, 101, 134, 138-139, 159
log jams 16
Los Angeles Trade Technical College 178
Lost Lake 10, 50, 51
lottery 101
Louisiana 22
Luxora, AR 76, 140
Lyell, Charles 73, 87

M

MacCarthy Geophysics Laboratory 179
Madison, Dolly 8
magma 22
Malden, MO xii, 6, 10, 29, 130
Malden Plain 29, 63 (also see Kennett-Malden Prairie)
Malden substation 6
Manila, AR 98, 140, 141, 145, 148
Marble Hill, MO xii, 9, 30, 179
marine rocks 31, 159
Marked Tree, AR xii, 24, 34, 95, 127, 154
Marmaduke, AR 38
Marston, MO 10, 13, 30, 75, 89, 106, 118, 122, 130
Marston-New Madrid Rest

Stop (see New Madrid Rest Stop)
Martin Lake 147
masonry 14, 125
Matthews, MO 10, 76, 85, 98, 127, 154, 155
meander loop 92
Meatte, Edward 90
Meatte, Modest 90
mechanically induced liquefaction (MIL) 8, 36, 42, 76, 87, 88, 97, 105, 107, 109, 135, 136, 159
mechanically induced liquefaction (def. of) 159
Memphis, TN xii, 10, 57, 134
Mercalli Scale 14, 16, 159
Mesozoic Era 20, 21, 22, 27
Metropolis, IL xii, 24
Metropolis Lowland 32
Mexico 16, 88
Michigan River System 18
Mid-Atlantic Ridge 23
midden (see kitchen midden)
MIL (see mechanically induced liquefaction)
mile-a-minute geologist 7
mima mounds (see prairie mounds)
Miner, MO 98, 112, 154, 155
mink 88
missing smokehouse 142
Mississippian Indians 147
Mississippian Period (or rocks) 25, 27
Mississippi Embayment 18, 26, 33
Mississippi-Missouri-Ohio River System 26
Mississippi River (formation of) 26-33, 79, 114
Mississippi River Observation Deck 5, 99, 104, 105, 106
Mississippi River ran backwards 10, 13, 56, 59-60, 67, 68, 72, 88, 101, 106, 132, 133, 137
Mississippi River waterfalls 10, 13, 53, 56, 59, 67, 68, 71, 72, 88, 104, 106, 133
Missouri River 26, 27
Modified Mercalli Scale (see Mercalli Scale)
moisture and visibility of seismic features 2, 145
Monkey's Eyebrow 10

Morehouse Lowland 29, 30, 32, 80
Morehouse, MO 29, 30, 33, 37
Morley, MO 33, 112, 114
morphoseismic features 2, 4, 39-43, 62, 88, 96-97, 119, 130-131, 134
morphoseismology (def. of) 6, 160
mosquito 3, 64
mound (see Indian Mound or prairie mound)
Mound Cemetery 108
murder 124
muskrat 87
Myers, Kim 124, 130

N

Natchez, MS 30
Native American artifacts 4, 128, 143, 147
Native Americans 8, 12, 42, 70, 79, 100, 105, 106, 108, 119, 142, 143, 147, 149, 150, 178 (also see Indian mound)
natural levees 42, 63, 91, 160
New Franklin Ditch (a good site for digging to see sectional views of sand features) 146, 148
New Hamburg, MO 10
New Hamburg quake 38
New Madrid Bend 66, 69
New Madrid Cemetery (see Evergreen Cemetery and Mound Cemetery)
New Madrid Central High-school 50, 87, 104, 108, 111
New Madrid County 30, 31, 91
New Madrid Fault 12-13, 67, 69, 70, 128, 154, 160 (also see New Madrid Seismic Zone)
New Madrid Golf Course 104, 107
New Madrid Historical Museum 3, 5, 59, 86, 99, 102, 104, 105, 106
New Madrid Island 75, 104
New Madrid, MO xii, 10, 13, 30, 34, 35, 37, 42, 52, 56, 59, 67, 68, 75, 76, 87, 98, 99, 104, 127, 129, 130,

132, 134, 137, 154
New Madrid Nursing Home 111
New Madrid (original site) 42, 59, 66, 104, 106
New Madrid Rest Stop 75, 76, 87, 90
New Madrid Rift Complex 18, 20, 21, 22, 23, 24 (also see New Madrid Seismic Zone)
New Madrid Seismic Zone (def. of) 160
New Madrid Seismic Zone (NMSZ) xii, 1, 2, 3, 7, 9, 18, 19, 20, 23, 24, 35, 39, 78, 95, 101, 135, 141, 160 (also see New Madrid Rift Complex)
New Madrid Source Zone 24
New Madrid Visitors Center 75, 76, 87, 90
New Orleans, LA 106, 111, 137
Newport, AR 62
Nicormy (see Lake Nicormy)
noncoherent landslide (see incoherent landslide)
Noranda Aluminum Co 75, 106, 110
normal fault 54, 69
North American craton 20
North Lilbourn 75, 104
Nuttli, Otto 13, 16, 60

O

oak trees 5, 65, 86, 109, 131, 132
Obion River 132, 133, 134
Obion, TN xii, 10, 132
Ohio River 26, 27, 29, 30, 33, 53, 76, 79, 96, 113
Ohio River, Falls of 53
Old Kingshighway (see El Camino Real)
omelet 126
Oran, MO 29, 33
Ordovician Period (or rocks) 25, 27
original site of New Madrid 42, 59, 104, 106
origin of New Madrid Seismic Zone 18-22
Osceola, AR 140, 144
otter 88
Ouachita Mountains 22
Ouachita Trough 20

overcup oak (quercus lyrata) 131
oxbow lake 51, 136, 160
Ozark escarpment 31
Ozark highlands 31, 78, 113
Ozark province (see Ozark highlands)

p

Painton, MO 37
Paleozoic Period (or rocks) 18, 20, 21, 31
Pan American Health Organization 179
Pancho's Restaurant 146
Pangaea 19, 22, 23
Pascola Arch 31
Pascola, MO 31, 76, 98, 122, 126, 127, 128, 140, 155
patty cakes 36
paw paw 160
peach pie 110
pecan trees 92, 142, 143, 147
Pemiscot (meaning of word) 142
Pemiscot Bayou 94, 103, 140, 141, 142
Pemiscot County 30, 31, 91
Pemiscot River 142, 143
Penick, James 53, 59, 60, 72
Peru 179
petroliferous nodules 4, 45, 128, 160
Phillippy, TN 75, 132, 137
physiographic features of the NMSZ 30
piano 179
PIggly Wiggly Store 141
Piggott, AR 10, 38, 130
Pineville, MO 178
plate lunch at a good price 89
plate tectonics 19-23
Pleistocene Epoch (or deposits) 26, 27, 57
Pliocene Epoch (or deposits) 27, 57
Point Pleasant 10, 13, 42, 66, 74, 75, 100, 118, 119, 121, 122, 132
poisonous snakes 146
Pomeroy, Lee (Stewart) xi, 179
pontoon boat cruise 136

Poplar BLuff xii, 10, 29, 30, 79
Portage Open Bay 66, 76, 90, 91, 100, 118, 119, 120, 121, 122, 123, 124, 131
Portageville, MO 75, 76, 90, 91, 100, 119, 121, 122, 123, 130, 132
possum 129
potential slope failures 115, 116
pot shards (Indian) 128
power lines 102
Powers Island 112
prairie mounds 33, 42, 62
Prakash, Shamsher 163
Precambrian 20, 21, 27
pre-earthquake sale 9, 177, 180
pre-1811 earthquakes 128
primates 27
Proctor, Elaine 80
Proctor landslide 76, 80, 96, 112, 113
Proctor, Roy 80
Proctor sand boil 76, 81, 112
property owners 5, 6
prophecy 11
Protoatlantic 22
pseudoseismic features 40, 42, 60

Q

quake burger 105, 111
Quaternary alluvium 31
Quaternary Period 27
quick clay 36
quick gravel 36
quick sand 3, 36
quick silt 36

R

raccoon 129
Race Track, The 93
radio 43, 102, 107
railroad tracks 8, 88, 97, 104, 107, 115, 135, 136
raised land (see uplift features)
Reelfoot Basin 20, 68
Reelfoot Bayou 132
Reelfoot Fault 24, 25, 53, 56, 57, 69, 72, 101, 132, 133, 135, 136, 137
Reelfoot Lake 3, 5, 7, 10,

13, 17, 30, 50, 51, 53, 57, 63, 67, 68, 72, 75, 76, 98, 101, 107, 117, 126, 130, 132, 133, 135, 146
Reelfoot Lake Visitors Center 3, 135
Reelfoot Scarp (see Reelfoot Fault)
refrigerator 107
refugees of the earthquakes 122, 129, 131
regional planning 5-6
Rend Lake Fault System 24
requirements for Certification as a Fault Finder 149-150
research trenching 136, 143
resonance 38
rest area (see New Madrid Rest Stop & Arkansas Visitors Center)
restaurants 78, 83, 86, 87, 89, 104, 105, 107, 110, 111, 126, 129, 131, 134, 135, 136, 141, 146
retrofit (see seismic retrofit)
retrograde motion of Mississippi River (see Mississippi River ran backwards)
reverse fault 54, 70
Reyno, AR 38
rice 8
rice hulls 88
Richard, Mr. & Mrs. 126
Richter, Charles F. 161
Richter Dip Stick 6, 84-85, 96
Richter scale (def. of) 159, 161
Ridgely Ridge 135
Ridgely, TN 98, 135
rift valley (see New Madrid Rift Complex)
rift zone (see New Madrid Rift Complex)
Riley, Robert 107
ring dike (see liquefaction ring dike)
Risco, MO, quake 39
River Bend Cafe 111
river ran backwards (see Mississippi River ran backwards)
Rocky Mountains 16, 88, 91
Roosevelt, Nicholas 8
Rosie's Restaurant 104, 105, 110
rotational slump 42, 101, 132, 138, 139

Roundhouse Restaurant 129
Russ, David 159, 161

S

safety in driving 7
sag 46, 48, 93, 122
sag pond 58
Samburg, TN 75, 132
Samford, MO 103, 143, 155
sand blanket 44
sand blow (see blow sand, channel blowout, earthquake pond, explosion sand & blow crater)
sand boil 4, 25, 40, 42, 44, 61, 76, 81, 83, 85, 89, 90, 91, 95, 96, 97, 99, 100, 101, 102, 103, 104, 107, 110, 111, 112, 115, 116, 118, 121, 122, 123, 127-129, 131, 133, 135, 140, 141, 142, 143, 145, 148, 154
sand dike 42, 46, 145
sand dune 32, 40, 42, 62, 80, 83, 84, 100, 110, 114, 115, 117, 161
sand features, sectional views of (see sectional views of seismic sand features)
sand fissure 42, 47-48, 61, 84, 89, 94, 95, 100, 101, 103, 122, 123, 125, 140, 141, 145, 147
sand mine 42, 64, 83
sand ridge 42, 48, 49, 101, 141
sand sill 42, 46, 145
sand slough 42, 48, 49
sand volcano 41
San Francisco quake 1906 37
Satan 12
satellite imagery 124, 130, 154
Scott City, MO 76, 77, 179
sea level 29, 31
Scientific American 2
scratch 'n sniff 4, 128
seasonal variation in appearance of seismic features 2-3
secondary fault 42, 52-53, 128
sectional views of seismic sand features (by digging

in sides of New Franklin Ditch near Cooter, MO, or ditch near Buckeye, AR) 140, 141, 145, 147
seep springs 88, 139
seiche 73-74, 161
seismically historic sites 39, 42, 66, 100, 104, 106, 121, 122, 124, 29, 131, 147
seismically induced liquefaction (SIL) 36-39, 40, 52, 121, 128, 145, 162
seismic building design 87, 99, 108, 111, 112, 116, 136
seismic dump 43, 104, 107
seismicity of NMSZ 77, 80, 95-96 (also see chances of an earthquake happening)
seismic liquefaction ring dike 46
seismic retrofit 99, 104, 105, 110-111 (also see seismic building design)
seismic river wave 71
seismic sand fissure (see sand fissure)
seismic sand traps 107
seismic sea wave 71
seismic tar balls (see petroliferous nodules)
seismograph 106
seismohydrology (def. of) 162
seismohydrology 4, 5, 8, 35, 38, 39, 41, 43, 52, 63, 88, 139, 145, 162
seismoluminescence 41
Self-Realization Fellowship 178
seven-acre sand boil (see Proctor sand boil)
shaking damage 38
shale pieces 4, 45, 95, 128
Shawnee 8, 12, 90
Shawneetown Fault Zone 24
Shinbone, MO 90, 121
shovel for digging (see sectional views of seismic sand features)
shrimp creole 126
Sikeston, MO xii, 6, 7, 10, 78, 83, 100, 112, 113, 115, 127, 154, 155
Sikeston Power Plant 85, 115, 117
Sikeston Power Plant fissure 6, 100, 112, 113, 116, 117
Sikeston Ridge 29, 32, 33,

49, 63, 79, 80, 81, 83, 84, 85, 86, 100, 106, 107, 112, 113, 115, 116
Sinclair Deli 107
Sinclair Sand Boil 105, 107
SIL (see seismically induced liquefaction)
sill (see sand sill)
Silo Island 112, 113, 114, 115, 117
skeletons 147
slaves 12
slide (see slope failure features)
slope failure features 3, 39, 40, 42, 76, 101, 133-134, 135, 138-139
slump (see slope failure feature)
Small New Madrid Source Zone 24 (also see Large New Madrid Source Zone)
smokehouse 142
smokestack (see Associated Electric Co. & Sikeston Power Plant)
snake 60, 129, 146
soda pop 145
solar eclipse 11
Southeast Missouri State University 90, 124, 127, 178, 179
southern red oak (quercus falcata) 5, 105, 109
Southwestern Bell Building 111
souvenirs 106 (also see Duckies)
Spanish 12, 79, 110, 119, 120
Spanish Mill 100, 121, 122, 124
Speed, Mathias 53, 56
spoil bank 42, 64, 91, 148, 162
SPT (see standard penetration test)
standard penetration test (SPT) 39, 162-163
Star, The 53, 122, 123, 124, 130
steamboat 100, 106, 129
Steele earthquake 141
Steele, MO 10, 12, 30, 61, 76, 93, 98, 101, 130, 140, 141
Ste. Genevieve Fault 24, 25, 78
Ste. Genevieve, MO 79
stew 107

Stewart, David 9, 37, 49, 60, 64, 92, 99, 125, 150, 61, 162, 178-179

Stewart Landing 118, 120

Stewart, Lee Pomeroy xi, 179

Stewart translational block slide 132

St. Francis River 16, 30, 32, 41, 52, 66, 91, 106, 119, 124

St. Johns Bayou 66, 67, 68, 69, 71, 74, 75, 76, 104, 106, 113 (also see St. Johns Ditch)

St. Johns Ditch 75, 76, 85, 112, 114-115, 117 (also see St. Johns Bayou)

St. Johns Fault 70, 72, 73, 74

St. Johns Lake (see Lake St. John)

St. Jude Industrial Park 13, 75, 76, 106, 118

St. Lawrence Seaway 22

St. Louis, MO 10, 37, 79, 106, 178

St. Martins des Cyprie (see des Cyprie)

St. Marys, MO 25

Stoddard County 30, 31

St. Peters sandstone formation 25

stream gradient (see altered stream gradients)

stressed vegetation (see distressed vegetation)

strike-slip fault 54, 154, 163

subduction 22

subsided channel 64

subsidence 64, 68, 73, 81, 85, 87, 101, 136 (also see differential subsidence features, sag & sunk land)

sun boil 42, 63

sunken Spanish boat 120

sunk land 42, 49, 76, 81, 85, 87, 100, 108, 112, 113, 114, 116, 136

supply vent 4, 44

Swilley, J.K. 90

Swilley Pond 76, 89

sycamore tree 143, 147

T

Taconic Orogeny 20

Teceikeapease 90

Tecumseh, Chief 8, 12, 90

tectonic plates (see plate tectonics)

Tennessee Prison Facility 75, 136

Tenskwatawa 12

terraces of the Mississippi 28, 29, 31, 79

Terra Haute, IN 24

Tertiary Hills 30

Tertiary Period (or deposits) 27, 31

Tex-Mex food 146

Thebes Gap 30, 32, 33, 80

Thebes, IL 30, 33

thrust fault 31, 70

ticks 3

tidal wave 71

Timms Point 140, 146, 148

Tiptonville Dome 51, 52, 53, 56, 69, 70, 72, 88, 133, 135

Tiptonville Horst 10, 25, 52, 63, 67, 68, 70, 72, 132, 135, 137

Tiptonville, TN 30, 75, 98, 135, 136

toll bridge 124

Tom's Grill 105, 111

tractors 8, 43, 88

traffic induced liquefaction (TIL) 8, 36, 87, 88, 97, 109 (also see mechanically induced liquefaction)

traffic safety (see safety in driving)

trains 8, 88

translational block slide 42, 132

trees broken (see forestland, destruction of)

trench research 136, 143

Trimble, TN 132

trumpet vines 94

T-shirts 106, 150, 175

tsunami 71, 151, 163 (see fluvial tsunami & seismic sea wave)

TV transmitting tower (see Richter Dip Stick)

TV set 43

Twell, Karen (Knox) xi, 178

Twin Borrow Pits 120

Tywappity Hill 80 (also see Benton Hills)

U

Union City, TN xii, 10

Union Soldiers 145

United Methodist Church 179

United Nations Disaster Relief Organization 179

United States Army Corps of Engineers 64, 71

United States Geological Survey 61, 103, 136, 154, 161, 179

University of Arkansas, Fayetteville 178

University of Iowa, Iowa City 178

University of Missouri, Rolla 179

University of North Carolina, Chapel Hill 179

unreinforced masonry 125

uplift features 42, 52, 68, 137 (also see Tiptonville Horst & Tiptonville Dome)

V

vacation, fault finding 3

variations in appearance of seismic features 2

vegetative cover and appearance of seismic features 2-3, 17 (also see distressed vegetation)

vibratory ground motion 38

vicarious field trip 3, 8, 9

Victoria, AR 140, 155

violent flooding 68, 71

visibility of seismic features in different weather 2

Volcano (see sand volcano)

W

Wabash River 18

Wabash Valley Fault Zone 24, 163

Walmart 178

walnut tree 127

Walton, Sam 178

Wardell, MO 76, 91

warm groundwater 41

Warrensburg, MO 178

Washington, DC 16

washing machine 107

washout 86, 108, 112, 113, 115, 163 (also see des Cyprie)

waterfalls on the Mississippi (see Mississippi River waterfalls)

water-loving plants (see hydrophytic plants)

water snake 146

wave harmonics 37, 125

Weaver, John 124

Webb, Dan 91

Webb, Joyce 91

weigh station 92

Western Lowland 32 (also see Advance Lowland)

western omelet 126

what to do in case of an earthquake 101-102

Whitewater River 32

Whizbang, MO 178

Wickliffe, KY 10, 29, 57, 134

Willard's Wood Shop 131

wind erosion 32, 114

Wine, Fault Finders 3

wireless TV tower (see Richter Dip Stick)

witness trees 5, 65, 76, 86, 99, 104, 105, 109, 131

Witness Tree State Park 109

wolves 129

world's largest sand boil (see Beach, The)

wump, the 87

Wyandot 178

Y

Yellowstone Park 88

Yum Yum Drive-In 141

GUTENBERG-RICHTER
PUBLICATIONS

THE EARTHQUAKE AMERICA FORGOT

2,000 Temblors in Five Months . . .
And it Will Happen Again

by Dr. David Stewart & Dr. Ray Knox
Cover by Don Greenwood, Illustrations by Anthony Stewart

You'll be an eye witness. An experience you'll never forget. This book will take you back to the times and places of the greatest sequence of earthquakes in the last 2,000 years of World History—the New Madrid earthquakes of 1811–12. From the safety of your favorite reading chair, you'll encounter River Pirates, Indians, Romance, War, Peace, Good Times, Tough Times, Slavery, Corruption, Heroes, Scoundrels, Bizarre Animal Behavior, Murder, Mystery—Political, Social and Geologic Upheavals all at the same time. Famous people were there—President Thomas Jefferson; Artist and Naturalist, John James Audubon; Explorer and Governor, Meriwether Lewis; Abraham Lincoln (age three at the time); Teddy Roosevelt's Grandfather, the fiery, charismatic Shawnee Chief Tecumseh, and his brother, the Shawnee Prophet Tenskwatawa. This is the most complete account of these earthquakes ever published. Dozens of incredible stories, fascinating first-person accounts, and here-to-fore unpublished facts—plus more than two-hundred photographs, figures, maps and illustrations, including pictures of seismic features still visible in the landscape of the New Madrid Fault Zone today. The definitive work on the Great New Madrid earthquakes. Reads like a novel. But this is not fiction. These fantastic events actually happened. Once you start you won't want to put it down. When you read this book you'll feel like you were there . . . and are glad you survived.

(EAF) First Edition 1995
376 pages, 8.5x11, 280 photos, maps and illustrations, index, bibliography, hardcover
LCCN 91-91492
ISBN 0-934426-45-7 $29.95

GUTENBERG-RICHTER
PUBLICATIONS

THE EARTHQUAKE
THAT NEVER WENT AWAY

The Shaking Stopped in 1812 . . . But the Impact Goes On

by Dr. David Stewart & Dr. Ray Knox

Get comfortable and take an armchair field trip to the greatest display of earthquake features in the world. See how a sequence of massive earthquakes long ago still effect the live and times of people living in and around the New Madrid Fault Zone now. When the shaking is over, the impact of a great earthquake is not. It's lasting effects can reach down through the centuries to touch people today—influencing engineering, agriculture, transportation, and the way people live and think. You will see seismic sand boils formed two centuries ago where farmers still get stuck with their tractors. You'll see 200-year-old seismic sand fissures under railroad tracks that cause train derailments today. You'll see modern houses built over old earthquake landslides whose foundations are cracking up and creeping down hill—a process started by seismic forces long before the town was settled. This book gives you a "vicarious visual tour," complete with the narrative you would hear from two leading world authorities as your personal guides. 138 original photos, 5 figures, and 3 maps of faults, fissures, and scars in the landscape still visible today from the great New Madrid earthquakes of 1811–12. (These same illustrations are also available as 35 mm color slides, see page 173). Carefully researched and scientifically rigorous, yet written with wit and entertainment for the enlightenment of the public. You will be amazed at what you can still see of these earthquakes—evidence permanently impressed upon the landscape of the unbelievable churning, boiling, cracking and splintering of the earth's surface from the unimaginable violence of the cataclysms that caused these lasting landforms that people must still deal with today.

(NWA) First Edition 1993
222 pages, 8.5xll, 138 photos, 5 figures, 4 tables, 3 maps, index, bibliography, quality paperback
LCCN 92-75133
ISBN 0-934426-54-6 $19.95

GUTENBERG-RICHTER PUBLICATIONS

150 EARTHQUAKE SLIDES ON THE NEW MADRID SEISMIC ZONE
by Dr. David Stewart & Dr. Ray Knox

It has been said that "an expert is someone more than twenty miles from home with a tray of slides." Now you can become an expert on the Great New Madrid Earthquakes of 1811-12—taking friends, civic groups, professional peers, and students of all ages on a fascinating picture-tour of the fault zone and its thousands of earthquake features. The New Madrid Fault Zone is the most extensive and outstanding display of landforms sculptured by earthquakes known on earth. Scientists, engineers, and visitors from all over the world come to see what is there and marvel. There are more sand boils, fissures, landslides, broken stream channels, seismic ponds, explosion craters, and earthquake lakes in this region than anywhere on earth. See the world's largest sand boil—over a mile long and 136 acres in size. (Most sand boils are less than 10 feet in diameter.) These slides will take you and your audience on a tour where you fly over, drive by, and walk on some of the world's greatest morphoseismic features. Step into a graben crevasse. Fly along the Bootheel fault. Climb up an earthquake landslide. Photos from five states—Arkansas, Illinois, Kentucky, Missouri and Tennessee. 150 color slides, 35 mm, two carousel trays full. Complete set of narrative notes, a glossary of definitions, and instructions for a smashing presentation to any group. The New Madrid Seismic Zone has a story to tell and you can be the one to tell it. All you need is this set of slides and the book that accompanies it. You will be awed by what you see—and so will your audiences.

Slide set comes in an attractive 3-D-ring binder with archival plastic sleeves for storage and easy previewing. Delivered shrunk-wrapped and ready to use. Binder contains a 3-hole punched copy of *The Earthquake that Never Went Away* (see p. 171) which serves as the narrative notes for the set.

(SET) First Edition 1993
150 color slides, 35mm, D-ring binder, 222 page book of notes with index, bibliography
ISBN 0-934426-51-1 $180.00 for complete set with book
Slides from set also available individually $4.00 each ppd

OTHER BOOKS Available from Gutenberg-Richter

DAMAGE & LOSSES FROM FUTURE NEW MADRID EARTHQUAKES
Dr. David Stewart

The New Madrid Fault has the capability of causing damage in 22 states. Do you live in one of them? What will happen in your area when the next major New Madrid quake hits? What is the probability in your lifetime? With this easy-to-use manual you can find out how many buildings will collapse, how many will be injured, how many will die, how many bridges will be out, and a host of other valuable information about the county where you live. Ideal for medical personnel, emergency planners, business owners, insurance personnel, school officials, government leaders, national guard units, Red Cross chapters, or anyone who wants to know what will happen during the next destructive New Madrid earthquake. Published jointly by Missouri State Emergency Management Agency and Federal Emergency Management Agency. (DAL) Fourth Printing 1994. 74 pp, 8.5x11, 16 maps, softcover
ISBN 0-934426-53-8   FREE ON REQUEST (postage & handling $3.00)

THE NEW MADRID EARTHQUAKE
by Myron Fuller (Foreword by Dr. David Stewart)

This is the book all researchers and serious students start with in studying the great New Madrid earthquakes of 1811-12. Originally released in 1912 as a U.S. Geological Survey publication, Written by a geologist, this is the first serious scientific study of these events to be put into print. Many photos and figures. Published by Center for Earthquake Studies, SE MO State University. (NMF) 1990 edition. 120 pages, 8.5x5.5, quality paperback
ISBN 0-934426-49-X $15.95

THE NEW MADRID EARTHQUAKES
by Dr. James Lal Penick Jr. (Foreword by Dr. Otto Nuttli)

A scholarly and authoritative account of the New Madrid earthquakes written by a historian. Meticulously documented. Photos and line drawings. Well written. Published by University of Missouri Press, Columbia. (NMP) Revised Edition 1981. 176 pages, 5x7, quality paperback.
ISBN 0-8262-0344-2 $16.95

EFFECTS OF EARTHQUAKES IN THE CENTRAL UNITED STATES
by Dr. Otto Nuttli (Foreword by Dr. David Stewart)

Dr. Nuttli was the leading world authority on this subject in his life-time. This was his last published work. Maps, figures, and photos. Considers all active faults in the Midwest. Clearly articulated. The perfect primer on earthquake risk in the central U.S.
(CUS) 1990 edition. 50 pages, 6x9, quality softcover.
ISBN 0-934426-50-3 $9.95

OTHER ITEMS Available from Gutenberg-Richter

NEW MADRID FAULT TOURS

Take a tour of the New Madrid Fault Zone with Dr. David Stewart and/or Dr. Ray Knox. If interested, send name, address and phone number to Dr. Stewart in care of Gutenberg-Richter Publications.

GUEST LECTURERS

David Stewart is available for a variety of public lectures or seminars suitable for any audience, profession, or age group. Address inquiries to Gutenberg-Richter Publications, address and phone given on page 177.

T-SHIRTS AVAILABLE WITH EARTHQUAKE ART

Don Greenwood's exquisite artwork displayed on the cover of the book, *The Earthquake America Forgot,* is available on a T-shirt. For information on prices and sizes, contact Gutenberg-Richter Publications, address and phone given on page 177. A great gift idea!

HOW TO MAKE YOUR OWN LIQUEFACTION MODEL
Free Booklet by Dr. David Stewart

Complete and simple instructions on how to make an earthquake liquefaction model. Make an earthquake (hit the table or stomp on floor) and watch the soil turn to quicksand. A great science fair project. Copies are free with book order. Otherwise, send $1.00 for postage and handling.

EARTHQUAKE GUIDE FOR HOME AND OFFICE
Free Booklet by Maria Dillard and Dr. David Stewart

Published in 1990 by Southwestern Bell Telephone Company and the Center for Earthquake Studies at Southeast Missouri State University, this excellent illustrated twelve-page booklet summarizes the hazards, what you should expect, and what you should do during an earthquake whether you are at home or at the office, in a vehicle, in an elevator or on the street. Also contains advice on earthquake preparation and what phone numbers you should post prior to an earthquake emergency. Copies are free with book orders. Otherwise send $1.00 for postage and handling. Available in bulk quantities to schools, civic organization, and others for cost of shipping.

GR
GUTENBERG-RICHTER
PUBLICATIONS

ORDERING INFORMATION

You may order Gutenberg-Richter Publications by directly from the publisher by remitting check or money order. A convenient order form is given at the end of this book on page 180 which may be photocopied, completed, and sent with your order. You may also use your VISA or Master Card, either by mail (see Order Form, p. 180) or by telephone via the toll free number given on the next page. You may also inquire at your local bookstore who can special-order these books for you should they not have them in stock. If your library does not have copies of Gutenberg-Richter publications, encourage them to order copies directly from the publisher. Purchase Orders Welcome.

MISSOURI SALES TAX: Missouri residents must pay 6% sales tax on all orders. For non-Missouri residents there is no tax.

SHIPPING INSTRUCTIONS

BOOK ORDERS: Please remit appropriate total for books desired plus shipping and handling as follows: For U.S.A., Mexico and Canada, add $3.00 for first book, plus $1.50 for second book, plus $1.00 per book thereafter. Other countries: Surface Parcel Post is $8.00 for first book, plus $4.00 for second book, plus $2.00 per book thereafter; Air Parcel Post is $15.00 for first book, plus $8.00 for second book, plus $3.00 per book thereafter.

SLIDE ORDERS: Complete set of 150 Colored Slides including book of narrative notes, $8.00 for Priority Mail within the U.S.A., $10.00 for Canada, and $35.00 for International Air Parcel Post in all other countries. Individual slides retail for $4.00 each which includes First Class Postage for U.S.A., Mexico, and Canada. All other countries include an additional $1.00 per slide for International Air Mail. Specify slides by numbers given in the book, *The Earthquake that Never Went Away.*

COMPLETE LIBRARIES: Books only, $8.00 (N. America), $15.00 (Other countries). Books plus Slide Set, $15.00 (N. America), $50.00 (Other countries)

✌ SPECIAL DISCOUNTS ✌

COMPLETE NEW MADRID EARTHQUAKE LIBRARY at SPECIAL PRICE
All seven books listed on Order Form on page 180 ($110 value) — Only $90
All seven books plus full set of 150 colored slides ($290 value) — Only $250
• **SAVE $20.00 ON BOOKS** • **SAVE $40.00 ON BOOKS & SLIDES** •

GUTENBERG-RICHTER PUBLICATIONS

• EXCLUSIVE EARTHQUAKE HAZARD WARRANTY •

Gutenberg-Richter Publications carry an exclusive "Earthquake Hazard Warranty" not offered by any other publisher. Any Gutenberg-Richter product you own that has been damaged by an earthquake will be replaced ABSOLUTELY FREE OF CHARGE. Simply return the damaged merchandise to Gutenberg-Richter and we will traded you for a new book or slide. We won't even charge you shipping and handling for this service. We just hope you won't personally ever suffer any injuries or losses from an earthquake. But if you do, you can know that your Gutenberg-Richter products are insured.

• MONEY-BACK GUARANTEE •

If at any time you, as the original purchaser, are not satisfied with a Gutenberg-Richter Publication, either book or slide set, please feel free to return it (or them) in good resellable condition for a prompt full refund.

VISA & MASTER CARD ACCEPTED

CALL THIS TOLL–FREE NUMBER ANY TIME NIGHT OR DAY TO PLACE YOUR ORDER

1-800-758-8629

"The Toll-Free Number with a Richter 8.8 in the Middle"

SEND ORDERS, REQUESTS, AND INQUIRIES TO:
Purchase Orders Okay · Bookstore Discounts Available
GR Federal EIN: 43—1165937

Gutenberg-Richter Publications
Rt. 1, Box 646
Marble Hill, MO 63764 U.S.A

Convenient Order Form Provided in Back on Page 180

ABOUT THE AUTHORS

DR. RAY KNOX

Burnal Ray Knox was born March 29, 1931, at Whizbang, Missouri, a country store and a post office and not much else. It no longer exists. Whizbang was in the Ozark hills of southwestern Missouri, "Not too far from Cyclone," he likes to say, "and actually not too far from Pineville and Huckleberry Ridge, either." He attended high school and "did most of his growing up" in Bentonville, Arkansas—better known as home of the late Sam Walton, founder of the Walmart Chain.

Dr. Knox is also part Native American. His great grandmother was a full-blooded Indian of the Wyandot Tribe. Her native name was "Missouri."

Presently, Dr. Knox is a Professor of Geosciences at Southeast Missouri State University and former Chairman of that Department. His major research interest is geomorphology, the scientific study of landforms and how they got that way. He earned his bachelors and masters degrees in geology from the University of Arkansas at Fayetteville and his doctorate from the University of Iowa in Iowa City.

In recent years he has become quite interested in morphoseismology—the study of how earthquakes mold and alter the landscape. Prior research had focused on the formation of the Ozark Mountains—especially its streams and caves. He is author of fifteen professional presentations and sixteen professional publications. He is coauthor of four books on the New Madrid Seismic Zone.

Dr. Knox is an avid fisherman and backpacker. He loves to involve his students in hiking trips that usually combine geology with such things as trail building and maintenance, wildflower admiring, bird watching, mountain goat observing, and fishing.

He is married to the former Karen Twell, his "bride" of 39 years, with whom he lives in Cape Girardeau, Missouri. Karen and Ray have three kids and two "extraordinary" granddaughters.

DR. DAVID STEWART

David Mack Stewart was born September 20, 1937, in St. Louis, raised in Crystal City, Missouri, graduated from high school in Jefferson City (1955), attended Central Methodist College in Fayette, Missouri, 1955-58 (majoring in philosophy, religion and English) and went to Los Angeles Trade Technical College, 1959 (to study photography). He was the photographer for Self Realization Fellowship, Inc., 1959-1962. He went to Central Missouri State University in Warrensburg, 1962-63 (majoring in social and life sciences), transferred to the University of

Missouri at Rolla where he worked his way through college as a piano teacher, and received a B.S. in Math and Physics (1965), graduating as Salutatorian of his class. After two years as a hydrologist and hydraulic engineer with the U.S. Geological Survey in Garden Grove, California, he returned to Rolla to earn an M.S. and Ph.D. in Geophysics in 1971.

Former Director of the Central U.S. Earthquake Consortium, Marion, Illinois. Former Director of MacCarthy Geophysics Laboratory and Assistant Professor at the University of North Carolina, Chapel Hill. Founder and former Director, Center for Earthquake Studies and Associate Professor at Southeast Missouri State University, Cape Girardeau. He is an Adjunct Instructor at the Emergency Management Institute, Emmitsburg, Maryland. He is a private consultant on seismic risk and damage assessment to government, insurance, and industry. He has given expert testimony for earthquake legislation on state and federal levels and has been an expert witness in many litigations.

He has given lectures, presented seminars, led field trips, or taught courses to thousands of people on virtually every aspect of earthquake seismology, mitigation and engineering. He has given international seminars on earthquake preparation for hospitals in Lima, Peru, and Bogota, Colombia, at the invitation of the Pan American Health Organization and the United Nations Disaster Relief Organization. He has been invited to conduct tours of the New Madrid Seismic Zone attended by scientists and engineers from many countries.

Dr. Stewart is author or coauthor of more than 200 publications, in ten languages, including thirteen books. Two of his works received the "Books of the Year" Award from the *American Journal of Nursing.* Two of his papers won national awards for clarity in technical writing. Two other publications have sold or circulated over a million copies each. In 1990-93 he served on the Editorial Board of *Earthquake Spectra*—the International Journal of Earthquake Engineering.

Dr. Stewart has been quoted in many journals and magazines, as well as by virtually every newspaper in the United States. He has appeared on national television in forty-four countries.

He and his wife, the former Lee Pomeroy, have five children ages 19 to 32—four sons and a daughter. Two are married. They have three grandchildren. (as of June 1995) David cannot claim any Native American blood, but Lee and his children are all part Cherokee. David and Lee celebrated their thirty-second wedding anniversary on September 1, 1994.

Dr. Stewart is a former licensed United Methodist Pastor who served the Illmo United Methodist Church at Scott City, Missouri, in 1993 and 1994. David and Lee are both members of the First United Methodist Church of Marble Hill, Missouri, where Lee is a choir director. David enjoys playing the piano, loves hiking and raises four-leaf-clovers for a hobby. David and Lee live on a farm in Bollinger County, Missouri.

(Please Photocopy This Form as Needed)

GR GUTENBERG-RICHTER PUBLICATIONS

ORDER FORM

ISBN	Code	Title	Author(s)	Price	Qty	Total
BOOKS:						
0-934426-45-7	(EAF)	The Earthquake America Forgot	Stewart/Knox	$ 29.95	_____	_____
0-934426-54-6	(NWA)	The Earthquake that Never Went Away	Stewart/Knox	19.95	_____	_____
0-934426-42-2	(FFG)	The New Madrid Fault Finders Guide	Knox/Stewart	16.95	_____	_____
0-934426-49-X	(NMF)	The New Madrid Earthquake	Fuller	15.95	_____	_____
0-8262-0344-2	(NMP)	The New Madrid Earthquakes	Penick	16.95	_____	_____
0-934426-50-3	(CUS)	Effects of Earthquakes in Central U.S.	Nuttli	9.95	_____	_____
0-934426-53-8	(DAL)	Damages & Losses from Future Quakes	Stewart	FREE*	_____	_____

* The book DAL is FREE, but Please enclose $3.00 shipping.

35 mm COLOR SLIDES:						
0-934426-51-1	(SET)	150 EQ Slides on the New Madrid Fault	Stewart/Knox	$180.00	_____	_____
	(SGL)	Single Slides (Specify by numbers given in NWA)		4.00 ea	_____	_____

OTHER ITEMS:						
	(EQG)	Earthquake Guide for Home and Office	Dillard/Stewart	FREE**	_____	_____
	(LIQ)	How to Make Your Own Liquefaction Model	Stewart	FREE**	_____	_____

**Please enclose $1.00 shipping unless request is accompanied with purchase.

GET A COMPLETE NEW MADRID EARTHQUAKE LIBRARY & SAVE $20–$40

(CLB) All seven books listed above (A $110 Value) • Save $20   ONLY $ 90.00 _____ _____

(CLS) All seven books plus full set of 150 slides ($290 Value) • Save $40   ONLY 250.00 _____ _____

SUBTOTAL _____

*YES! I WISH TO TAKE THE 5% PRE-EARTHQUAKE SALE DISCOUNT   95% of Above = _____

SHIPPING CHARGES: (complete international shipping info on p. 360 of EAF)

Books: (for USA , Mexico & Canada) $3 for first book, $1.50 for 2nd book, $1.00 per book thereafter.

150 Slide Set: (for USA) $8.00. (For Mexico & Canada) $10.00 (Other Countries) $35.00 for Air Parcel Post.

Single Slides: (for USA, Mexico & Canada) No additional charge. (Other Countries) Add $1.00 per slide.

Complete Libraries: (for USA, Mexico & Canada) Books only, $8.00. Books and Slide Set, $15.00.

SHIPPING _____

☞ **MONEY-BACK GUARANTEE**   6% SALES TAX (MO Residents Only) _____

NOTE: Prices Subject to Change Without Notice   **TOTAL**

NAME _____ COMPANY _____

ADDRESS _____

CITY _____ STATE _____ ZIP _____

COUNTRY (if outside the U.S.A.) _____ PHONE _____

❑ Enclosed is Check, Cash or Money Order in Amount of _____

❑ Please Charge to my VISA or MASTER CARD

❑ VISA   ❑ MASTER CARD   Expiration Date _____   **VISA**   **MasterCard**

Card Number _____ Signature _____

PURCHASE ORDERS OKAY • **Standard Discounts to Bookstores** • **Federal EIN: 43-1165937**

• Please Make Checks or Money Orders to: Gutenberg-Richter. Enclose with Order and Send To: •

Gutenberg-Richter, Rt. 1, Box 646, Marble Hill, MO 63764 USA

☎ **For Telephone Orders Use Toll Free Number: 1-800-758-8629** ☎